A CITIZEN'S GUIDE TO GOVERNMENT

Second Edition

C. Richard Tindal, Ph.D

McGraw-Hill Ryerson

Toronto Montréal New York Burr Ridge Bangkok Bogotá Caracas Lisbon London Madrid Mexico City Milan New Delhi Seoul Singapore Sydney Taipei

McGraw-Hill
Ryerson Limited
A Subsidiary of The McGraw-Hill Companies

A Citizen's Guide to Government
Second Edition

ISBN: 0-07-086416-0

2 3 4 5 6 7 8 9 10 W 0 9 8 7 6 5 4 3 2 1

Printed and bound in Canada.

Care has been taken to trace ownership of copyright material contained in this text; however, the publisher will welcome any information that enables them to rectify any reference or credit for subsequent editions.

Assistant Vice-President, Editorial Director: Pat Ferrier
Associate Sponsoring Editor: Marianne Minaker
Senior Marketing Manager: Jeff MacLean
Copy Editor: Erin Moore
Production Coordinator: Madeleine Harrington
Cover Design: Greg Devitt
Cover Image Credit: © Mark Hess/The Image Bank
Printer: Webcom Limited

Canadian Cataloguing in Publication Data

Tindal, C.R., 1943 —
    A Citizen's Guide to Government
    2nd ed.

Includes index.
ISBN 0-07-086416-0

1. Canada-Politics and government. I. Title.

JL81.T56 2000   320.471   C00-930366-9

Table of Contents

vi

> Many services that we supposedly can't afford from government, we buy from the private sector.

What this list reveals is that many of the services and programs that we supposedly can't afford from government, we are instead buying from the private sector. There are now more than twice as many private police as public one. For every apparent deficiency in the public sector, a private, profit-making alternative is offered. Those concerned about public safety can live in gated communities. If public schools are lacking, send your children to private school. Instead of waiting for tests or surgery from Canada's public health system, jump the queue and get attention today, at a private health clinic.

The wealthy in society can afford to access these private sector substitutes, and the more they do, the more they resist paying the level of taxation needed to provide these same services through the public sector. Without these tax dollars, however, public social programs continue to erode. Somehow a balance must be struck in the resources allocated to the public and the private sectors. This can be achieved only through sufficient intervention by government; it will never happen on its own as a result of the interplay of market forces. As Stewart argues, "we must have a government active enough and muscular enough to right the imbalances created by our marvellously efficient, monumentally unfair economic system."[3]

Who Wields Power, For Whom?

Ultimately, the issue comes down to the exercise of power, by whom and for whom. In oversimplified terms, we are facing a struggle between the political and economic spheres over the exercise of power.

Governments exist to make collective decisions for a country, including decisions about the provision of public goods. Only government is sanctioned to enforce its decisions, even through the use of force if necessary. In many countries, including Canada, the institutions

[3] *Ibid.*, p. 16.

Preface and Acknowledgements

This is not a conventional political science text book. As the title suggests, it is a basic primer on government, intended to encourage greater public understanding, interest and involvement. It is a "citizen's guide," designed to inform Canadians about their governments and how they work, and about the fundamental changes underway in the role of government and in key areas of Canadian public policy. It is unabashedly pro-government in the sense that it argues for a continued important role for government in our lives. Much more than the first edition, it draws attention to the constraints under which our governments operate, and it challenges the presumption that the so-called global economy leaves us no other option. Ideally, this book can serve as a call to action, motivating the reader to become an informed participant in our government system.

This Guide was also originally prepared for use with a general education course which I had developed and was teaching at St. Lawrence College (until my recent retirement). There is an accompanying Instructor's Manual which complements the use of the Guide for that purpose. In addition, each chapter of the Guide (except the first and last because of their introductory or summary nature) concludes with definitions of key terms and concepts (highlighted in **bold** where they first appear in the chapter), points to ponder for class discussion, and suggested additional sources, including web sites. The latter can be accessed from the web site for the book, which is found at *www.mcgrawhill.ca/college/tindal*. In preparing both the Guide and the Instructor's Manual, I have drawn upon almost 30 years of experience in teaching government courses at the community college level.

I am indebted to my colleague and close friend, Ian Wilson, of St. Lawrence College, for actively encouraging this project and for his many helpful comments and suggestions in connection with the first edition. Dr. Craig Jones of Queen's University provided valuable feedback based on his use of the first edition. For providing helpful suggestions at various stages of the revision exercise, I am grateful to the following: Geoffrey Booth, Georgian College, Harvey Brown, Fanshawe College, John Fakouri, Algonquin College, Randy Knapp, Sir Sandford Fleming

College, Ed Ksenych, George Brown College, and Joan Vinall-Cox, Sheridan College. Their comments were much appreciated.

It was a pleasure working with staff at McGraw-Hill Ryerson Limited, including Kelly Dickson and Erin Moore, and especially Veronica Visentin and Marianne Minaker.

For those interested in the technical side, this Guide was printed from a "camera-ready" original I prepared for the publisher using WordPerfect. The font used for the body of the text (including this Preface) is Garamond, 12 point.

Richard Tindal
Inverary, Ontario
January 2000

Chapter 1

Canada at the Crossroads

Objectives and Highlights

◆ To highlight key changes in Canadian society and in the role of government.

◆ To illustrate the economic influences on government decision making.

◆ To preview fundamental choices facing Canadians today.

Just over 100 years ago, Wilfrid Laurier proclaimed that the 20th century belongs to Canada. In some respects at least, he was correct. Canada came of age during this century, shaking off the last vestiges of its colonial ties to Britain, playing an important role in two world wars, and enjoying prolonged economic growth and prosperity during much of the second half of the century. The century ended with Canada being ranked first, for the sixth consecutive year, in the Human Development Report of the United Nations—a remarkable achievement.

Yet as the 21st century begins, there are sharply divided opinions on the role now being played by government and on the way that Canadian society is evolving. The same United Nations report that ranked Canada first overall, placed it ninth with respect to the 12% of its population living below the poverty line and noted that inequality between rich and poor is higher in Canada than in many industrialized countries. More than a decade of efforts to reduce government debt and deficits has seriously eroded the social safety net. As public disillusionment with government grows, so does the underground economy and tax avoidance. This withdrawal of public support, moral and financial, further undermines the legitimacy of government and creates a mutually-reinforcing downward spiral.

1

Why Are We at the Crossroads?

The overworked cliché which serves as the title of this introductory chapter does not refer to the beginning of a new millennium—another overworked term. But it does serve to describe the series of choices and challenges facing Canada after the pivotal decade of the 1990s.

That decade began with the federal Conservatives, led by Prime Minister Brian Mulroney, basking in the glory of a second successive majority government and the completion of a Free Trade Agreement (FTA) with the United States. The Prime Minister's other major initiative was a package of constitutional amendments known as the Meech Lake Accord. It was intended to gain the approval of Québec, which had refused to give its blessing to the patriation of the Canadian constitution in 1982. But as the decade began, time was running out on the approval of the Accord by all provinces. At the beginning of the 1990s, Canada still boasted a comprehensive social safety net which was a matter of national pride and which was held to distinguish it from the less compassionate and caring society south of the border. However, Canada was also experiencing ever-increasing annual budget deficits which were pushing its total national debt to worrisome heights.

The decade of the 1990s ended with the annual budget deficit converted into a budget surplus of some $10 billion. This turnaround was largely achieved because of low interest rates and strong economic growth, both the product of a booming economy in the United States. But Canada's fiscal solvency was also gained at the expense of its social programs. Federal expenditure cuts and reduced transfer payments to provinces produced a chain reaction of downloading responsibilities and costs and an era of fend-for-yourself federalism. An unravelling social safety net was reflected in such developments as reduced welfare payments, restrictive requirements on unemployment insurance, a burgeoning two tier health care system, and sufficient homelessness to constitute a national disgrace.

The so-called "Québec problem" remained unresolved at the end of the 1990s. The Meech Lake Accord died in June 1990, without receiving approval from two provinces (Manitoba and Newfoundland). A follow up Charlottetown Accord was rejected by voters in six provinces, including Québec, in October 1992. The inability to reach agreement on a constitutional deal presumably influenced the ominous referendum results of October 1995, in which Québécers rejected separation from Canada by a margin of less than 1%. Lucien Bouchard galvanized the separatist forces during that referendum, and in 1998 he was reelected Premier of Québec as head of the Parti Québécois.

The Canada-United States Free Trade Agreement of 1988 led to a further agreement including Mexico in 1993, known as the North American Free Trade Agreement or NAFTA. Both of these agreements extended the liberalization of trade which had been underway for most of the postwar period. As a result, governments, including Canada's, must contend with transnational corporations which have no particular or permanent home base or domestic market. Since modern technology allows them to deploy their resources wherever the bottom line can be maximized, much mass production, labour-intensive work is shifting to low wage areas of the world. Governments feel pressured to accommodate business interests to avoid losing them to other jurisdictions.

> National governments find themselves constrained by global economic forces.

On the political front, the 1990s ended with the Liberal party enjoying its second successive majority government, and contemplating the likelihood of a third. The confident Conservative party which began the decade in power was all but obliterated in the 1993 federal election, emerging with only two seats. It ended the decade with only 19 seats, but has rejected overtures to merge with the upstart Reform party to form a United Alternative which might combine the forces on the right to defeat the Liberals. What makes the task especially difficult is that the Liberals themselves have moved considerably to the right and arguably have done little more than implement the policies of Brian Mulroney (more effectively) since gaining power. As discussed in Chapter 3, even the New Democratic party (NDP), at its national policy conference in August 1999, moved toward the centre with respect to a number of its economic policies.

What Role Should Government Play?

Canadians are at a crossroads as they enter a new century because they face some very fundamental choices about the roles of our governments and the relationships they should have with one another and with the Canadian people. Those roles, and our perception of them, have fluctuated over time.

Historically, we were largely self-reliant. Problems were solved through individual effort and/or support from families and neighbours. For example, "welfare," such as it was, was essentially a form of local charity largely provided by the church. Individual landowners maintained the portion of road across the front of their properties. With the shift from a rural and agricultural society to an urban and industrialized one, individual and community self-sufficiency declined and the role of government increased. The extended family living off the land was replaced by the individual working in a factory and living alone in a city apartment. In response to the new economic uncertainties, the "positive state" developed, with governments establishing minimum standards to protect the public and enforcing numerous rules and regulations. By the mid-20th century, government accepted responsibility for managing the economy and promoting full employment, stable prices and economic growth. As a variety of social programs were introduced, the positive state became the welfare state.

Ironically, as government moved in, much of the remaining volunteer and community self-help activity died away. When problems arose, the attitude became "why doesn't the government do something about it." The more government did for us, the less people seemed able (or willing?) to look after themselves. They took less and less self-responsibility and relied more and more on government—even as they complained about the size of government and the burden of taxation.

In recent decades, however, the feeling developed that governments had grown too large, became too intrusive, encouraged too much dependency, got into too much debt, and had no choice but to scale back dramatically. Underlying this view was a belief, held by many, that governments were wasteful—perhaps inherently—and were involved in too many activities which could better be left to the private sector.

So pervasive was this point of view that it appeared to cut across the political spectrum. As previously noted, the federal Liberals embraced government downsizing and cutbacks with greater fervour than the Conservative Party they replaced. Provincially, this agenda was not only embraced by Conservative governments in Alberta and Ontario, but also by the New Brunswick Liberal government of Frank McKenna and the Saskatchewan NDP government of Roy Romanow. The summer of 1999 saw the reelection of the Conservatives in Ontario and the return to power of Conservative parties in Nova Scotia and New Brunswick.

Yet there is a profound inconsistency in the public's view of government and its role. People are against "big government," but they are very much in favour of many of the programs provided by government. They accept the argument that programs must be cut to eliminate deficits and, perhaps, to reduce taxes. But they consistently rank maintenance of Canada's publicly funded health care system as a number one priority. They also express concern about the erosion of government support for other social programs such as education and public housing. They worry about environmental pollution and about security from crime in their homes and neighbourhoods. In short, Canadians simultaneously want governments to do less as a general principle but they want it to do more, or at least as much, in terms of specific programs and services.

> Canadians want government to do less, in principle, but more, in specific programs.

What Are Your Concerns?
(Rank the items below, with 1 being the most important)

____	Health care
____	Dealing with unemployment
____	National unity
____	The economy
____	Education
____	Government debt
____	Poverty
____	Tax reform (tax cuts)

Surprise! These choices are listed exactly as they were ranked by Canadians in a January 1999 poll by Angus Reid. It is interesting that tax cuts ranked last in spite of the incessant demand by some politicians and business groups that they must come first. Of course, everyone would like to have a tax break, but apparently not if it has to be financed by further cuts to other programs they value, more debt, or increased poverty.

A Question of Priorities

Canada is a wealthy nation, with ample resources to address the needs of its citizens. One of the key issues with which we have been struggling, one of those crossroads we currently face, is the basis on which these resources will be allocated. How much will they be converted into public goods, financed by tax dollars, and available to the public at large, and how much will they remain as private goods, offered in the market place, and only available to those who can afford the price?

> Ironically, we must have adequate public goods to enjoy our private goods.

One of the greatest ironies about the current cutback mentality is that unless sufficient resources are allocated for the provision of public goods, our enjoyment of private goods can be seriously curtailed. With taxes kept sufficiently low, people can afford increasingly fancy automobiles, even if the streets and highways on which these cars must travel are not well maintained. Children have ready access to television and various forms of entertainment, even if their schools are deteriorating and plagued by violence. People have no shortage of food, alcohol, cigarettes, and other "creature comforts," but lack adequate medical and hospital care when health problems arise from the excesses of consumption. The signs of this dichotomy are increasingly prevalent today, but the book which raised this issue of public-private imbalance is more than 40 years old! It is *The Affluent Society*, by Canadian John Kenneth Galbraith, published in 1958.

Another perceptive analyst of government, Jim Sharpe of Oxford University, provides a vivid illustration of the value of public versus private goods in the local government context when he writes that:

> ... although the local government bill is not small, it provides education, public health, social services, highways, libraries, fire, police, refuse collection, and a whole range of other public services which most people need and demand, at a total cost that is no larger than the amount we collectively spend on such things as wine and beer, cigarettes, eye shadow, tennis rackets and a flutter on the horses.[1]

According to various published reports, some $6 billion has been spent on products related to the Pokémon craze during the last three years of the 20th century, much of it in North America. Yet we continue to debate whether or not we can afford welfare, public housing, public health, environmental programs and other services which form part of a basic standard of living in a civilized society. Obviously, we can afford public services if we believe in them and are prepared to support them with our taxes. What does the following list say about our priorities?[2]

Things We Can Afford	Things We Can't Afford
private health care	universal health care
hockey salaries in the millions	pay equity
private drug testing	public drug testing
lawsuits without number	free legal aid
RRSPs	Canada pension plan
toll roads	funding a national road system
hundreds of new car models	public transit
expense account lunches	school lunches
corporate subsidies	welfare programs
private schools	public schools
product research	scientific research
million dollar condos	public housing
$3 billion on Bre-X shares	securities watchdogs

[1]L. J. Sharpe (ed.), *The Local Fiscal Crisis in Western Europe, Myths and Realities*, London, Sage Publications, 1981, p. 224.

[2]Walter Stewart, *Dismantling the State*, Toronto, Stoddart, 1998, pp. 286-87.

> Many services that we supposedly can't afford from government, we buy from the private sector.

What this list reveals is that many of the services and programs that we supposedly can't afford from government, we are instead buying from the private sector. There are now more than twice as many private police as public one. For every apparent deficiency in the public sector, a private, profit-making alternative is offered. Those concerned about public safety can live in gated communities. If public schools are lacking, send your children to private school. Instead of waiting for tests or surgery from Canada's public health system, jump the queue and get attention today, at a private health clinic.

The wealthy in society can afford to access these private sector substitutes, and the more they do, the more they resist paying the level of taxation needed to provide these same services through the public sector. Without these tax dollars, however, public social programs continue to erode. Somehow a balance must be struck in the resources allocated to the public and the private sectors. This can be achieved only through sufficient intervention by government; it will never happen on its own as a result of the interplay of market forces. As Stewart argues, "we must have a government active enough and muscular enough to right the imbalances created by our marvellously efficient, monumentally unfair economic system."[3]

Who Wields Power, For Whom?

Ultimately, the issue comes down to the exercise of power, by whom and for whom. In oversimplified terms, we are facing a struggle between the political and economic spheres over the exercise of power.

Governments exist to make collective decisions for a country, including decisions about the provision of public goods. Only government is sanctioned to enforce its decisions, even through the use of force if necessary. In many countries, including Canada, the institutions

[3] *Ibid.*, p. 16.

and responsibilities of government are set forth in a constitution. The way that a government exercises its power is evaluated through periodic elections, thus providing a legitimacy for government actions.

Throughout much of the 20th century, political power was exercised in ways that constrained or limited economic power. As the scope of government activity expanded, more of society's resources were consumed for public goods rather than being left for private consumption. In addition, big government was usually synonymous with intervention and regulation of the economy—as a result of the pervasive influence of Keynesian theories.[4] As discussed in Chapter 10, there were also a number of international arrangements and institutions put into place at the end of World War II which exercised some control over the movement of capital and international economic activity.

The situation has rapidly reversed over the past quarter century, and governments now play a more limited role and one increasingly constrained by economic forces. This new reality is reflected within Canada in the abandonment of Keynesian economics, a downsized federal government which is less of a force in fiscal policies, a push for deregulation, and the promotion of privatization of public services. But it is at the international level where the shift in power is most dramatic. While governments still exercise political power, they have become convinced that they must do so in ways that reassure international currency speculators or that satisfy the needs of large corporations. The significance of the latter is evident from the fact that 51 of the 100 biggest economies in the world are now corporations. Walmart, the 12th largest corporation, is bigger than 161 of the world's 191 countries.[5]

Moreover, the international arrangements which have been introduced in recent years are devoted to facilitating free trade and impose restrictions on government actions which are seen as impeding this objective. Chapter 10 discusses the Canada-U.S. and North American Free Trade Agreements and the World Trade Organization set up in

---

[4]According to the writings of British economist John Maynard Keynes, governments could (and should) take a variety of actions to manage the economy.

[5]Sarah Anderson and John Cavanagh, "The Top 200: the Rise of Global Corporate Power," Washington, Institute for Policy Studies, as cited in the *CPPA Monitor*, Canadian Centre for Policy Alternatives, February 1997, p. 12.

1995, and provides examples of the ways in which they constrain the operations of Canada's governments. Clarkson and Lewis go so far as to characterize the various new trade agreements as "an external constitution that establishes new limits on the permissible actions of Canadian governments."[6]

What Is Your Role?

Canada is a democracy, a country in which government institutions supposedly exist to respond to public views and concerns. Yet government actions seem to be responding more to the needs of the marketplace and the dictates of international capital. This Guide will discuss a variety of ways for citizens to make their views and concerns known. Are you an active participant in your government system? Can you answer yes to all of the following questions?:

Measuring Your Participation

1. Do you vote regularly in federal, provincial and municipal elections?
2. Do you attend council meetings in your municipality?
3. Have you written to your MP or MLA or phoned your councillor?
4. Have you watched council meetings or Question Period on television?
5. Have you signed petitions on public issues?
6. Have you ever campaigned on behalf of a candidate for public office?
7. Have you ever run for office yourself?
8. Have you joined any organized groups as a way of trying to influence government actions?
9. Have you ever marched or joined in a demonstration about government actions or inaction?
10. Do you keep yourself informed on the activities of government?

---

[6]Stephen Clarkson and Timothy Lewis, "The Contested State," in Leslie Pal (ed.), *How Ottawa Spends 1999-2000*, Toronto, Oxford University Press, 1999, p. 315.

If you had to answer no to a number of these questions, you are unfortunately not alone. There appears to be a great deal of public disillusionment and cynicism about governmental matters—a perception that politicians don't listen and that our concerns won't be addressed. The percentage of people who think that "MPs lose touch" with voters and that "government doesn't care" about their opinions has steadily increased since at least the mid-1960s.[7] It is significant, however, that even though Canadians have doubts about their government, they do not see such alternatives as the marketplace, the family, or the volunteer sector as an adequate replacement. "[G]overnments are still identified as the prime agent for achieving societal goals."[8] When asked how to redress the balance of power, Canadians don't call for a reduction in government power. Rather, they want the power of big business and the media reduced and the power of small business and the average citizen strengthened. They believe the economy is important—but not viewed narrowly in terms of dollars and markets; they want "the economy harnessed for the well-being of average citizens...."[9]

After two decades of neoconservatism which attempted to diminish greatly the role and significance of government in our lives, there are signs that Canadians are receptive to a more active role for government —

> Canadians may be ready to support a more active role for government again, under certain conditions.

albeit under considerably changed conditions. The deficit and debt appear to be less of a threat, but there are growing concerns about the social costs of deficit reduction and of globalization, and fears of a loss of Canadian identity and autonomy. These feelings have prompted support for an increased role for government generally and the federal

---

[7]William Mishler and Harold D. Clarke, "Political Participation in Canada," in Michael S. Whittington and Glen Williams (eds.), *Canadian Politics in the 1990s*, 4th Edition, Toronto, Nelson, 1995, p. 145.

[8]The following discussion is largely based on Frank Graves, "Rethinking Government," in Leslie A. Pal (ed.), *How Ottawa Spends 1999-2000*, Toronto, Oxford University Press, 1999, which draws upon public attitudes measured by Ekos Research Associates.

[9]*Ibid.*, p. 47.

government in particular.[10] But it is support for a new style of government and governance that emphasizes fiscal discipline, sets measurable targets and is held accountable for their achievement, and promotes partnerships with other players rather than building traditional bureaucratic empires. Canadians are not in favour of a return to big, free-spending governments, but they also do not believe that problems such as child poverty and the growing gap between rich and poor can be solved by tax cuts and a minimal role for government.

The Case for Government

There is no doubt that many aspects of our government system could be improved. Among those aspects to be examined in this Guide are:

- how well do members of parliament represent the interests of their constituents?
- who finances the high cost of election campaigns?
- how effectively does parliament act as a "watchdog" in holding the government accountable for its actions?
- can the Senate's continued existence be justified?
- does the Monarchy play any role in our government system today?

There is nothing wrong with being critical of government when it does not appear to function effectively. It is also appropriate to question government priorities when they appear misguided or misdirected or insensitive to public views and concerns. This Guide will not hesitate to offer suggestions for improving both the governing machinery and its policy output. But whatever their shortcomings, we need our governments. They are the vehicle we use to decide how our scarce resources will be allocated among the wants and needs we have as a society. These decisions are never easy because our wants and needs are always greater than the resources available to fill them. Governments manage the conflict inherent in this situation, they provide a wide range of public goods available to the entire population, and they redistribute wealth in an attempt to ensure a minimum standard of living for all. Without the

---

[10]*Ibid.*, p. 54.

civilizing influence provided by government, we would be reduced to "the law of the jungle" and "the survival of the fittest."

The bias of this Guide is in favour of a continuing significant role for government. The current push for governments to be lean can all too easily result in a society which is

> This Guide favours a continuing significant role for government.

mean. It is all very well for politicians to talk about encouraging individual self-reliance and independence, but this can simply be a code word for abandoning individuals to their own devices. There has been a growing sense of insecurity among Canadians, not only because of the eroding social safety net but because so many jobs now are contract or temporary work, and because the prospect of downsizing frequently looms in the background.

It is fine for government to pursue greater efficiency, to talk about operating in a more business-like fashion. But constant reference to "business plans" and determining "what kind of business you are in," doesn't change the fact that government is *not* business. It exists to serve fundamentally different purposes. In many cases, it provides the kinds of services and programs that business does not provide and would not provide—because they are not profitable. Government's role is to serve the public interest, elusive as that may be; whereas business, especially big business, seems increasingly concerned only with maximizing profits for current shareholders. Even though they often say it, it is doubtful that most people would really want government to act just like a business—"making quick decisions behind closed doors for private profit."[11]

Too often, people turn against government because they hear of Senator absenteeism, MP grandstanding during Commons question period, or civil service "junkets" to high-priced conferences. What must be realized is that government consists of much more than these activities—to the extent that they happen at all. Governments are also the organizations that provide or financially support hospitals and

---

[11]David Osborne and Ted Gaebler, *Reinventing Government*, New York, Penguin Books, 1993, p. 22.

universities, provide policing and fire protection, maintain highways and public transit systems, protect the environment, and provide many other public services which Canadians need and want. Rather than calling for a reduced role for government, as is currently the fashion, this Guide takes the position that we need our governments to play a larger role, not necessarily in terms of their expenditure levels, but in promoting domestic policies which protect the interests of Canadians within the global economy.

Concluding Observations

Much of the material in subsequent chapters will focus on the basic government machinery in Canada, at all levels, and how it operates, as well as on the relationships among those levels of government. A familiarity with these matters is a prerequisite to informed participation by Canadians in their government system. But participation within the existing system may be of limited benefit. As this introductory chapter has attempted to convey, the ability of national governments to pursue policies and programs desired by their citizens has been increasingly constrained by international economic and financial influences. It is important, therefore, that this Guide examine not only the governments we have, but also the priorities they have been pursuing—as will be done in two chapters on economic and social policy. In the same vein, any suggestions about improving the health of Canadian democracy must extend beyond participation within our governing system to the kinds of actions which are needed at the international level if national governments and their citizens are to remain masters of their destiny.

Appendix A on the following page provides a very brief summary of some of the historic highlights of Canada's political and economic life. It may serve as a useful point of reference, especially for those without much prior background in government, and may be worth reviewing when you get to later chapters dealing with the economy and intergovernmental relations.

Appendix A

Historical Highlights

1867 ←→ **2000**

Political:

1867		1919–1957	1957–1963	1963–84	1984	1993–?
Conservatives rule most of 19th century, led by Sir John A.	Laurier's Liberals from 1896 to 1911; defeat on free trade	From 1919–1957, mostly Liberal King/St. Laurent	PCs under Diefenbaker	Pearson Trudeau	Mulroney	Chretien

Intergovernmental:

1867		1919–1957	1963–84	1984 – 2000
Federal government dominant in early years	Before end of 19th century, provinces demanding more say	Centralization during Depression and war years	Provincial and local levels more important with urbanization	Federal role reduced with decentralizing, downloading, and cuts in grant payments

Economic:

1867	1919–1957	1963–84	1984
Government role limited to enterprises such as railways	Economic management based on Keynes after WWII	By 1970s Keynes being abandoned for monetarism	Inflation and deficit reduction focus of '80s and '90s

Trade and International:

1867		1919–1957	1984	2000
National Policy of 1879, including higher tariffs	Economic ties shifting from Britain to U.S.	Trade barriers worsen conditions in Depression; IMF and World Bank set up in 1944	Freer trade negotiated under GATT	Free trade deal with U.S. and Mexico

The Last Word

Definition of Terms and Concepts

This chapter introduced some terms or concepts which may not be all that familiar to the reader. Examples might be Keynesian economics or patriation of the constitution. No definitions are provided herein, because the ideas introduced in this chapter are developed more fully in subsequent chapters and the terms and concepts can be better explained in the broader context found in these later chapters. Definitions will be found in this section at the end of each subsequent chapter.

Points to Ponder

1. When you hear the word "government," is your first reaction negative and critical? Has this chapter caused you to change your view of government at all?

2. What do you think of Galbraith's argument that insufficient public goods can prevent us from enjoying our private goods, however plentiful and pleasant the latter may be?

3. How did you score on the public participation questions? In what areas is your participation most lacking?

For Further Reading

In addition to footnote references, limited in this chapter, each subsequent chapter will include suggestions for additional readings and, where appropriate, web sites related to the topics covered.

Chapter 2

What Are Our Many Governments and What Do They Do?

Objectives and Highlights

◆ To introduce the structure and operation of government at all levels.

◆ To illustrate the varied and valuable services provided by government.

◆ To develop your personal government directory.

While there are many possible causes of the widespread public disillusionment with government, it seems clear that two reasons are that: **(1)** citizens aren't sure which level of government is responsible for what, and **(2)** even if they find the right level of government, they don't know whom to hold accountable or where to pursue their concern. They do, however, often feel that they are over-governed, a sentiment that may arise from the fact that most Canadians are under the jurisdiction of at least three levels of government, and often four. These are:

1. The Government of Canada, usually referred to as the federal government.

2. A provincial or territorial government, such as the Government of Manitoba or the Government of the Northwest Territories.

3. A municipal government, such as a village, town, city or township. [In addition, there may be an "upper tier" municipal government, such as a county, regional or district government, found mainly in Ontario, Québec and British Columbia.]

A good starting point is a list of names and phone numbers, such as the one you can compile using the *Guide to Government Directory* provided at the end of this chapter. Once completed, it will provide you with a

17

convenient checklist of contacts for your future interaction with government.

Also in this chapter is a whimsical description of *A Day in the Life* of college student Frank N. Earnest, whose adventures serve to illustrate many of the important services and programs provided by the various levels of government in Canada.

We begin with a brief overview of the general structure of government found at the federal, provincial and local levels in Canada.

Introduction

Knowing which level of government looks after what is quite a challenge—especially when so many responsibilities are shared among two or more levels. Later chapters will shed more light on who does what, why responsibilities have become so intertwined, and what the implications are of efforts to disentangle responsibilities in recent years. This is the first of several chapters (see also Chapters 5 and 6) examining the organization and functioning of government at all levels.

The Federal Government

It is customary to discuss the organization of the federal (and provincial) government in terms of two separate branches, executive and legislative, and how they are interrelated—as depicted in Chart 1 on the next page. Most texts also identify a third branch, the judiciary or court system, about which more will be said in Chapter 7 of this Guide.

For most Canadians, their main personal interaction with the federal government occurs approximately every four years[1] when they have an opportunity to elect from their riding one member of parliament (MP) to the **House of Commons**.

---

[1]The maximum term for a parliament is five years (except for a possible extension during an extreme emergency such as wartime), but the party in power usually calls an election toward the end of the fourth year. The timing depends on the party's assessment of when it is most likely to get re-elected.

Chart 1

Government of Canada

Executive Branch   **Legislative Branch**

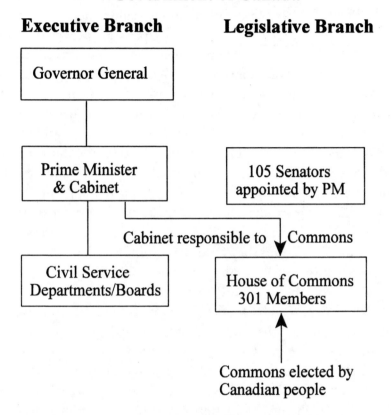

The Commons consists of 301 members elected from 301 geographic areas (ridings) into which Canada is divided. These members are chosen to represent and make decisions on behalf of the Canadian population. This arrangement for **representative government** is found in virtually every democratic governing structure. As will be seen, it is present in the election of legislative assemblies at the provincial level and of councils at the municipal level. It is also found in the election of student unions or student councils in colleges and universities.

Besides its representative role, the House of Commons has two other key roles: **(1)** to pass laws, in the form of acts or statutes, for the governing of Canada, and **(2)** to act as a "watchdog" keeping an eye on

> The three main roles of the House of Commons are representative, legislative and watchdog.

the Cabinet and the civil service. The watchdog role is mainly carried out by the opposition parties in the Commons, since members of the governing party are expected to support their Cabinet, not to criticize it.

While the House of Commons receives most of the media and public attention, Canada's Parliament has two Houses. In this **bicameral legislature**, the **Senate** is the upper chamber. It shares the law-making role of the Commons and must also give its approval before a bill can become a law. In addition, it plays a kind of watchdog role by giving "sober second thought" to actions taken by the Commons. This mature reflection was supposed to come from the appointment of leading Canadians from all walks of life, who would bring experience and sound judgment to the task. To be appointed, Senators must be at least 30 years of age, and they hold office until age 75. However, an appointed Senate gradually lost legitimacy as notions of democracy and accountability took hold in the 20th century.

Turning to the executive branch, the **Governor General** represents the Queen in Canada, reflecting the fact that Canada is a constitutional monarchy. The Governor General is appointed by the Queen (but on the advice of the Canadian Prime Minister), to act on her behalf when she is not in Canada. The Queen is the Head of State, whereas the Prime Minister is the head of government. These governing arrangements distinguish Canada from a republic like the United States, in which there isn't a separate Head of State different from the President.

The Governor General has many official duties, in Canada and abroad. A number of the duties are automatic and simply carry out the "advice" given by the Prime Minister. This is true, for example, of the appointment of Cabinet ministers. Many of the duties are social and ceremonial in nature and could presumably be carried out by the Prime Minister, as they are by the President or other Head of State in countries which are republics. But the Prime Minister is a partisan, political figure, less suited to representing the country as a whole and is sufficiently burdened with other duties. For these reasons, there is much to be said for having a separate Head of State. Moreover, there are a limited number of discretionary powers vested in the Governor General/Queen which are rarely required but can be important in the operation of our system of government. These discretionary duties are explored in Chapter 5, but they help to make the position of Governor General more valuable and relevant than is commonly appreciated. That later chapter will also consider the merits of recent suggestions that the monarchy should be abolished in Canada.

The key members of the executive branch are the **Prime Minister** and **Cabinet**. While the government of Canada consists of the various elements of governing machinery outlined in the preceding chart, when people refer to "The Government," they are usually thinking of the Prime Minister and Cabinet, which highlights the central position they hold. The main responsibilities of the Cabinet include: **(1)** developing policies to deal with the issues facing the country, **(2)** introducing bills to carry through these policies into law, and **(3)** supervising the civil servants who apply these policies and administer the laws on a day-to-day basis.

Given the central importance of the Prime Minister and Cabinet, it is perhaps surprising that they are not directly elected by the Canadian people—although it can be said that they are indirectly chosen. This is true in the sense that by voting for the candidate of a particular party, we are helping to elect members of that party to the Commons. Normally, the party which elects the most members is deemed to have won the election. The leader of that party will become the Prime Minister of Canada and a number of other victorious candidates from that party will be chosen by the Prime Minister to serve as ministers in the federal Cabinet and to share in running the government.

The principle of **responsible government** holds that the Cabinet is responsible to the House of Commons (from which its members come) and can only stay in office so long as it is supported by a majority

> The Cabinet readily finds the support it needs when a majority of the Commons belongs to the same party.

of the members of the Commons. However, when a majority of the members of the Commons belong to the same party as the members of the Cabinet, as is usually the case, this principle ceases to have much practical value. In such a situation, the governing party can almost always count on sufficient support in the assembly when required, and will continue to govern until the Prime Minister decides that the time is right to call an election—sometime before the maximum term of five years draws near to completion.

The actual day-to-day work of the government of Canada is carried out by full time employees who are known as the **civil service** or public service. The majority of these employees work for government departments (like Agriculture, Fisheries, Environment, Health and Welfare, Revenue, and Transport), and each department is headed by a minister of the Cabinet. Through this structure, the appointed civil servants are answerable to the Canadian people through elected politicians in the Cabinet. Through the long-standing principle of **ministerial responsibility**, ministers are held accountable for the performance of the civil servants within their departments.

Cabinet

M   M   M   M

▲   ▲   ▲   ▲

The Provincial and Territorial Governments

Canada is a **federation**. A federation is a system in which the functions of government are divided between two or more levels: a national government and provinces or states. In Canada's case, the federation is made up of one national government, ten provincial governments and three territorial governments—the Yukon, the Northwest Territories, and the recently created territory of Nunavut, which came into existence on April 1, 1999. The latter's small population of 25 000, 85% of whom are Inuit, are scattered across a vast area of the Eastern Arctic, an area roughly twice as large as Ontario.

The Government of the Provinces

If you understood the structure of the government of Canada, the governing arrangements at the provincial level are much the same, as is evident from the chart which follows.

Chart 2

Government of a Province

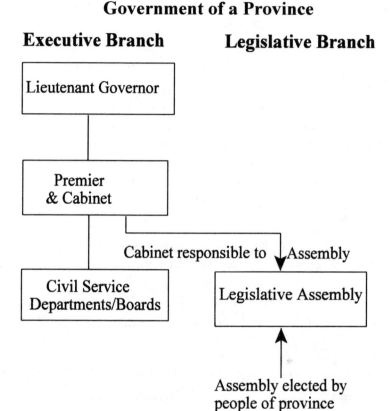

Executive Branch   **Legislative Branch**

Lieutenant Governor

Premier & Cabinet

Cabinet responsible to ↓Assembly

Civil Service Departments/Boards

Legislative Assembly

↑

Assembly elected by people of province

The public's main participation is again through the election of a representative body, in this case called the **Legislative Assembly** (or National Assembly in the case of Québec). The number of members varies by province and ranges from a high in Quebec of 125 members to only 32 in Prince Edward Island. All provincial legislatures are **unicameral**; there aren't any upper chambers like the Senate found at the national level. The Legislative Assembly has the same responsibilities as the House of Commons: to represent the people, to pass laws, and to act as a watchdog.

The party winning the most seats in the Assembly makes up "The Government," consisting of the **Premier** and Cabinet. The Cabinet is responsible to the Assembly and must have the support of its members; but here again, party loyalty usually ensures that support. The Cabinet has the same key roles as its federal counterpart: to develop policies, introduce laws, and supervise the administration of those laws.

The day-to-day running of the government is again carried out by civil servants, mostly organized in departments headed by Ministers who sit in the Cabinet.

The **Lieutenant Governor** is the official head of the provincial government (representing the Queen). He or she is appointed by the Queen on the advice of the federal government, which really means appointment by the Prime Minister. The roles of the Governor General also apply to the Lieutenant Governor. In addition, one of the traditional roles of the office was to act as an agent of the federal level in "keeping an eye on" provincial actions which might be contrary to the national interest. Given the strength of provincial governments today, however, any intervention of this sort by a Lieutenant Governor would not be tolerated.

Overall, the government of a province operates on the same principles of representative and responsible government, and has much the same governing machinery—except that:

- it has a Legislative Assembly instead of the House of Commons.

- it doesn't have any second chamber like the Senate.

- it has a Lieutenant Governor instead of a Governor General.

In all provinces but Ontario and Québec, the members of the legislative assemblies are known as MLAs. Ontario members are officially known as MPPs, even though there is only one Parliament in Canada. Québec members are known as MNAs, or members of the National Assembly. Québec refers to its legislative assembly in this manner to reflect the independent, nation-like status it has attempted to project. But in spite of the change in name, the Québec assembly operates under exactly the same principles of representative and responsible government.

Government of the Territories

Another significant difference from the federal governing arrangements is evident with respect to the government of the Northwest Territories (and now Nunavut as well), and reflects the influence of their large aboriginal populations. Before the division of the northern territories, aboriginals made up 60% of the population, as compared to only 25% in the Yukon.[2] Governing traditions among aboriginals rest on the achievement of consensus. As a result, while the NWT government observes the principles of representative and responsible government, it operates quite differently. A 24 member Legislative Assembly (now reduced to 14) is elected. The Premier and Cabinet are responsible to the Assembly and only govern with its support. But there aren't any political parties—yet. The NDP ran six candidates in the December 1999 election, but they received very little support. After each election all MLAs choose, by secret ballot, which of them will serve as Premier and as Ministers. The result is a great deal more discussion of issues among all members and a much less divisive, confrontational style of decision making. While this may sound appealing to Canadians tired of the constant bickering among political parties, these arrangements also mean that it is very difficult for voters to pass judgment on a government's performance. The absence of parties also means the lack of a clear focus of accountability.

Aboriginals are even more dominant in the new territory of Nunavut, with Inuit making up 85% of is population, and it has the same nonpartisan arrangements for its new 19 member assembly.

Municipal Governments

By comparison to the federal and provincial levels, the organization of government at the municipal level is simpler. There aren't two separate

---

[2]According to Graham White, "Canada's Most Distinctive Region: The Northwest Territories," in Paul Fox and Graham White (eds.), *Politics: Canada*, 8th Edition, Whitby, McGraw-Hill Ryerson Limited, 1995, pp. 182-190, on which this section is based.

branches, executive and legislative. Nor is there any separate governing group like a Cabinet. Instead, all governing responsibilities are centred on one body—the elected **municipal council**.

The size of the council varies depending on the type of municipality. Small and rural municipalities such as Ontario's villages and townships have only five members. Alberta villages may be governed by as few as three members and the councils of its municipal districts (rural municipalities) normally have between four and nine members.[3] On the other hand, large cities and county and regional municipalities may have 20 members or more. The head of the council is variously known as the mayor, reeve, warden or chair and is either directly elected (in most instances) or chosen by the members of the council.

> There aren't separate executive and legislative branches at the local level.

The council combines both executive and legislative responsibilities. It proposes policies, passes laws (by-laws), appoints staff and supervises their work as well. In other words, it carries out within one body the work that is divided between separate executive and legislative branches at the provincial and federal levels.

In smaller municipalities, members of council are usually elected **at large** or by **general vote**. Under this method, they run for office across the whole municipality and voters have an opportunity to choose from among all candidates in selecting their preferences. In larger municipalities, the head of council is still elected at large, but it is common for councillors to be chosen on a **ward** basis. This means that the municipality is divided into a number of separate geographic areas or wards, with one or more councillors elected from each ward. This arrangement is not unlike the process we use in electing members to the provincial legislature or House of Commons from separate ridings.

Whether by general vote or by ward, however, councillors are normally elected as independents. Organized parties are not much in evidence at the municipal level in Canada, even though they are com-

---

[3] Jack Masson with Edward Lesage Jr., *Alberta's Local Governments, Politics and Democracy*, 2nd Edition, Edmonton, University of Alberta Press, 1994, pp. 90 and 106.

mon in the United States and Britain. The main exceptions are some of the larger Québec municipalities. 1999 saw the death of the colourful Jean Drapeau, whose Civic Party controlled a majority of seats on Montreal's council for almost three decades until he retired in 1986.

Without parties, there is no governing group within a municipal council; nor any official opposition or "watchdog" for that matter. Unlike the Prime Minister or Premier, a big city mayor has no bloc of party votes to call upon in support of measures to be passed. Canadian municipalities are governed by what is often termed a "weak-mayor system," in which the head of council has to rely upon his or her persuasive powers to try to mobilize support for actions to be taken. Even so, many mayors have played a strong leadership role. Examples include David Crombie in Toronto, Stephen Juba in Winnipeg, Allan O'Brien in Halifax, and Hazel McCallion in Mississauga.

One of the most colourful mayors in Canadian history has to be Charlotte Whitton, who became the first woman mayor of a major Canadian city with her election in Ottawa in 1951. She held that position until 1956, and then again from 1960 to 1964. Her antics were legendary and well documented, including the time she threatened the Board of Control (Ottawa's executive committee) with a gun—only a cap pistol as it turned out. Typical of her irreverence was the following exchange with the Lord Mayor of London.[4] It was a formal occasion, with the Lord Mayor resplendent in his robes and chains of office and Charlotte wearing a fine gown and a corsage.

Lord Mayor: *"If I smell your flower, will you blush?"*
Charlotte: *"If I pull your chain, will you flush?"*

The day-to-day running of government is handled by staff, the municipal civil service, organized into departments which reflect the responsibilities being exercised by the municipality.

The basic governing structure of a municipality, therefore, consists of just two components—the elected council and the municipal staff. There are many variations on this basic governing structure, of course,

---

[4]This anecdote has long made the rounds and is repeated in Allan Levine (ed.), *Your Worship* (The Lives of Eight of Canada's Most Unforgettable Mayors), Toronto, James Lorimer and Company, 1989, p. 132.

especially in larger municipalities. Two of the most common variations are: **(1)** to establish a number of standing committees of council, to assist the council in discharging its responsibilities; and **(2)** to establish a chief administrative officer (CAO) to act as the senior coordinating officer for all staff matters. A standing committee system is depicted in the chart below.

Chart 3
Government of a Municipality

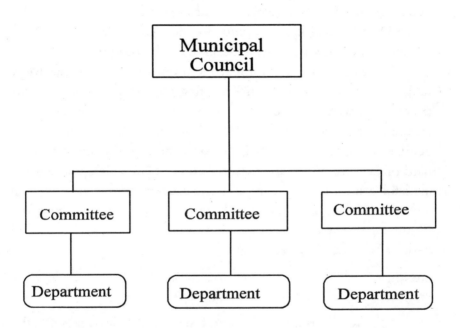

While the structure of government in any one municipality is relatively simple, the overall system of municipal government is far from being so. There is only one federal government in Canada, along with ten provincial governments and three territorial governments. In contrast, there are over 4000 municipalities in Canada, although their numbers have been sharply reduced in recent years because of extensive municipal amalgamations promoted by several provincial governments.

Ontario has been the most aggressive in this regard, with the result that very soon the number of municipalities in that province will be fewer than the 539 which it had at the time of Confederation.

Municipalities are classified into a number of different categories: cities, towns, villages, rural municipalities (also termed townships, parishes, and rural districts), counties, and regional, district and metropolitan municipalities. In addition, there are thousands of agencies, boards and commissions which also form part of local government in Canada. These bodies include boards of education, health units or agencies, electricity and utility commissions, conservation authorities, police commissions, parks boards, and library boards. Most of these bodies are appointed, not elected, they provide a number of important services that are (or ought to be) closely coordinated with municipal services, and they claim a substantial portion of the revenues raised by the municipalities within their jurisdiction. The latter feature is especially true of school boards, whose expenditures may claim a greater proportion of the property tax yield of its member municipalities than expenditures on municipal services.

The net result of all these local governing bodies is a local government system characterized by considerable fragmentation and potential confusion, even if the governing arrangements for any one municipality may be relatively simple and straightforward.

Summary: You and Your Governments

So where do you fit into the picture, after this admittedly very brief introduction to the levels of government in Canada?

You and your fellow Canadians decide who will make up these various levels of government through exercising your voting rights. You get to choose the head of your municipal council and all the council members, or at least the members representing your area if there is a ward system of election. You also elect one member of the legislative assembly in your province or territory, from the particular riding or constituency in which you reside, and you similarly elect one member of the House of Commons.

Understanding Who Does What

There is no simple way of describing the division of responsibilities among the various levels of government in Canada—especially since many responsibilities are actually shared by two or more levels. Perhaps the simplest approach is to describe a day in the life of a mythical college student in the Township of Bountiful. The story which follows is rather fanciful, but it does serve to illustrate the relevance of government in our lives, something which we too often take for granted or fail to appreciate.

A Day in the Life

Scene 1: A Morning Eye-Opener

The day does not begin well. Our student, Frank N. Earnest, is attempting his morning shave, still rubbing the sleep from his eyes. Suddenly, to his mounting horror, the following things happen:

- the water stops running in the sink, and the lights go out.
- when he goes to the living room window to see if there has been a power failure in the neighbourhood, he discovers that the road in front of his house has disappeared.
- squinting in the early morning light, he realizes that the park across the street has vanished, as has the school down the street.
- he races to the phone to call the police—but there is no answer. He gets the same result when he tries to call the fire department.
- Frank wakes up in a cold sweat. A dream. It was only a dream. No more anchovies on his bedtime pizza, he resolves.

Frank's wild dream isn't that far-fetched. What it describes is nothing more than the disappearance of a number of the basic services provided by local government. This contrived scenario is just a way of illustrating how important those services are to us in our everyday lives. While most of these services are financed with assistance from the senior levels of government (mainly the provinces), they are provided by municipalities and local boards (such as the school board).

Scene 2: Just a Few Errands

After recovering from this morning adventure, Frank goes about his daily activities.

- Still not finished with local governments, he visits the branch library in his neighbourhood to return *Local Government in Canada*, a riveting story which he had finished late last night.
- Back in his car, Frank heads toward the adjacent city of Plentiful. Without even noticing, he leaves a township road and drives for several miles on a county road and then a provincial highway. From there, he goes on to Highway 401 (a federal-provincial highway) and travels the last few miles to the city.
- Frank's next stop is to get a new sticker for his licence plate. He goes to the Ontario Government building in Plentiful and pauses in the lobby to get his bearings. Looking down the list of offices on the wall by the bank of elevators, he notices:[5]

  ❑ The Assessment Division of the *Ministry of Finance*, where his parents had gone recently to appeal the assessed value of their home. (They had first blamed the municipality, before learning that it was the Province which assessed properties.)
  ❑ The *Ministry of Colleges & Universities*, with which he is familiar from his years as a student.
  ❑ The *Ministry of Community and Social Services*—an office Frank had seen more than he wanted to during a long period of unemployment before he had decided to increase his job prospects by taking a college diploma.
  ❑ The *Ministry of Environment*, to which his father had taken a water sample from the cottage, to have it tested.
  ❑ The *Ministry of Health*, to which he had come to get his new photo health card (now a collector's item?).
  ❑ The *Ministry of Labour*, where his uncle had gone for literature on collective bargaining, in anticipation of a union being certified to represent his plant workers.
  ❑ The *Ministry of Municipal Affairs*, which has just begun an investigation into the financial affairs of Bountiful after receiving a petition from concerned taxpayers.

---

[5]The names which follow are illustrative of the government departments which are typically found at the provincial level. These names are modified periodically as the result of provincial restructuring.

□ The *Ministry of Natural Resources*, from which Frank gets his annual hunting permit.

□ The *Ministry of Solicitor-General*, with which his cousin Marty was familiar, having been an unhappy guest in a provincial detention centre.

□ The *Ministry of Transportation*—finally the Ministry he wanted today. This shouldn't take long he thought as he entered the elevator, unless the staff are all out on the highways catching unsafe trucks and transports again!

Scene 3: Frank and the Feds

A few minutes later, Frank is on his way again, pleased with the prompt and courteous service he has received. His next stop is the Post Office (an outlet of *Canada Post*, a crown corporation which is part of the executive branch of the Government of Canada) where he buys a stamp and mails his income tax return to *Revenue Canada*.

With only a couple of months until the end of his school year, Frank then heads off to the *Canada Employment Centre* of the federal government to check again on job postings. As he reviews the limited listings, he wonders again if he should consider a career in the *Armed Forces* (another part of the executive branch of the federal government). He has a friend who is getting his university education paid for while in the forces; Frank wants to find out more about what this involves. He wouldn't mind pursuing a university degree after finishing his college diploma, but he would need government financial support to do it. His father recently took an early retirement buy-out from the *Department of Fisheries and Oceans*, as part of the downsizing underway throughout the federal government. His parents both seem concerned about keeping up the mortgage payments on the home they purchased a few years ago, although they are relieved that the *Bank of Canada*, another agency of the Executive Branch of the federal government, has moved away from its high interest rate policies.

A few years ago Frank had thought of a career in the federal civil service. A posting in some foreign embassy of the *Ministry of External Affairs* had seemed exciting and exotic—until embassy bombings and hostage-takings became far too common. The *Ministry of Indian and Northern Affairs* had also interested him, especially with all the land claim disputes flaring up between the federal government and Canada's native peoples. However, Frank had come to terms with the fact that government, including the military, was no longer a promising source of new jobs.

Downsizing had become a more familiar term than job security for government workers.

Scene 4: Frank Faces Reality

Shrugging off a vague feeling of discouragement, Frank turns the car toward home and an evening of studying for his government course. Thinking back over the day's activities (and that crazy dream he'd had), Frank is struck by how much government is involved with his everyday life. He resolves to get a better understanding of the various governments affecting him and to work on ensuring that they are serving his needs.

Who Are You Going To Call?

The best starting point for Frank—and you—is to know *where* you are from, "governmentally speaking" and to know *who* your main contacts are and *how* to reach them if you have problems or concerns relating to any level of government. Make up your own special Government Directory using the form on the following page. It may take you a few minutes to track down all of the information  you need, but completing this list is your first step in taking responsibility for your relationship with government.

Concluding Observations

So far, so good. You now have a general grasp of the various levels of government in Canada, how they are organized in terms of basic governing machinery, and the kinds of services they provide. These governments exist to give us a vehicle through which we can identify and address our collective concerns as Canadians. How well our governments fulfil this role is a matter for your personal assessment, but the ensuing chapters will provide you with additional background on which to base that judgment.

Your Guide to Government Directory

A: LOCAL

1. Name of your municipality   _____

2. Head of municipal council   _____

3. Councillors from your area
    (if elected by wards)   _____

4. Clerk or CAO of municipality   _____

5. Treasurer of municipality   _____

6. Phone # of municipal office   _____

7. Phone # of school board office   _____

8. Director of Education   _____

9. School trustee for your area   _____

10. School principal (if applicable)   _____

B: PROVINCIAL

11. Name of provincial member   _____

12. What political party?   _____

13. Phone # of riding office   _____

14. Location of riding office   _____

15. Provincial Ombudsman   _____

C: FEDERAL

16. Name of federal member   _____

17. What political party?   _____

18. Phone # of riding office   _____

19. Location of riding office   _____

20. Federal Ombudsman   _____

The Last Word

Definition of Terms and Concepts

At Large Elections: (Also known as General Vote elections.)
Candidates for office run over the entire municipality and all voters in that municipality choose from among all the candidates—in contrast to ward elections, described below.

Bicameral Legislature:
A legislature with two houses of parliament, an upper chamber and a lower chamber—as in the case of Canada's Parliament.

CAO (Chief Administrative Officer):
The senior coordinating officer who heads up the public service in municipalities which use this system.

Cabinet:
A committee of ministers chosen by the Prime Minister (or Premier) to lead and coordinate the activities of government.

Civil Service:
The employees of the government (at all levels), who are responsible for implementing the decisions of government, administering the laws, delivering the programs and services, and looking after day-to-day operations.

Federation:
A government system in which powers are divided between two or more levels: a national government and provinces or states.

Governor General:
The representative of the Queen, who acts on her behalf as the Head of State for Canada when she is not in this country.

House of Commons:
The lower house in Canada's bicameral Parliament, a body whose members are elected by Canadians from ridings across Canada.

e Assembly:

ovincial equivalent of the federal House of Commons, whose members are elected from ridings across the province.

Lieutenant Governor:

The provincial equivalent of the Governor General with respect to acting as the Queen's representative in the province. The Lieutenant Governor also represents the federal government.

Ministerial Responsibility:

The principle that a minister is responsible for the actions taken by those in the department of government which he or she heads.

Municipal Council:

The governing body elected to exercise the powers granted to a municipality.

Premier:

The head of government for a province, who attains this position (normally) by virtue of being leader of the political party which wins the most seats in the Legislative Assembly in a provincial election.

Prime Minister:

The federal equivalent of a Premier, who attains his or her position in exactly the same way.

Representative Government:

The election of members to represent and make decisions on behalf of the larger population. This principle is reflected in the election of the House of Commons at the federal level, of legislative assemblies at the provincial and territorial level, and of municipal councils at the local level.

Responsible Government:

The principle that the executive branch of government is responsible to, and must be supported by, the legislative branch. More specifically, this principle means that the Cabinet can only continue governing as long as it is supported by a majority of elected members in the Commons or Provincial Assembly.

Senate:

The upper House in the Canadian Parliament, consisting of 105 appointed members.

Unicameral Legislature:

Term to describe a legislature which has only one House, such as is found in all provinces today. In contrast, a bicameral legislature like the Canadian Parliament has two Houses: a House of Commons and a Senate.

Ward Elections:

This occurs when a municipality is divided into geographic areas or wards, with candidates running for office from within these wards rather than over the whole municipality. The latter arrangement is known as election at large or by general vote.

Points to Ponder

1. How long did it take you to compile your *Guide to Government Directory*? With which level of government were you most familiar when you began working on your Directory?

2. Do you now understand how the same voters (including you) elect different members (usually from areas with differing geographic boundaries) to make up governing bodies at the municipal, provincial and federal levels?

3. Try re-enacting the adventures of our student in the "Who Does What" section of this lesson (leaving out the fanciful nightmare). In other words, try to keep track of your activities for one day, noting how many times you come in contact with services, activities or regulations provided by one of our levels of government. The resulting list should help to demonstrate why you need to know more about government.

For Further Reading

A number of short and readable articles on the executive and legislative branches are found in Paul Fox and Graham White, *Politics: Canada*, 8th Edition, Whitby, McGraw-Hill Ryerson Limited, 1995, or any of the earlier editions edited by Paul Fox.

An introduction to the basic machinery and operating principles of government is found in a number of political science texts. Examples include W. White, R. Wagenberg and R. Nelson, *Introduction to Canadian Politics and Government*, 6th Edition, Toronto, Harcourt Brace & Company, 1994, Chapter 1 and James John Guy, *How We Are Governed*, Toronto, Harcourt Brace & Company, Canada, 1995, Chapter 1.

A number of readings on more detailed aspects of the various levels of government will be found at the end of Chapters 5 and 6, which explore these governments in more depth.

Obviously, information on our governments and their operations is readily available from news programs on radio and television. But you may not realize that using these media can also be quite entertaining. Topical political issues and personalities are regularly satirized in both *Double Exposure* and the *Royal Canadian Air Farce*, programs found on both CBC radio and television. *This Hour Has 22 Minutes* also includes a good deal of political satire in its "off-the-wall" antics. Reruns of the British series *Yes, Minister* and *Yes, Prime Minister* provide a very amusing examination of relations between senior civil servants and their political "masters."

Chapter 3

Left, Right, or Just Plain Wrong?

Objectives and Highlights

♦ To distinguish among Canada's political parties and their place on the political spectrum.

♦ To demonstrate the valuable roles played by parties in our government.

♦ To examine the nature of pressure groups and the roles that they play.

It is common to use the terms **left wing** or **right wing** as a short form for particular political philosophies or approaches to governing. These terms are also employed, not always with much definition or explanation, to differentiate among Canada's **political parties**. The first task, therefore, is to provide some clarification of their meaning. The key distinction relates to the extent of the role which government should play in our economy and society. Those on the left support a substantial role for government, believing it is needed to remove barriers to equal opportunity and to protect individuals from economic uncertainty. Those on the right prefer a distinctly limited role for government, less regulation of the economy, and more individual freedom. The ultra-right or **neoconservative** view advocates tax cuts, reduced social programs, and more community and self-responsibility. A second distinguishing feature which has come to the fore in the past couple of decades relates to the issue of law and order and security in our neighbourhoods. It is really a subset of the first distinction, however, in that those on the right insist that individuals must accept more responsibility (and punishment) for their actions and misdeeds, while those on the left argue that government should take more steps to improve social conditions and to prevent misdeeds from arising in the first place.

Canada's Political Parties

Only two parties have ever held power in Canada at the national level. The Conservatives dominated the 19th century, largely because of the leadership of Sir John A. Macdonald. The Liberals have dominated much of the 20th century, notwithstanding the success of the Conservatives in the 1980s. Because of this pattern, Canada has historically been characterized as having a two party system—even though there are obviously other political parties which run candidates and enjoy some support across the country.

What's in a Name?

To avoid confusion, a brief explanation is in order concerning the name of the Conservative Party. It was officially changed to the Progressive Conservative Party in the 1930s as one of the conditions required by John Bracken, then the Premier of Manitoba, to accept the party leadership. While earlier references are quite properly to the Conservative Party, the correct name today is Progressive Conservatives or the PC Party.

The New Democratic Party (NDP)—and its forerunner, the Cooperative Commonwealth Federation (CCF)—has consistently elected federal members for over 60 years. The CCF/NDP has also enjoyed considerable success at the provincial level over the years, forming governments in British Columbia, Saskatchewan, Manitoba, and Ontario. They currently (at the end of 1999) hold power in Saskatchewan, British Columbia and Manitoba.

A few other parties have also held power provincially, but in most cases their success was long ago and related to particular circumstances. For example, the United Farmers of Alberta held power for one term in the early years of the Depression[1] and the Union Nationale held

---

[1] A coalition of United Farmers parties from the Western Provinces and Ontario known as the Progressive Party enjoyed earlier, but very brief, success at the federal level, electing 65 MPs in 1921.

power in Québec for several terms in the 1940s and 1950s, largely thanks to the leadership of Maurice Duplessis. The Social Credit Party enjoyed prolonged success in Alberta between 1935 and 1970 and has also formed governments in British Columbia on several occasions since the 1950s. As will be discussed, the Reform Party is, in some respects, a federal variation of the Social Credit Party.

Distinguishing Among the Parties

To party faithful, the merits of their particular party are self-evident, as are the deficiencies of opposing parties. But to the average citizen, it is usually much less clear what a party stands for and why one should be supported over another. We begin with a brief summary of the only two parties ever to form a national government.[2]

The (Progressive) Conservatives

The first of these to emerge was the Conservative Party, which was formed by Sir John A. Macdonald out of a coalition of local interests under the label the Liberal-Conservatives. This alliance of eastern commercial interests, conservative French Canadians and Ontario Tories was committed to bringing about Confederation and then developing the new country through constructing a national railway and promoting commerce behind tariff walls.[3]

Under the leadership of Sir John A., the Conservatives went on to dominate the national scene until almost the end of the 19th century. Macdonald was a very astute politi-

> The Conservatives were the dominant party in the 19th century.

cian and a leader with a national vision which he pursued effectively. He remains one of Canada's best known Prime Ministers, not least because of the stories of his legendary drinking bouts.

---

[2]The summary of the Conservative and Liberal Parties which follows is largely based on Robert Jackson and Doreen Jackson, *Politics in Canada*, 3rd Edition, Scarborough, Prentice-Hall Canada Inc., 1994, Chapter 10.

[3]Tariffs are essentially taxes on imported goods, designed to raise their prices and, therefore, to encourage Canadians to purchase domestic products.

Turning More Than the Other Cheek

One such occasion saw Macdonald attending a function where he was to speak against an opposition candidate in a Northern Ontario riding. Too much strong drink and a rough train ride on the way to the meeting caused him to throw up on the platform during his opponent's speech. Even Sir John's supporters were disgusted. When his turn came to speak, Macdonald began as follows: "Mr Chairman and gentlemen, I don't know how it is, but every time I hear Mr. Jones speak it turns my stomach." The audience dissolved in laughter and were back on side.[4]

The pro-business stance of the Conservative Party did not endear it to Western farmers. Western disaffection was eventually reflected in the formation of the Progressive Party of the 1920s, one of many such Western protest parties, of which the present Reform Party is in some respects the latest. Nor were French Canadians supportive, because of the party's strong ties to Britain. The weak "French connection" was shattered when Conservative governments executed Riel[5] in 1885 and imposed conscription (mandatory military service) in 1917. These factors combined to help ensure the electoral success of the Liberal Party throughout much of the 20th century.

Conservative fortunes improved, temporarily, under John Diefenbaker, who delivered strong support from his native Prairies and even picked up 50 seats from Québec in a sweeping 1958 election victory. Diefenbaker was in his own way as much a "character" as Sir John A., whom he greatly admired. He was a masterful story teller and excelled in the cut and thrust of parliamentary debate.[6] On one occasion an up-and-coming MP made the mistake of trying to interrupt Diefenbaker in full flight. Without breaking stride, "the Chief" snapped: "When a hunter is after big game, he doesn't stop for rabbit tracks." The member subsided, to lick his wounds.

[4]This example is from Jack McLeod, *The Oxford Book of Canadian Political Anecdotes*, Toronto, Oxford University Press, 1988, p. 28.

[5]Louis Riel was a Métis leader in Manitoba who led a rebellion protesting land losses and other grievances arising from an influx of English settlers.

[6]The example which follows is from Thomas Van Dusen, *The Chief*, 1968, as quoted in McLeod, *op. cit.*, p. 174.

The skills which made him an intimidating opposition leader, however, did not translate well into the role of leader of the Government. In the memorable words of Donaldson, "he had stormed the ramparts of power; now he didn't know how to work the draw-bridge."[7]

Diefenbaker's forced departure created deep divisions which plagued his successor, Robert Stanfield, for years after. The selection of Joe Clark as leader in 1976 further secured the party's support in Western Canada, but it continued to lose ground in most other areas of the country. Under Brian Mulroney, the party won its first election majority in more than a quarter century in 1984.[8] It scored a major breakthrough in his home province (Québec), and also received strong support across the country. This success was substantially repeated in the election of 1988. By the spring of 1993, however, Mulroney's unpopularity was sufficient to prompt his resignation. He made much of the fact that he was the first Conservative leader to turn over the reins of power while still forming the Government. It didn't help. His successor, Kim Campbell, led the party to a crushing defeat in 1993, squeezed in the West by Reform, in Québec by the Bloc Québécois, and everywhere else by the resurgent Liberals.

The road back from near oblivion has been a difficult one for the Conservatives. Under Jean Charest's leadership, the party managed to win 20 seats in the 1997 election, but that result still left it in last place among the five parties in the House. The following year (1998), Charest left to take on the leadership of the Québec Liberal Party, responding to widespread insistence that he was the one person who could defeat the separatist government of Lucien Bouchard (he didn't) and "save" Canada. The party's choice for a new leader turned out to be an old one—Joe Clark, first elected leader in 1976. Since his election, Clark has spent much of his time rebuffing efforts by the Reform Party to join with it to form a United Alternative on the right (discussed below) which can defeat the Liberals.

---

[7]Gordon Donaldson, *Fifteen Men*, Toronto, Doubleday Canada Limited, 1969, p. 192.

[8]Its last majority victory had been in 1958 under Diefenbaker. The party also won in 1962 and 1979 but only with short-lived minority governments.

The Liberals

Notwithstanding their ascendancy in the 20th century, the Liberal Party was much slower to develop on the national scene. While the party did win an election in 1873, its success was almost entirely due to the Pacific Scandal which engulfed Sir John A. Macdonald's administration. The party did not really take shape as a unified force until Laurier became leader in 1887. As Canada's first French-Canadian Prime Minister (from 1896 until 1911) Laurier solidified the party's position in Québec.

The Liberals were badly split by the conscription crisis of 1917 which saw many of their English members join with the Conservatives to form a coalition government to continue the war effort. The party emerged from the election of that year as largely a Québec "rump." However, it was soon rebuilt under the crafty if distinctly uncharismatic leadership of Mackenzie King. In an age before television and experts on make-up, dress and speaking skills, this short, balding undistinguished looking man who few claimed to like and even fewer admitted to voting for, managed to win more elections and serve longer in office than any Prime Minister in the British parliamentary system.[9] He did so partly by displaying, in a period before polling and sample survey techniques, an almost uncanny sense of what the Canadian people wanted or would accept and where he should take his party. While his shifts in policy and position were undeniably successful, they earned him (and the Liberals) the criticism of being without consistent principles. In the colourful words of John Diefenbaker: "The Liberals are the flying saucers of politics. No one can make head nor tail of them and they are never seen twice in the same place."[10]

Liberals
"out of this world?"

---

[9]King won in 1921 and 1926, then was "lucky" enough to lose in 1930 and give the Conservatives the thankless task of governing during the Great Depression. He returned to power in 1935 and won two further elections before retiring in November 1948 and turning over the leadership of the Liberal Party to Louis St. Laurent.

[10]Diefenbaker in 1962, quoted in David Olive, *Canadian Political Babble*, Toronto, John Wiley & Sons, 1993, p. 114.

The Liberals retained their power base in Québec throughout much of the 20th century—although there was (as noted above) a temporary defection to the Conservatives during the Diefenbaker landslide of 1958 and also a partial shift (largely in the form of a protest vote) to the Ralliement des Créditistes[11] during the 1960s. However, the party steadily lost ground in Western Canada, to the point that there were frequent jokes about party meetings being held in phone booths. Trudeau's election victory in 1968 brought some upsurge in Western support, but only temporarily.

Just as Mulroney overstayed his welcome and left his party to face an overwhelming defeat, Trudeau experienced a somewhat similar fate ten years earlier. When John Turner replaced Trudeau in 1984, he almost immediately called an election. The result was a massive defeat for the Liberals who received their lowest support ever, at only 28% of the popular vote. Fortunes change quickly, however, and in 1993 the Liberals enjoyed one of their biggest victories, capturing 178 seats and receiving support from all areas of the country. Jean Chrétien led the Liberals to a second successive majority government in 1997, but with only 38% of the popular vote and only 155 seats out of an expanded House of 301. Once again the Liberal success was attributed, at least in part, to the fact that those on the right split their support between the Conservatives and the Reform Party.

The Reform Party

The Reform Party was created in 1987 by disgruntled Western Conservatives, whose slogan, "The West Wants In," summed up their view that Canada suffered from too much Ottawa and too much Québec.[12] Western alienation and prairie-based protest parties have been in evidence throughout much of the 20th century. A variation of the Reform Party has been active at the provincial level for more than 50 years, primarily in Alberta and British Columbia, under the name of the Social

---

[11]This Québec-based wing of Social Credit won support partly as a protest vote against both the Liberals and Conservatives and also because of the popularity of its fiery leader, Réal Caouette.

[12]Thomas Walkom, "Right a victim of own success," *Toronto Star*, February 13, 1999.

Credit Party.[13] Indeed, the Social Credit Party formed the government in Alberta from 1935 until 1970, for most of that time under the leadership of Ernest Manning. It is his son, Preston, who now heads the Reform Party.

The Reform Party burst onto the national scene with 52 seats in the 1993 federal election, just missing out on becoming the official opposition because of the 54 seats, all from Québec, won by the Bloc Québécois. Reform increased its standing to 60 seats, and gained official opposition status, in the 1997 election. This success, however, was tempered by the fact that the party again failed to make inroads in Ontario or eastward and that the Liberals benefited from right wing support dividing between Reform and the Conservatives.

Reform leader Preston Manning responded to the situation by launching plans for a new United Alternative which would see the Reform and Conservative parties merging to create a unified right which could defeat

> Reform tried to create a United Alternative with the Conservative Party.

the Liberals. While Manning received the endorsement (albeit lukewarm) of his own party to proceed with this plan, Joe Clark has consistently rejected the idea, claiming that any merger will only occur when Reform supporters rejoin the Conservative Party. His uncompromising stand was endorsed at a party convention in late 1999, when delegates voted to run PC candidates in all ridings in the next election.

While it is possible that a new United Alternative Party may eventually be formed, especially if the Liberals continue to win reelection more because of a divided right than because of their own merits, it is unlikely to be created from a formal merger of Reform and the Conservatives. The fact is that the two parties do not have that much in common. Many of them share a conservative view on economic matters, believing in the virtues of free enterprise, in less government regulation, and in lower taxes. But Reformers differ in their social conservatism and their explicit set of moral values. Often religious fundamentalists, they

---

[13]As already noted, the Social Credit Party elected a substantial number of members from Québec in the 1960s, mainly as a protest vote against the two old line parties and as a response to its very colourful leader.

generally disapprove of many things, "from drugs to short skirts, to abortion, to working mothers,"[14] and aren't reluctant to use the state to impose their own morality. Many traditional Conservatives are uncomfortable with the more radical elements of the Reform Party. Even if the Conservative Party were to disband (an increasingly unlikely prospect), there is no assurance that Reform would gain appreciably, since polls indicate that the majority of Conservatives would vote Liberal, with whom they share a moderate, middle-of-the-road philosophy, rather than Reform.

The New Democratic Party

By far the most prominent and enduring of the third parties has been the New Democratic Party (NDP). It was first formed in 1933 as the Cooperative Commonwealth Federation (CCF), which brought together an assortment of Fabian socialists, Marxists and farm and labour groups under the leadership of J. S. Woodsworth. The party's origins gave it a mainly Western rural support base which limited its electoral support (and its financial stability) over the almost 30 years of its existence.[15] In 1961 the CCF was dissolved and replaced by the New Democratic Party. This move was designed to embrace organized labour, thereby broadening the support base of the party, extending it more into urban Canada, and ensuring it of a more stable financial future based on union contributions.

As a party of moderate socialism, the NDP has wrestled over the years with how to maintain its founding principles and its commitment to extensive government intervention in the economy and society without being overly dogmatic and ideological and thereby losing possible electoral support. This internal tension triggered a split by the "Waffle" group in the late 1960s—an incongruous name, since their position was that the NDP must not waffle on its socialist principles. The party had popular and respected leaders in Tommy Douglas, David Lewis and, especially, Ed Broadbent, who in 1988 led the party to its best showing ever with 20% of the popular vote and 43 seats. However, his successor,

---

[14]Walkom, *op. cit.*

[15]The description of the CCF/NDP in this section is largely based on Jackson and Jackson, *op. cit.*, p. 432.

Audrey McLaughlin, was only able to hold nine seats for the party against the Liberal landslide in 1993. This reduced standing meant that the party lost its official status in the House and the research funds that went with it. McLaughlin's successor, Alexa McDonough, led the party back to 21 seats in the 1997 election, many of them from her power base in the Maritime provinces.

The party continues to struggle, however, with the policies it should follow today. At its national policy convention in August 1999, the NDP shifted its economic vision significantly to the centre of the political spectrum, adopting a number of policies characterized as pro-business. In some respects, this might appear to be a realistic response to the new world order. However, this move not only runs the risk of alienating hard core NDP supporters, it also moves the party into an already very crowded centre and centre-right position on the political spectrum. With Reform still trying to unite the right, and with the Liberals masquerading very successfully as Conservatives, it is arguable that the NDP should have stayed on the left to offer Canadians a real alternative.

> Is the NDP right to move from the left?

The Bloc Québécois

The Bloc is the newest party on the national stage, and its longevity is very much in doubt. It was formed after Lucien Bouchard defected from the Conservative Cabinet of Brian Mulroney in 1990, and joined with a few other Québec members in the Commons (mostly from the Conservative Party) to work for separation. The Bloc shocked the country by capturing 54 seats in the 1993 federal election, enough to create the bizarre situation in which "Her Majesty's Loyal Opposition" was made up of a party dedicated to the break-up of Canada.

When Bouchard left the federal scene at the end of 1995 to become leader of the Parti Québécois and Premier of Quebec, there was speculation that a number of the Bloc members might abandon federal politics as well. The new leader, Michel Gauthier, stepped down at the end of 1996 as a result of internal dissent in the party. The Bloc managed to hold on to 44 seats (again all from Québec) in the 1997 federal election, but it is increasingly difficult to see what role it now has. Barring a major change in public opinion in Québec, there is very little support for another referendum on separation. Bloc leader Gilles Duceppe attempts to show his party's relevance by arguing that it also discusses a variety of other issues such as foreign affairs, defence and financial issues.[16] But if the party is now concentrating more on broad, national issues, how does that advance the separatist cause? If it reverts to its separatist objectives, how relevant are they with the current mood in Québec? Increasingly, it looks to many that the Bloc is merely marking time.

The Parties and the Political Spectrum

How do Canada's political parties compare when placed on the left-right political spectrum? The Bloc is omitted from the chart depicted below only because it does not fit a conventional left-right distinction. It includes members from all parts of the political spectrum, united mainly by their common objective of Québec independence.

Left	Centre	Right
NDP	Liberals and	Reform
(Liberals in a hurry)	Conservatives	(Ultra Conservatives)

The political spectrum can be useful in analyzing and understanding political developments, especially if one bears in mind that the whole spectrum shifts to the left or right over time. From World War II until the 1980s, most Western nations supported a prolonged shift to the left, reflected in a marked increase in the role and size of government, in the range of programs and services provided, and in the number of rules and regulations put into place. The federal government led the way in Canada.

Postwar period saw a prolonged shift to the left.

---

[16]"Whither, Mr. Duceppe?" Editorial, *Ottawa Citizen*, September 17, 1999.

- It gave a commitment to full employment, price stability and other economic goals even before the end of World War II. This marked the first time any Canadian government accepted responsibility for our economic health.
- It used the "federal spending power" to promote national standards in areas such as health, education and social services. This is the power of the federal government to spend money in areas in which it cannot legislate. During the first three decades following World War II, these initiatives shaped the modern welfare state.

Partly through the support of federal transfers, most provinces also greatly expanded expenditures on such areas as highways, education and social programs. For example, close to 70% of the annual operating budget of the Ontario government by the beginning of the 1990s was taken up by expenditures on just three areas: health, education and social services.

Last two decades have seen a pronounced shift to the right.

Over the past couple of decades, there has been a pronounced shift to the right. Politicians promising to "get governments off the backs of people," enjoyed success in countries like the United States (under Reagan) and Britain (under Thatcher). Deregulation, downsizing, and privatization became "buzz words." Governments that were smaller and less obtrusive became the goal. This shift back to the right became sufficiently pronounced that it affected all political parties, at both the federal and provincial levels, as these few examples illustrate:

- The federal PC Party talked a lot about downsizing and deficit reduction during Mulroney's two terms in office, but it was the Liberal Party, after taking office in 1993, which acted more right wing in terms of its attack on the deficit, downsizing of the public service, and cuts in transfer payments for various social programs.
- The Ontario NDP government began the 1990s with traditional left wing policies which included increased welfare payments and an expansionary budget designed to create jobs through various public works programs. As its term progressed, however, it became increasingly right wing in its policies in response to growing concerns about the provincial debt. This shift was highlighted, in April 1993,

by the introduction of a Social Contract and Expenditure Control Program which imposed cuts in transfers to schools, hospitals, and municipalities.

A "Rae" of Light?

The then leader of the NDP in Ontario, Bob Rae, has since publicly mused that we must all accept the reality of the global economy. Rather than railing against its excesses, we must work to mitigate them. In pursuit of this objective, Rae concludes that the traditional left wing solutions such as bigger centralized government, higher taxes, more intervention, and public ownership, are no longer acceptable to the electorate.[17]

- The Progressive Conservative governments in power in Alberta and Ontario in the 1990s have pursued an agenda very much on the right side of the spectrum, introducing major spending cuts to social programs in order to reduce debt and to be able to offer tax cuts. More surprisingly, governments of other political stripes, such as the Liberals in New Brunswick and the NDP in Saskatchewan, also introduced right wing policies in their pursuit of fiscal restraint. For example, the NDP closed large numbers of rural hospitals in Saskatchewan, the birthplace of medicare.
- Further insight into the shift to the right in Canadian politics was evident when the Progressive Conservative Party held a national convention in Winnipeg in August 1996. This was a vitally important gathering, designed to start the party back on the road to recovery from its devastating defeat in the 1993 federal election. There was strong pressure, especially from the youth wing of the party, for a commitment to substantial tax cuts. There were also calls for privatization of medicare, abolition of the Canada Pension Plan, the establishment of boot camps for young offenders, and restoration of the death penalty.[18] Some of the right wing positions could be interpreted as positioning the PC Party to woo back disaffected supporters who had gone over to the Reform Party. But

---

[17]See Bob Rae, *The Three Questions*, Toronto, Penguin Books, 1998.

[18]David Vienneau, "Hardliners, moderates staking out Tory ground," *Toronto Star*, August 24, 1996.

it is also evident from various comments made by delegates that many believed that government had become the enemy, that money should be shifted from government to private hands.

As Canada enters a new century, there is some indication that the pendulum may be swinging again, this time back to the left—or at least back toward the centre and more moderate policies. The alleged virtues of free enterprise and the unfettered global economy look more suspect in the face of the economic turmoil in recent years in countries like Russia, Indonesia, Japan, and South Korea. The abuses of "cowboy capitalism" in the former Soviet Union, and the growing inequities around the world fuelled by excessive individualism, provide evidence that governments still have an important role to play. Britain, Germany and Italy have all elected "**Third Way**" leaders, an increasingly fashionable term to describe a moderate approach which acknowledges that neither socialism nor conservatism is working.[19] The popularity of ultra-conservative Newt Gingrich has steadily faded in the United States, with American voters rejecting the far right views of Republicans in the 1998 congressional elections.

Less Me and More "Hugh"

The far right views of conservatism in Canada have been rejected by a very prominent Conservative, Hugh Segal, in a book entitled *Beyond Greed*. Rather like Bob Rae's call for moderation from the other side of the spectrum, Segal criticizes neoconservatives who value individual freedom to an extreme, and far more than responsibility to each other or to the common good. He argues that traditional conservatism does not dismiss or denigrate the importance of government (and other institutions) in the larger cause of equality of opportunity and some measure of fairness.[20]

The success of the Liberal Party throughout the 20th century is at least partly attributable to its ability to place itself at or near the middle of the political spectrum, no matter where that middle might be! Thus,

---

[19]Cecil Foster, "The failure of political extremism," *Toronto Star*, November 23, 1998.

[20]Hugh Segal, *Beyond Greed*, Toronto, Stoddart, 1997, p. 3.

the party moved sharply to the left in the early postwar period, so as to undercut the growing popularity of the policies of the CCF. In the 1990s, it moved just as markedly to the right, embracing—and implementing more aggressively—the policies which had been advocated by the previous Conservative regime. As the pendulum begins to swing back toward the centre at the beginning of the 21st century, the Liberals are talking more about their traditional values, and the need to shore up and even expand social programs. Critics may dismiss the political astuteness of the Liberals as evidence that they lack principles and are willing to embrace whatever views are politically expedient. [Remember John Diefenbaker and his flying saucer analogy.] But parties which are perceived to be too far to the left (the NDP) or the right (Reform) face an uphill battle in gaining widespread support. If they moderate their position and move toward the centre (as the NDP has recently decided to do), they run the risk of becoming indistinguishable from the Liberals, who almost always seem to be occupying that centre area, wherever it is.

Tweedledum and Tweedledee

It is not only the Liberal Party which has shifted its position over the decades. Both of Canada's ruling parties have reversed themselves over the years, making it very difficult to

> Both of Canada's ruling parties have reversed their positions over the years.

identify what distinguishes them. This lack of substantial and continuing party differences has led some to characterize the parties as tweedledum and tweedledee or, in the words of less kind observers, tweedledum and tweedledumber. How do we compare the Liberals and Conservatives, and how do these comparisons fit on the political spectrum?

The traditional view has the Conservative Party stressing stability and respect for the established order, and the Liberals more readily embracing change and reform. But that doesn't get us very far; nor does it always jibe with past experience. The Conservatives attach great importance to the freedom of the individual, although still within a framework provided by government. The Liberals are equally concerned with the human condition, but they often see the need for somewhat greater government intervention to support and ensure individual development and progress.

Consider, however, these rather striking examples of shifts in party position and philosophy:

- The Conservative Party introduced tariffs as part of Sir John A.'s "National Policy" of 1879, and defeated the Liberals under Wilfrid Laurier in 1911 by playing on fears that the Liberal proposal for reciprocity or free trade with the United States would undermine Canadian independence. In 1988, however, it was the PC Party which pursued and achieved free trade agreements, first with the United States and then with Mexico, while the Liberals vigorously opposed them.

- The Conservative Party was traditionally very pro-Britain and was not overly anxious to see closer ties between Canada and the U.S. (as in the free trade example already given). The Liberals were much more anxious to sever the ties with "the mother country" and to expand dealings with the Americans. It was Liberal governments which presided over the massive American investment in (critics would say buyout of) the Canadian economy in the post-war period. Yet it was also the Liberals in the 1970s who introduced the Foreign Investment Review Agency and other initiatives designed to limit foreign ownership of Canada's economy. Meanwhile, it was the Progressive Conservatives, especially under Brian Mulroney, who became preoccupied with fostering the closest possible ties with the United States—symbolized by the spectre of Mulroney and President Reagan warbling "When Irish Eyes Are Smiling" at the so-called Shamrock Summit meeting in Canada not long after Mulroney became Prime Minister.

- Historically, the Liberals have been seen as a party which favours more government intervention in the economy and society than the Conservatives. But it was the Conservatives who set up the Bank of Canada and the CBC. It was a Progressive Conservative leader, Robert Stanfield, who proposed wage and price controls to deal with runaway inflation in the early 1970s. Moreover, it is the Liberals, since their victory in 1993, who have pursued the downsizing of government in a much more forceful way than the preceding two Progressive Conservative administrations.

The Roles of Political Parties

Whatever their particular policies, parties in general seem to suffer from the same negative image that Canadians tend to have of most things governmental. Those dubious about the motives of a politician are unlikely to feel any better when they contemplate a larger group of the same species. Parties are criticized for indulging in mindless attacks and counter-attacks, playing out some ritual game without any particular regard for the real merits of the issue under debate. This pattern is all too evident to those who have seen "Question Period," whether live or on late night television. What we see, most of the time, is empty posturing, polarization, and insults hurled across the floor on the basis of little more than the fact that the other speaker sits on the opposite side of the House. Parties are also criticized for demanding rigid loyalty from their members, who, as a result, often seem quite unresponsive to the demands and preferences of those who elected them.

What must be understood, however, is that political parties are an integral part of the government system at the provincial and federal levels of government. They are organizations devoted to fielding and electing candidates for office, with the objective of capturing the most seats and thereby forming the government. They serve a number of very practical purposes in our system of government.

1. They tell us who won the election and will form a "government." Imagine the chaos and confusion if 300 independent members turned up on Parliament Hill the morning after an election, attempting to decide who should govern.

2. They provide a watchdog and an alternative government in the form of the Official Opposition.

3. They provide a relatively clear focus of accountability. There is a governing group, usually with a majority of the elected members, and it will have to answer for its performance. Contrast the situation on most municipal councils, where all members sit as independents. There isn't any governing group or any official opposition. Everyone is responsible for everything, which also means that no one is really responsible for anything.

4. They allow for a smooth transition of power, since any new party which takes office has already formulated its plans about governing while serving on the opposition side. The amount of preparation may be less, of course, for a party that wasn't expecting to win. But it will still be greater than would exist if a group of independent members with no common background or allegiance were suddenly asked to form a government.

5. Parties also simplify the election process, narrowing down the range of candidates and the choice of issues. Instead of just a list of names which may not mean much, the voter sees names *with party affiliations*, and the parties offer some more or less clear choices each election. Once again, the contrast with the municipal level is quite striking. Municipal voters face multiple ballots (for council positions, for head of council, for school board trustees, and— often— for public utility commissioners) which may add up to 30 or 40 names. Most of these individuals are unknown to the voter, and there isn't any party label to provide at least a basic identifier. Voting in such circumstances is a challenge and often a guessing game.

    Parties also fulfil other more intangible, philosophical roles.[21]

6. They attempt to simplify the vast range of interests and choices available in society today and to organize public support around selected issues.

7. Parties help educate the public through debate on the issues of the day. Much of the public awareness and understanding of current issues, however superficial or imperfect, is derived from the party exchanges—as reported by the media. An example is the much wider public awareness of Canada's deficit and debt problems after a number of political parties made this a key issue in the 1990s.

8. Parties are often described as "gatekeepers," because they allow certain public demands through to decision-makers, while they eliminate others or combine or modify them.

9. Partly because of their gatekeeper role, parties are central players in the formulation of public policy, as noted in later chapters.

---

[21]Jackson and Jackson, *op. cit.*, pp. 414-416.

10. Parties also *can be* important players in the process of political socialization. This refers to the need for parties to play special roles as "agencies for the creation of national symbols, experiences, memories, heroes, and villains."[22] The failure of Canadian parties to bind regional cleavages by building strong national bases of representation limits their effectiveness in this area.

Clearly, parties play a wide range of important roles. It is difficult to imagine our parliamentary system functioning without them. But it is functioning differently as Canada moves increasingly to a multi-party system. Even after third parties began to make their appearance in the Commons in 1921 (in the form of the Progressives), the two old-line parties remained dominant until the late 1950s. Elections usually resulted in majority governments, offset by a large opposition party, an alternative government-in-waiting. The next two decades, however, saw six minority governments (in 1957, 1962, 1963, 1965, 1972, and 1979). By the 1990s, five political parties were represented in the Commons, but instead of producing minority governments, they have fragmented and weakened the opposition, Given their regional limitations, neither the Bloc (especially) nor Reform have been credible as alternative governments-in-waiting.

> As we move increasingly to a multi-party system, the main effect seems to be a divided, weaker opposition.

Some, like John Meisel, suggest that political parties are in decline, and that their functions are being taken over by other institutions.[23] Among the factors he cites are:

- the growth and complexity of government activities, which shifts power to expert civil servants and reduces the role of parties to observing and then criticizing or rubber-stamping the advice received.
- the increasing reliance on federal-provincial diplomacy—both at high level conferences of first Ministers and at scores of meetings

---

[22]John Meisel, as quoted in *ibid.*, p. 426.

[23]John Meisel, "Decline of Party in Canada," in H. G. Thorburn (ed.), *Party Politics in Canada*, 5th Edition, Toronto, Prentice-Hall Canada Inc., 1985.

between federal and provincial officials—resulting in decisions which legislatures and parties have little choice but to accept.

- the growing influence of the media, as television filters the public perception of politics and politicians and as investigative journalism supplements, or even seems to supplant, the watchdog role of the opposition parties.

- the lack of significant policy differences between the main, old-line parties (as in tweedledum and tweedledee), and the increasing inclination of people to turn to more specialized interest groups or pressure groups as a means of advancing their particular concerns.

Interest Groups and Their Activities

What are we to make of the expansion of interest group or pressure group activity in Canada?

◆ Something to Think About

Does the proliferation of interest groups undermine political parties and reflect a decline in the legitimacy of our existing political institutions? Or are these groups a positive development, providing increased access to government and decision making for Canadians?

Distinguishing Groups and Their Activities

Before we can attempt to answer these questions, some clarification of terminology is in order, since the terms interest group, pressure group, and lobbyist are often used interchangeably.

Interest Groups

As the name suggests, **interest groups** bring together people who share a common interest or concern. The interest may range from bird watching to preservation of world peace. Interest groups can be described as **pressure groups** when they attempt to exert pressure on government to do (or to refrain from doing) something. Some groups rarely go beyond being interest groups. For them, political activity "is often a minor and unwelcome addition to the concerns that have brought them together."[24] For example, a group of bird watchers may meet regularly over many months or years for nothing more than the pure pleasure of searching out and enjoying their feathered friends. Then urban sprawl into a forested area, development encroaching on wetlands, or some other environmental threat to the habitat of birds, may transform them into a pressure group, seeking action from their governments to protect the environment. After fighting this battle, the members may again return to their original interest without paying much further attention to government.

Pressure Groups

In contrast to interest groups which only occasionally and very temporarily indulge in political activity are those pressure groups whose main raision d'être is to attempt to influence government decisions. These are usually long-standing national organizations with ample resources and access to government. Examples would include the Canadian Manufacturing Association, Canadian Labour Congress, Canadian Petroleum Association, Canadian Bankers Association, Canadian Federation of Agriculture, and Canadian Medical Association. However, they may also include temporary or short term groups formed in response to a particular issue, and usually devoted to blocking something which is viewed as undesirable. Good examples would be citizen or neighbourhood groups set up to oppose the location of a high rise building or an expressway or a landfill site near their area. These latter groups are equally devoted to applying pressure on government, but they usually lack the resources available to the national organizations, and rarely endure beyond the crisis which brought them into existence.

Lobbyists

While pressure groups "lobby" the government to advance their cause, the term **lobbyist** refers to individuals and organizations which special-

---

[24]A. Paul Pross, *Group Politics and Public Policy*, 2nd Edition, Toronto, Oxford University Press, 1992, p. 5.

ize full time in the "art" of influencing government. These professional lobbyists are available for hire and their main value has been described —in a remark attributed to Senator Keith Davey—as helping clients "to tiptoe through the Ottawa tulips." This colourful phrasing refers to the fact that lobbyists are well plugged in to the policy process in Ottawa; they earn their money by keeping on top of what is breaking in government and whom to contact on a given item.

In fact, many lobbyists are retired public servants or former political advisors who retain an impressive network of contacts within government. Consider these examples:[25]

- Paul Martin's former parliamentary secretary, Barry Campbell, now heads the Canadian arm of the giant Washington-based lobbying firm known as APCO, where his financial background and connections are clearly valuable to clients such as the Bank of Nova Scotia and J. P. Morgan.
- Former Transport Minister Doug Young, who helped to privatize Canadian National Railways, now lobbies his old department on behalf of CNR.
- Paul Pellegrini, a former aide to Defence Minister Art Eggleton was a member of the team that lobbied successfully on behalf of an Anglo-Italian consortium seeking a contract for military helicopters.
- Leslie Noble is one of the closest advisors to Premier Harris and co-author of the Common Sense Revolution which first brought him to victory. She also runs the leading lobbying firm dealing with the Ontario government.[26]

Organizations concerned about policy developments which may affect them often decide that these interests can be better protected by purchasing the services of someone "on the scene" and well connected. Some large organizations hire their own full time lobbyists, but most work for public relations or government consulting firms and have a number of organizations as clients.

---

[25]Except as specified, these examples are from Edison Stewart, "Back in Town," *Toronto Star*, May 30, 1998.

[26]Kevin Donovan and Moira Welsh, "Queen of the Park," *Toronto Star*, March 13, 1999.

Since 1989, lobbyists have been required to register with the Ministry of Consumer and Corporate Affairs Canada, as a result of which we have information on some 1000 professionals who lobby on behalf of others and another 2000 who are employees of organizations and associations that lobby the government.[27] There was much criticism of the 1989 legislation, which did not require information on the names of those who were lobbied or specifically what kind of lobbying activity took place. Since only paid lobbyists had to register (and not even all of them bothered to do so), a large number—perhaps 100 000 or more—of those involved in lobbying were not covered by the register.

While a parliamentary committee made several recommendations to toughen the legislation in 1993, these were not implemented before the defeat of the Conservative government that year. The Liberals had promised in their famous red book to reform the lobbying business but, once in power, appeared to lose some of their enthusiasm for the task, especially when faced with fierce lobbying against reform by the lobbyists. Amendments adopted in 1995 were much weaker than had been recommended, but did require that more information be provided. "Rather that just the general object of lobbying, the specific legislative proposal, bill, resolution, regulation, policy, program, or contract in question had to be identified, along with the name of each department or other governmental institution lobbied."[28]

Ontario is the only province with a lobby registry, set up under the province's Integrity Commission under legislation proclaimed in January 1999.[29] Under this legislation, anyone who lobbies government, whether a consultant or an employee of corporations or associations, is required to sign up and identify for whom he or she is working, whether or not the client body relies on government funding, and the subject matter of the lobbying activity.

---

[27]James John Guy, *How We Are Governed*, Toronto, Harcourt Brace & Company Canada, Ltd., 1995, p. 304.

[28]Rand Dyck, *Canadian Politics*, Scarborough, Nelson, 1998, p. 199.

[29]This section is based on Caroline Mallan, "Harris cohort among first on lobby list," *Toronto Star*, January 30, 1999.

Social Movements

Yet another variation is found in **social movements**, which bring together individuals and groups to press for greater government action on what are felt to be neglected or mishandled issues. Examples would include the feminist, animal rights, gay rights, and environmental movements. The latter would include not only a large number of specific environmental groups but also others such as students, cottage owners, anglers and hunters, community groups, and professional associations—both organized and unorganized. These social movements can be distinguished from pressure groups by their structure, or lack thereof. They are not "organizations," but informal networks of interaction among a large number of often diverse individuals and groups who share a common cause.[30]

The Voluntary Sector

Many interest groups are part of the 175 000 non-profit groups and organizations concerned with social, economic, cultural, environmental, and political issues which constitute the **voluntary sector**.[31] This sector plays an extremely important role, both with respect to its activities and services and because it provides a means for citizens to engage in community and public issues. Organizations in the voluntary sector are praised for their innovative approaches, their long-term perspective, and their holistic view of the needs of citizens.[32] The voluntary sector undertakes extensive private fund raising, through organizations such as the United Way and community foundations that create endowments to invest in local activities in social, cultural and environmental areas. Governments also provide funding for many of the voluntary organizations, especially those in the health and social areas which deal with such matters as child care and home care.

---

[30]This discussion of social movements is based on Michael Whittington and Richard Van Loon, *Canadian Government and Politics*, Whitby, McGraw-Hill Ryerson Limited, 1996, pp. 441-442.

[31]The discussion in this section is based on Sherri Torjman, *Unravelling the Threads of Democracy*, Caledon Institute of Social Policy, June 1999.

[32]*Ibid.*

In spite of the important role it plays, the volunteer sector has been under siege from governments in recent years. As programs have been cut or abandoned to deal with the deficit, more and more services have been offloaded to the voluntary sector, sometimes through formal agreement but more often by default. This is occurring at the same time as governments have been cutting their financial support to these same organizations. There have also been attempts by government to impose greater control over the operations of voluntary organizations.[33] This is being done by imposing greater conditions over the money provided to the organizations, through the kinds of members appointed to their boards, and through less than subtle suggestions that the organizations refrain from inappropriate advocacy roles.

"Flower Power" Curtailed?

Illustrative of the changing times is the experience of Ontario's Trillium Foundation, which, since its establishment in 1982, has distributed more than $200 million in grants generated through lotteries.[34] Following its election in June 1995, the Conservative government undertook a review of all provincial agencies, partly to ensure that they were sufficiently effective and accountable. The government claimed that the Trillium Foundation did not have a fixed business plan or a concrete vision. It is clear that the government and some of its supporters also felt that too many of the Foundation's funds were being allocated to left wing groups critical of the Conservative agenda. Particularly irksome was a grant made in 1996 to the Metro Network for Social Justice, to be used to increase public awareness about economic and social issues facing Torontonians. But the Network was also a major player in the "Days of Action" rotating strikes held in various cities across Ontario to protest government cutbacks. Since 1997 the government has appointed 22 new people to the board of the Foundation. At present only 6 of the 20 board members have *not* contributed to the Conservative Party, and a number of them are well known Conservative supporters.

---

[33] *Ibid.*

[34] This summary is based on Kellie Hudson, "$190,000 grant that angered Tories," *Toronto Star*, January 9, 1999.

◆ Something to Think About

What do you think of the apparent attempt by the Ontario government to rein in the Foundation and discourage it from "inappropriate" funding activity? Isn't it reasonable to expect a government to balk at funding groups which attack its actions?

Yes, it is understandable that governments might act in this manner, as they have in other jurisdictions as well. But as a former board member of the Trillium Foundation has pointed out, "many of the organizations who work on behalf of the most vulnerable in our society have no choice but to be advocates.... So banning funding for advocacy groups is a very effective way of shutting down the only voice of the most vulnerable."[35]

Pressure Group Activity

Pressure groups are by no means new to Canadian politics and Pross notes that even in pre-Confederation days it was common for groups to lobby authorities in Britain or France for public policy concessions that would advance their interests.[36] They have now become so prominent, however, that according to Jeffrey Simpson,[37] modern politics is interest group politics, "a giant bazaar where parties try with increasing desperation to satisfy interest groups which, by definition, have a stake in being dissatisfied."

> A number of factors encouraged the proliferation of interest groups.

The diversity of Canadian society contributes to the proliferation of interest groups, and our federal system of government stimulates the organization of interest groups on various levels to apply pressure on several fronts. In addition, our parliamentary system of government provides multiple contact and pressure points,

---

[35]Pauline Couture, quoted in *ibid.*

[36]Pross, *op. cit.*, p. 20.

[37]Jeffrey Simpson, *Globe and Mail*, September 5, 1990, quoted in *ibid.*, p. 1.

further encouraging the development of pressure groups.[38] Moreover, operating departments have often found it useful to forge alliances with outside interest groups (and even to encourage and foster their development). These links have provided helpful allies when the departments need to defend their programs and budgets, especially with the cutback mentality which has prevailed in recent years.

Whatever their other purposes, these groups do provide a vehicle through which citizens can participate in public affairs. Many Canadians are disillusioned with political parties, which seem to avoid taking a clear stand on the issues that concern them, or reverse that stand when it suits their purpose. In contrast, interest groups—almost by definition—have clearly defined objectives which are pursued in a more consistent fashion. By joining groups which advocate positions similar to their own, individuals feel able to participate more effectively in society. Pross takes the view that the competition provided by pressure groups is not the problem; rather it is a symptom of the decline in the policy role of political parties and of our elected representatives.[39] This view would suggest directing efforts to improve our governing institutions rather than to restricting pressure groups.

The existence of widespread pressure groups is central to the pluralistic view of policy making, which sees government decisions essentially emerging as a result of the interaction of these groups and their demands. Not all Canadians belong to groups, however, and not all groups have equal resources or equal access to government. In particular, the poor and the less educated are much less likely to join together in concerted efforts to influence government action. In the classic words of E. E. Schattschneider, "the flaw in the pluralist heaven is that the heavenly chorus sings with a strong upper-class accent...."[40]

Many believe that the front row of that chorus is occupied by business leaders and corporations. They certainly have the resources to

---

[38]These explanations for the prevalence of pressure groups are provided by Guy, *op. cit.*, p. 292.

[39]Pross, *op. cit.*, p. 16.

[40]E. E. Schattschneider, *The Semi-Sovereign People*, New York, Holt, Rinehart and Winston, 1960, p. 35.

promote their point of view, and they appear to have ready access to government as well. The fact that so much of the funding for the Liberal and Progressive Conservative parties has come from business has certainly helped to ease that access. A recurring theme in this Guide is the strong influence exerted by the business community over the economic policies and objectives pursued by our governments.

> A number of business or business-backed organizations exert considerable influence over government.

Particularly influential are a number of business-backed "think tanks" which purport to offer research and recommendations on public issues, but which do so from a markedly right-wing, pro-business perspective. Leading the list is the Fraser Institute, which has been unceasing in its attacks on government interference in the market economy and in its promotion of the importance of freeing society so that people can pursue wealth. The C. D. Howe Institute claims to be less ideological than the Fraser Institute, but it has been very influential in emphasizing the dangers of Canada's public debt and the need to cut social programs. One of its studies, calling for the elimination of inflation as a top government priority, was used by the government and the Bank of Canada to justify the harsh zero inflation policy pursued by the Bank in the 1980s and discussed in Chapter 10.[41]

Another prominent player has been the Business Council on National Issues (BCNI), headed by Tom d'Aquino, which was very effective in promoting the free trade agreements with the United States and Mexico. The extent of the influence wielded by this body, and its leader, became the subject of a series of amusing—if not terribly revealing—media reports in 1998. Allan Fotheringham sparked the debate in his regular column in *Macleans*. According to Dr. Foth, Peter Newman's new book, *Titans*, contained quotes from an interview with Tom d'Aquino in which he took credit for an extraordinary degree of influence over the policies pursued by the federal government, under both Mulroney and Chrétien. If one is to believe Fotheringham quoting

---

[41]For a highly critical discussion of the role played by these and other business organizations, see Murray Dobbin, *The Myth of the Good Corporate Citizen*, Toronto, Stoddart, 1998, especially Chapter 8.

Newman quoting d'Aquino, the latter met Mulroney while out for a stroll one day and talked him into supporting free trade, and then in 1993 met with newly elected Prime Minister Chrétien for three hours and convinced him to implement the BCNI's agenda. Veteran political commentator Dalton Camp, who was in the Privy Council Office during part of the Mulroney period, offers a tongue-in-check rejection of this interpretation of events.[42] According to Camp, d'Aquino is a mild, unassuming, humble, dutiful servant to the free enterprise system and the Canadian way, and, as the best dressed lobbyist in Ottawa, is not the kind of person who runs countries on the sly. Camp expresses doubt that either d'Aquino or Chrétien is responsible for the Liberal policies of the 1990s, suggesting instead that it might be Paul Martin or a reporter for the Wall Street Journal!

It should be noted that there are those who argue that business groups don't have nearly as much decisive influence as is usually attributed to them. They face competition from other strong groups, representing the interests of labour, the environment, consumers and others. The Canadian Centre for Policy Alternatives and the Caledon Institute of Social Policy, for example, both provide effective critiques of the business agenda and make the case for strong social programs. The Council of Canadians, headed by Maude Barlow, has provided a strong voice against what it perceives as the excesses of the business agenda and the dangers facing Canadians from such developments as the free trade agreements and the proposed MAI (Multilateral Agreement on Investment).[43] In addition, as discussed in Chapter 7, the Charter has shifted some power in our system to interests and groups which had previously been relegated to the sidelines, but which now can use the courts to pursue their objectives. Competition between political parties and the need to appeal to the general public are also felt to prevent businesses from "having their way" with governments. The fact that some government policies are adopted over the strong objections

---

[42]See Dalton Camp, "Snappy dressers like d'Aquino don't run countries," *Toronto Star*, December 30, 1999, on which this section is based.

[43]All three of these bodies maintain extensive web sites which are, respectively, *www.policyalternatives.ca*, *www.caledoninst.org*, and *www.canadians.org*.

of business is cited as further evidence that business influence has been overstated.[44]

In this regard, the unsuccessful merger efforts of Canada's big banks provide an interesting example. Finance Minister Paul Martin rejected the merger plans of the Royal and the Bank of Montreal and of the Toronto Dominion Bank and CIBC in December 1998. On the surface, this action would appear to demonstrate that even such large business interests as the banks represent don't necessarily have their way with government.

Don't Bank On It

However, it is widely believed that other factors explain this particular government decision.[45] For one thing, the banks badly mishandled the whole issue, by announcing their merger plans—and forcing Martin's hand—before a government study on the banking sector had been completed. Second, Martin has taken a tough line on government spending, including social spending, in his successful quest to balance the federal budget. It is plausible to see his rejection of the banks as a way of softening his image, of demonstrating his concern for ordinary Canadians. At the same time, by leaving the door open for the banks to apply again in the not-too-distant future, Martin need not lose the Bay Street (big business) support which he would also like to retain. If these speculations are valid, the bank merger rejection may have more to do with timing and political strategy than with the extent of business influence over government.

Lobbyists at Work

Further insight into a number of issues discussed above can be seen from an examination of the activities of the tobacco lobby in response to government efforts to ban tobacco advertising. When legislation was

---

[44]For a very good discussion of both sides of this issue, see the articles by William Coleman and W. T. Stanbury in Mark Charlton and Paul Barker (eds.), *Crosscurrents: Contemporary Political Issues*, 2nd Edition, Scarborough, Nelson, 1994, pp. 336-363, on which the above summary is based.

[45]This discussion is based on William Walker, "Why Martin will say no to banks," *Toronto Star*, December 13, 1998.

first introduced in 1987, the tobacco manufacturers
hired a prominent lobbyist, Bill Neville, to work on
their behalf, and mounted a campaign of newspaper
advertisements and direct mailings. Various health
groups, including the Canadian Medical Association
and the Canadian Cancer Society countered with
their own campaigns, including black-edged post-
cards to MPs to symbolize the cancer-related deaths
in their ridings.[46] Rather than trying to kill the legislation, the tobacco
lobby concentrated, successfully, on delaying its passage for a considerable time. Moreover, when the Tobacco Products Control Act was
passed in June 1988, opponents appealed to the Supreme Court which
ruled, in 1995, that the Act was unconstitutional because its nearly total
advertising ban violated the tobacco industry's right to free speech.[47]

When the Liberal government announced plans to introduce new
legislation to control tobacco advertising in the spring of 1996, those in
the tobacco industry employed several tactics.[48]

- They hired influential former civil servants, including chiefs of staff
  to two former Prime Ministers, for advice on making their case.
- They hired professional lobbyists with Liberal connections to lobby
  the public service and the office of the Minister of Health.
- They helped to establish and to fund an alliance of arts and sports
  groups, which had become dependent on millions in annual cigar-
  ette sponsorships for their events, to lobby politicians.
- They pointed out that economically depressed Montreal, home to
  the country's largest tobacco company and site of many cigarette-
  sponsored festivals, would be hard hit by the government's plans.
- They even found a national unity link, reminding the government
  that the President of Imasco (Imperial Tobacco), one of Québec's
  leading companies, is a strong federalist voice in that province.

---

[46]This discussion is based on Robert Jackson and Doreen Jackson, *Canadian Government in Transition*, Scarborough, Prentice-Hall Canada Inc., 1996, p. 238.

[47]*Ibid.*

[48]The description of this round of lobbying is based on Mark Kennedy, "Health issue entangled in issues of jobs and national unity," *Kingston Whig Standard*, November 19, 1996.

The tobacco industry also relied upon the close political ties it had built up over the years. It donates substantial funds to mainstream parties, including $63 000 to the Liberals in 1995 and $92 000 the previous year.[49] A number of Senators sit on tobacco boards, as did Finance Minister Paul Martin until he became an MP in 1988. Presidents and other executive members of various riding associations have strong ties to the tobacco industry, and tobacco companies have made substantial campaign contributions to individual candidates.

The tobacco story offers a number of insights into pressure group activity in Canada. It illustrates how influential and well connected business groups can be, as previously discussed. But it also demonstrates, in support of pluralist views of policy making, that other interests—in this case from the health field—can also mobilize and make an effective case. Even with all of its connections, the tobacco lobby was unsuccessful in blocking a second attempt at government legislation banning advertising, introduced in late 1996 and passed in April 1997.

But continued pressure did succeed in weakening the resolve of the Liberal government, especially as the time drew near for the 1997 election. When the tobacco companies threatened to cancel their sponsorship of Montreal's Grand Prix, the Health Minister announced that limited tobacco advertising would continue to be allowed in connection with racing events. This move was apparently sparked by the Prime Minister's concern that the controversy with the tobacco companies might hurt Liberal candidates in Montreal ridings in the impending election. The Tobacco Act was amended in 1998 (Bill C-42) to provide a two year extension (to October 1, 2000) for tobacco sponsorships of existing events and groups (not just related to racing). For three years thereafter, sponsorship will be permitted freely on the site of events only, and effective October 1, 2003 all promotion of tobacco sponsorship will be banned.

---

[49]*Ibid.*

Concluding Observations

This chapter has provided an extremely brief overview of political parties and the political spectrum. It in no way constitutes an adequate examination of this topic. It is up to you to build from this introduction. Find out more about the political parties and where they stand on the issues that concern you. When the next federal or provincial election occurs, be sure that you have an informed basis for exercising your democratic rights.

When you look at the parties and the promises they make, you should also consider carefully the assumptions they are making about the role of government—in other words, where they fit on the political spectrum. Where you want them to fit is your call. But this Guide offers a reminder that—as with all things in life—a balance must be maintained in the size and scope of government. It may well be that government had grown too large and too intrusive. If we over-react to this perceived situation, however, we may pay the price for scaling back too much the role and contribution made by government. We may aggravate social divisions and widen the gap between the haves and have-nots. We may find ourselves with not only a leaner government but a meaner society. It's up to you, and all Canadians, to monitor the actions of our governments and our political parties, and to maintain a desirable balance between the scale of government operations and that of the private sector.

Besides participating through political parties, you may wish to join pressure groups that deal with issues that concern you. But recognize that governments can't always respond to the interests of your particular group(s), no matter how well expressed. Nor would such a response necessarily be desirable, unless one assumes that the "public interest" is little more than the sum total of the various, separate pressure group interests. Since many of the most influential pressure groups seem to represent the interests of big business, their combined perspective is unlikely to accord with the public interest, which suggests that you should also pay more attention to the activities of these pressure groups and the kind of influence they wield over government.

The Last Word

Definition of Terms and Concepts

Interest Group: (See also Pressure Group.)
A number of individuals who come together because of their common interest in a particular issue or activity.

Left Wing:
Term to describe political views which support a major role for government in the management of the economy and the provision of programs and services to support individuals and families.

Lobbyist:
Someone who specializes in attempting to influence government, either as an employee of a particular organization or as a professional who works for a variety of different clients.

Neoconservatism:
Term to describe ultra-right wing views which advocate minimum government, tax cuts, cuts in program spending (especially on social programs), more self-responsibility, and the benefits of competition and market forces.

Political Party:
Organization dedicated to recruiting candidates and electing members, with the objective of forming a government and carrying out their policies and objectives.

Pressure Group:
An interest group which interacts with government in an attempt to influence its policies. All pressure groups are interest groups, but not all interest groups become (or stay) pressure groups.

Right Wing:
Term to describe political views which hold that minimum government is best in terms of individual freedom and development. Also a term used to depict a strong (punitive?) position on matters of crime and punishment.

Social Movement:
Not an organization but an informal network of interaction among a large number of often diverse individuals and groups who share a common cause.

Third Way:
Term applied to moderate political position assumed by leaders like Britain's Tony Blair which acknowledges that neither socialism nor conservatism has worked.

Voluntary Sector:
Non-profit groups and organizations concerned with social, economic, cultural, environmental, and political issues.

Points to Ponder

1. Where do you place yourself on the political spectrum, and why? [Don't be surprised if you decide that you are left wing in some respects and right wing in others. This doesn't mean that you are schizophrenic. You might, for example, hold right wing views on law and order (such as favouring the return of capital punishment) but left wing views on social programs and their importance.]

2. In considering which party you support, is that support based on:
   a) a positive view of the leader of the party,
   b) a negative view of the alternatives, or
   c) positive feelings about specific policies of the party?

3. Identify any current political issue, observe how it is handled, and attempt to identify the pressure groups involved, their activities, and their apparent degree of success in promoting their viewpoint.

For Further Reading

For a good overview of political parties and the philosophies of conservatism, liberalism and socialism, see Robert Jackson and Doreen Jackson, *Canadian Government in Transition*, 2nd Edition, Toronto, Prentice-Hall Canada Inc., 1999, Chapter 10. There is also a more extensive treatment of this topic by these authors in *Politics in Canada*, 3rd Edition, Toronto, Prentice-Hall Canada Inc., 1994, Chapter 10. See also C. Campbell and W. Christian, *Parties, Leaders and Ideologies in Canada*, Whitby, McGraw-Hill Ryerson Limited, 1996, and Michael Whittington and Richard Van Loon, *Canadian Government and Politics*, Whitby, McGraw-Hill Ryerson Limited, 1996, Chapters 13 and 14.

A series of short articles on Canadian political parties and their roles and philosophies is found in Paul Fox and Graham White (eds.), *Politics: Canada*, 8th Edition, Whitby, McGraw-Hill Ryerson Limited, 1995.

For an overview of the much more limited activity of organized political parties within local government, see C. Richard Tindal and Susan Nobes Tindal, *Local Government in Canada*, 5th Edition, Scarborough, Nelson, 2000, Chapter 10.

Pressure groups are discussed in many texts including A. Paul Pross, *Group Politics and Public Policy*, 2nd Edition, Toronto, Oxford University Press, 1992, the previously-cited Whittington and Van Loon text, Chapters 16 and 17, and the previously cited texts by Jackson and Jackson.

A good discussion of whether or not business groups enjoy privileged access to government is found in the articles by William Coleman and W. T. Stanbury in Mark Charlton and Paul Barker (eds.) *Crosscurrents: Contemporary Political Issues*, 2nd Edition, Scarborough, Nelson, pp. 336-363.

Information on three prominent pro-business organizations can be found at their web sites, *www.fraserinstitute.ca*, *www.cdhowe.org*, and *www.taxpayer.com*. The first two are self-explanatory and the third is the site of the Canadian Taxpayers Federation. For a contrary point of view, check out web sites for the Canadian Centre for Policy Alternatives, the Caledon Institute of Social Policy, and the Council of Canadians, all cited earlier in this chapter.

Chapter 4

Don't Fight Them, Join Them

Objectives and Highlights

◆ To describe various ways you can participate in government activities.

◆ To identify factors which limit public participation.

◆ To examine the roles played by the media in our system of government.

Notwithstanding its shortcomings, few would dispute that Canada's system of government is democratic. But the quality of Canadian democracy in practice depends on the extent to which citizens make use of the various means of participation available to them and the extent to which that participation influences the decisions made by government.

As mentioned in Chapter 1, many Canadians appear disillusioned with government and alienated from it. In this regard, the provincial election results in Ontario in June 1999 were quite remarkable. The preceding four years had been filled with turmoil as the ruling Conservatives aggressively implemented a series of radical policies in support of their "Common Sense Revolution." Widespread hospital closings were announced. Welfare payments were cut and workfare was introduced. More than 200 municipal governments were "persuaded" to amalgamate. Education decision making was centralized within Queen's Park. These and other measures prompted widespread public protests, including a series of "days of action" by organized labour and a teachers' strike. Even those who supported the general approach of the government conceded that it was moving too fast.

Given the extent to which Ontario was polarized during the first term of the Conservative regime, one might expect a fiercely contested election in 1999, and a high degree of public involvement. The fact that the Conservatives were reelected (with 45% of the popular vote) suggests that a substantial portion of Ontarians supported the Common Sense Revolution. But what is astounding is that only 62% of the eligible voters in Ontario cast their ballots in the June 1999 election. It is true that the low turnout is not much different from results in other recent Ontario elections. In the three previous elections, for example, the turnout was 62.9% in 1995, 64.4% in 1990 and 62.7% in 1987.[1] But it is hard to imagine an election which mattered more, which offered such a fundamental choice about the direction in which Ontario society should proceed. That more than one-third of Ontario's voters could not be bothered to exercise their democratic rights in this situation is disappointing and disturbing—not only for those opposed to the Conservative agenda, but also for the Conservatives themselves. While

> A low voting turnout can mean that a majority government is actually backed by less than one-third of eligible voters.

they hold a majority of the seats in the provincial legislature and will proceed as if they have a strong mandate from the citizens of Ontario, their 45% support from the 62% who bothered to vote actually represents the endorsement of fewer than one-third of Ontario citizens.

The primary purpose of this chapter is to explore various ways in which Canadians can participate in government, in the hope that this information may stimulate more Canadians to do so. Consistent with its purpose as a "Guide," it includes information on requirements for voting and candidacy, as well as information on the laws governing election financing. It also explores participation through such direct democracy concepts as the referendum and recall. Consideration is also given to the media, given the key role they play in linking people and their governments.

---

[1]These figures are from Charles Gordon, "The secret of the Harris win is foes failing to vote," *Ottawa Citizen*, June 17, 1999, whose observations helped to inform the discussion in this section.

Voting

It may surprise you to learn that the **franchise** (that is, the right to vote) has been universal only since 1960.[2]

At the time of Confederation, the franchise was based on provincial laws and was restricted to male property owners. As a result, in 1867 only 11% of the population was eligible to vote in federal elections.[3] Plural voting was allowed in that citizens could vote in each area in which they owned property. There was no single election day and the government staggered voting so that results came in first from their strong areas to develop a bandwagon effect. There wasn't any secret ballot in the early years; electors had to state publicly the name of the candidate they supported. Elections in the early years in this country were tumultuous affairs which sometimes dragged on for months, with bribes of food, drink and money, violence, and occasional loss of life.[4]

In 1885, balloting was brought under federal jurisdiction, but a new restriction was added with the disenfranchisement of Asians. In 1917, Canadians of Central European descent lost their vote. Females, if relatives of soldiers, were given the right to vote, along with native Indians serving in the Armed Forces. The following year, all women were granted equal voting rights. Canadians of Asian descent, however, were not granted normal voting privileges until 1948, and Inuit—who were disenfranchised in 1934—didn't have the right restored until 1950. Religious conscientious objectors, mainly Mennonites, who had been disenfranchised as early as 1920, did not regain voting rights until 1955. The last group to receive voter status was reservation Indians, and that as late as 1960.

---

[2]The summary which follows is partly based on Robert Jackson and Doreen Jackson, *Politics in Canada*, 3rd Edition, Scarborough, Prentice-Hall Canada Inc., 1994, p. 479.

[3]Elections Canada Online, *A History of the Vote in Canada*, at web site *www.elections.ca/gen_info/history_book*.

[4]*Ibid.*

Today, we enjoy a universal franchise at all levels of government. Every Canadian citizen, 18 years of age or older by polling day, who meets the specified residency requirements, and who is not otherwise disqualified, is eligible to vote.

Amendments to the Canada Elections Act in 1993 broadened the *federal* franchise[5] by removing disqualifications for several groups, including judges, persons who are "restrained of their liberty of movement or deprived of the management of their property by reason of mental disease" and inmates serving sentences of less than two years in a correctional institution. Provision was also made for Canadians to vote if they are absent from Canada for less than five consecutive years and intend to return to reside in Canada, or if they are temporarily outside of the country or outside of their electoral district.

There are very few persons still prohibited from voting. These include the Chief Electoral Officer, returning officers in each riding, and individuals disqualified by law for corrupt or illegal practices. Inmates of penal institutions serving a sentence of more than two years were disqualified until a successful court challenge just before the 1997 election.

Ontario legislation states that persons are eligible to vote if they have resided in Ontario for twelve months prior to polling day, and are ordinarily resident in the electoral district in which they intend to vote. A 1984 amendment to the Election Act gave the vote to judges, returning officers, election clerks, and inmates of mental hospitals or homes for the mentally incompetent.

To be an elector at the *municipal* level, one must be a Canadian citizen, 18 years of age or older by polling day, and a resident in the municipality—or an owner or tenant of land in the municipality or spouse of same.[6] It is possible to vote in more than one municipality. For example, someone may live in one municipality, own a business in a second municipality, and have a summer cottage in a third one.

---

[5] Jackson and Jackson, *op. cit.*

[6] These are the provisions with respect to municipal elections in Ontario. A number of amendments to the Municipal Elections Act were passed in December 1996 as part of Bill 86, the Better Local Government Act.

Voting Turnout

The fact that there are very few limitations on the right to vote doesn't translate into a high voting turnout in Canada. The average turnout in federal elections in the 20th century has been about 73%, but it varies considerably from one province to another. The more than one quarter who do not vote have consistently been shown to be alienated from or uninformed about government, and found primarily in the poor and working classes.[7] While Canada's turnout in national elections is well ahead of the United States (which has been steadily falling to 50% or below), and is similar to that of Britain, it lags well behind many other countries.

Some of the public disillusionment with voting may stem from a feeling that their vote is wasted or badly distorted as a result of the "first-past-the-post" electoral system used in Canada. Under this system, in which the winning candidate does not have to receive 50% plus one of the popular vote but simply more votes than any other candidate, the proportion of seats won by a party may bear little relation to the proportion of popular vote it receives. The absence of members representing the

> The seats a party wins may not accord with the popular vote it receives.

Liberal Party in the West or the NDP in the Maritimes seems to disenfranchise the substantial numbers of people who voted for these parties (in vain) in these areas. These discrepancies, and the possible use of a proportional representation system to address them, are discussed in the next chapter.

Another troubling issue, for those who vote as well as those who don't, is the very passive and limited nature of this participation. The opportunity to vote arises approximately every four years at the senior levels (and exactly every four or three years in the case of municipal elections, depending on the province involved). Many people feel that once an election is over, the politicians pay little attention to them, or their views, until the next election is called. Those not content with this very limited involvement sometimes express an interest in more direct

[7]Rand Dyck, *Canadian Politics*, Scarborough, Nelson, 1998, p. 114.

participation through such tools as the referendum and the recall, which are discussed later in this chapter.

The turnout for provincial elections has been both higher and lower than the federal average, depending on the province and the year. But the real contrast is found at the municipal level, where only about 40% of eligible voters cast their ballots. Among the reasons offered for this low turnout are the following:[8]

- the turnout tends to be lower in larger municipalities than smaller ones, where there is election by general vote (over the whole municipality) rather than by ward, amongst those with lower educational levels, and amongst tenants as opposed to home-owners (who pay the municipal property tax).
- it is lower when there is less competition for seats on council and especially when there is an acclamation (no election contest) for the position of head of council.
- it is also felt that the turnout is lower because of the complexity of the municipal election process, with the possibility of several separate ballots (for head of council, council, school board, and utility commission), several names per ballot, and no party affiliations to differentiate these names.
- the limited scope of municipal activities, the extent to which municipalities are controlled by their provincial governments, is another factor cited.

Becoming a Candidate

Most Canadians would probably never consider becoming a candidate for political office. This reservation is not because of legal requirements, which are fairly minimal. Rather, it is because of a number of other "unofficial barriers" which tend to limit the availability of candidates. Before examining these barriers, let's look at the legal requirements involved.

---

[8]The summary which follows is based on C. Richard Tindal and Susan Nobes Tindal, *Local Government in Canada*, 5th Edition, Scarborough, Nelson, 2000, pp. 299-301.

Legal Requirements for Candidacy

The federal requirements are outlined below. Provincial requirements are similar, but you should consult the legislation in your particular province for the specifics.

1. You must be eligible to vote.

2. You must be a resident of Canada, but not necessarily a resident of the riding in which you seek to be a candidate—although candidates who are "parachuted" into a riding with which they have no past association are often rebuffed.

3. You must not be disqualified from seeking federal office by the provisions of the Canada Elections Act. This category includes persons guilty of corrupt election practices and members of a provincial legislature.

4. You must have the signatures of 100 fellow electors. [But, if you decide to run some day, be sure to get 102 or 105 signatures while you're at it. If you have only 100 names and it then is determined that one of those people is not an eligible voter in your riding, and the nomination period has closed, you are out of luck! Don't take that chance. Have some margin for safety.]

5. You must pay a deposit of $1000. This payment is intended to discourage frivolous candidates. Half of this deposit is returned when the candidate files the required financial statement following an election and the other half is refunded to those who receive at least 15% of the votes cast in the election. An Ontario judge ruled, in March 1999, that the 15% requirement with respect to the refund was an unconstitutional barrier to the participation of smaller political parties.[9] However, this ruling is binding only on political parties within Ontario, and is subject to possible appeal.

As mentioned, the provisions for provincial elections are very similar. For example, the requirements for Ontario include the same 100 signatures. A financial deposit has only been required since 1984 and it is for $200, not the $1000 required at the federal level.

---

[9]Theresa Boyle, "Elections Act found to be unjust," *Toronto Star*, March 12, 1999.

In the case of municipal elections (again using Ontario as the example), you must be eligible to vote, must not be disqualified from being a candidate (such as by being a member of the Legislative Assembly of Ontario or the Federal House of Commons) and you must not be an employee of the municipality or of defined local boards—unless you obtain a leave of absence. In a change very much in line with federal and provincial provisions, candidates for municipal office in Ontario must now provide a financial deposit of $100, which is refundable if the candidate withdraws, receives more than a prescribed minimum of the vote, or is elected.

> The main barriers aren't legal, but involve socio-economic constraints and party nominations.

So far, so good. There aren't many legal barriers to becoming a candidate for office at any level in Canada. But we have been ignoring two significant hurdles which have to be overcome, even though they are not legal requirements. First, there are a variety of what might best be termed socio-economic variables which tend to reduce dramatically the potential pool of candidates. Second, those seeking office at the federal and provincial levels have the added task of becoming nominated by a political party—since there is little chance of being elected as an independent candidate. A closer look at both of these types of barrier will reveal the real limitations on public participation through standing for office.

Socio-Economic Limits on Candidacy

Perhaps as little as 20% of the Canadian population would ever consider themselves "candidate material" or would be accepted as such by their fellow electors. What are the factors which so severely restrict the pool of potential candidates?

a) **Age**

   Once elected, a candidate can be reelected any number of times, without too much attention being paid to the advancing years. However, a first time candidate who was a senior citizen might be considered too old by the electorate. At one time, first time candidates also faced the possibility of being rejected as too young, but over the past couple of decades we have seen a dramatic increase in the number of youthful candidates being elected at all three levels.

b) Sex or Gender

This has been a factor, but it too appears to be lessening. In the recent past, Canada has had a female Prime Minister, albeit for a brief period. The federal NDP replaced one female leader with another in the fall of 1995. Women have also been gaining more prominent positions in provincial politics. BC had Canada's first female Premier in 1991, a female Premier was elected in Prince Edward Island in the mid-1990s (although she stepped down from that position not long after), and the leader of the NWT government until the fall of 1995 was a woman. Perhaps most dramatic of all has been the number of women heading municipalities, including (in Ontario alone) present or recent past Mayors of Mississauga, London, Kingston, Ottawa, Toronto, Vaughan, Kanata, and Vanier.

On the other hand, there is some evidence from the provincial and federal levels to suggest that the gains by women are not always sustained and that, in particular, they have more difficulty than men in retaining support when they are in leadership positions. For example, the mid-term resignation of PEI Premier, Catherine Callbeck, is blamed by some on pressure from "back-room boys," Lynda Haverstock was forced out as Opposition Leader in Saskatchewan by a caucus revolt in 1996, and Lynn McLeod stepped down as Liberal leader in Ontario after that party's failure in the June 1995 provincial election.[10] In all cases, they were replaced by men. The pattern of reversal has been particularly striking in Ontario, which not long ago featured an NDP government in which 40% of the members were female. By contrast, the Conservative Cabinet which replaced it had only four women members, and almost 85% of the legislature elected in 1995 was male.

---

[10]This discussion is based on "Why don't female leaders last in Canadian politics?" *Ottawa Citizen*, November 29, 1996.

c) Race and Religion

Historically, these factors almost always related to the French-English and Catholic-Protestant features of the "two founding races" of Canada. However, Canada, especially in its urban areas, has become increasingly cosmopolitan. Many races and religions are now to be found and may influence a candidate's chances for success in particular ridings.

d) Type of Employment

There is a widespread, if ill-defined and even subconscious, perception that shift workers, labourers, semi-skilled workers and others in what used to be termed "blue collar" jobs would not be suitable candidates as elected members. Conversely, those in "white collar" positions like lawyers, bankers, business managers and other professionals are regarded as better qualified.

e) Educational Level

This is, to some extent, a perception issue like the preceding one. It refers to the fact that people are likely to question the suitability of a high school dropout, especially if the alternative is a college or university graduate. The requirements of elected office will mean that most members will be called upon to communicate with the public frequently. Whether fair or well founded, the perception is that the higher the educational level, the more likely a member will write and speak in a polished and articulate manner and will present an image in keeping with what most people think an elected member should be.

f) "Social Class"

This factor is similar in some respects to the "blue collar-white collar" distinction made earlier and also reflects one's educational background. However, it can be much more. While Canadians like to think of themselves as a classless society, there is still a strong sense of living on the "right side of the tracks." Some families are prominent in a community; they have enjoyed social standing for decades—perhaps back through several generations. Other people are felt to come from uncertain or dubious origins. They lack the same pedigree. Much of this, of course, is little more than snobbery. It may be quite inaccurate and unfair. But, perception is reality, and nowhere more so than in politics.

g) Money

The income level a candidate for office enjoys is largely a product of the preceding three factors: type of employment, educational level, and social class. It can influence the availability of candidates in two contradictory ways. If those with limited incomes should consider running for office (in spite of all the other barriers listed above), they may be attracted by the prospect of the salary and expense allowance paid to an elected member. The majority of prospective candidates, however, are likely to hold reasonably well paid positions already; for them, the politician's salary is likely to offer a reduction in income and a disincentive.

Whatever their existing income, most prospective candidates think twice when they contemplate the expenses that they face— first in contesting the election itself, and second if they should win the election. Campaign expenses, and sources of funding for these expenses, are discussed later in this chapter. The extra expenses which arise after an election victory come particularly from the need to maintain two households (in the riding and in the national or provincial capital) and from the unending list of charities and worthy causes which will expect (demand) financial support from a public figure.

Municipal politicians who operate businesses in their municipality often face two further difficulties relating to finances. They may lose business opportunities with the municipality because of a perceived conflict of interest. They may also find that some ratepayers shun their business if unhappy about some municipal policy or service. This may sound petty, but it is all part of the "gold-fish bowl" atmosphere of municipal political life.

h) Impact on Personal Life

This impact can be expressed very simply—you won't have a "personal" life. It has been said that public figures can't have private lives. It is true that the public is entitled to know about private matters which may affect the public performance of an elected

Your life will be under a microscope

member or may place the member in a conflict of interest situation. But, they do not need to know personal details of a member's private life or of the private lives of the member's family. Yet with increasingly aggressive investigative journalism now in vogue, "health records, past academic performance, youthful peccadillos, friendships, family life, holiday activities, entertainment preferences, and all else are now fair game...."[11] The thought of being placed under a microscope, or of having one's family background probed by overzealous media investigators, may be enough to eliminate many potential candidates.

The demands of the job also take their toll on one's personal life. Members are separated from their families throughout much of the year. They are not present to share in the important events in their children's lives—from school plays to sporting events to first dates. When members are home (mostly on weekends), they are expected to be "out and about"—being seen in the riding and available to take calls from constituents who have some problem which the member should solve. It has been said that "politics is a demanding mistress" and one of the unfortunate consequences of elected office is a number of broken marriages, presumably fuelled by the long separations of partners and the constant demands on the time and energies of the elected partner.

These eight points are not a definitive list of the factors which tend to inhibit people from becoming candidates for political office. Some may dispute the validity of some of these points and the way they are described. The fact remains that factors such as these dramatically limit the pool of Canadians who would ever give serious consideration to becoming a politician—and who would be taken seriously by the rest of the public if they decided to run. One result, as discussed in Chapter 5, is that the make-up of the House of Commons does not represent the

---

[11]John Meisel, "Decline of Party in Canada," in Mark Charlton and Paul Barker (eds.), *Crosscurrents: Contemporary Political Issues*, 2nd Edition, Scarborough, Nelson, 1994, p. 241.

characteristics of the overall Canadian population. If it did, it would have more members under the age of 35, far more women members, and many more unskilled workers. We sometimes decry the fact the House of Commons is not more representative of "ordinary" Canadians, but it is uncertain that we would elect significant numbers of such Canadians if they could be persuaded to stand for office.

The Limitations of the Party Nomination

There is no legal requirement to obtain the backing of a political party to run for office at any level of government. Official party endorsement is not even an issue at the municipal level, except in the handful of Canadian cities in which political parties vie for seats on council. Even though they run as independents, however, many candidates for municipal council benefit from the fact that they are known to be associated with one political party or another. They also benefit from the campaign support they may receive from "the party machine." In fact, Canadians have a rather perverse view about party politics in municipal government. They accept quite willingly that municipal councillors are actively involved with political parties. They just don't accept that councillors should make this fact official by running on a party label.

However, elections for the federal and provincial level are fought on party lines. The political parties raise and spend large sums of money on behalf of their platforms and their candidates. The chances of an independent candidate being elected are extremely slim—almost non-existent. But as the following two examples indicate, victory by an independent candidate is not impossible.

Mission (Im)possible?

In 1974, a former Mayor of Moncton, New Brunswick, Leonard Jones, was elected as an independent MP. The circumstances were most unusual. He had originally been chosen as a Conservative candidate, but the leader of the Conservative Party, Robert Stanfield, refused to sign his nomination papers—which meant he could not contest the election on

continued over

behalf of the party. Stanfield refused on the grounds that certain anti-French sentiments and statements expressed by Jones were unacceptable and unwelcome in the Conservative Party. The response of Jones was to run anyway, as an independent candidate. Because of the high profile and personal popularity which he enjoyed, as a former Mayor, he was elected. However, he served only one term. Being an independent member in the House of Commons is a pretty lonely life.

John Nunziata was expelled from the Liberal Party for his outspoken criticisms of the government, but ran in his old riding as an independent in the 1997 federal election and was successful. He continues to sit in the House as an independent.

If success at the provincial and federal levels presupposes a party affiliation, how does a prospective candidate go about obtaining a party nomination?

Party candidates are selected at nomination meetings called by each local **riding association**. This means that the decision on a candidate is usually made locally, by the party members in a particular riding who attend the nomination meeting. On the surface, this is a very democratic process, in which the candidate who attracts the largest number of supporters to the meeting carries the day. Some riding associations dictate that party memberships must have been held for some defined time period prior to the meeting—in an attempt to guard against some group packing the meeting with "instant members." The candidate who sells the most memberships (before any such deadline), and who gets out the votes, wins the nomination.

Most ridings are large and diverse. To become well known across such a riding, a candidate may have to spend several years working with the riding association and assisting in election campaigns. Parties like candidates to have "earned" the right to represent them.

While special issues may dictate some riding outcomes (for example, an ethnic candidate or an anti-abortion takeover), normally the local riding will select someone well established in the community and in the party. Obtaining the nomination, therefore, is to a large extent a matter of good timing and good luck. For example, if you would like to seek the nomination in a riding in which your party has a sitting member, you have almost no chance. If you are a Conservative seeking election in a riding which has returned Liberals since Confederation, your prospects aren't great. But, if you are a Liberal, living in a riding which has had a popular Liberal member who is not seeking re-election, your timing could hardly be better. There is an opening for you to win, in a riding which your party holds. Lucky you.

Changes in the Canada Elections Act have increased the role of the federal party leaders. Revisions in 1970 require that each candidate's party affiliations appear on the ballot. It is necessary for parties to identify their own candidates so that they will qualify for benefits under the legislation, including expenditure reimbursement (discussed below). A statement signed by the party leader or designate confirming the party's endorsement must be filed with a candidate's nomination papers. This provision allows party leaders to reject candidates nominated by the local riding. (As discussed above, it was this provision that allowed Robert Stanfield to block the candidacy of Leonard Jones.)

At its 1992 national convention, the Liberal Party went further and gave its leader the authority to hand-pick (prior to a nomination meeting) a number of candidates for the upcoming (1993) federal election. The rationale was that this discretion would allow the leader to ensure a good balance among candidates and to field a strong team to attract the voters. It was also felt that this appointing power could be used to avoid disruptive challenges to incumbents, such as when riding redistributions might leave two members fighting over one seat. There was also a feeling that some method was needed to reassert some central control over local nomination processes which were often quite unruly. For example, Liberal nomination meetings in 1984 and 1988 in a number of urban ridings in the Toronto area had been hijacked, defeating so-called star candidates that the embarrassed party had gone to some effort to recruit.[12]

Jean Chrétien used this power on several occasions leading up to the 1993 election. One early example was his selection of former Toronto Mayor Art Eggleton as the candidate for a Toronto-area riding. Eggle-

---

[12] Joan Bryden, "Not only women benefit when PM appoints candidates," *Ottawa Citizen*, March 18, 1997.

ton was elected and became a member of the Liberal Cabinet. Chrétien received a good deal of criticism (even from within the Liberal Party itself) for what was perceived as high-handed and undemocratic actions. Critics claimed that these actions denied to constituents the democratic right to choose the candidate, and also denied to other possible candidates the right to seek the nomination. The uproar caused the Prime Minister to back away from plans to appoint a series of "star" men. Instead, 11 of the remaining 13 appointments he made were women, with the justification being the need to ensure some measure of gender balance in the House of Commons.[13]

While this shift in emphasis reduced the criticisms of interference by the Prime Minister in 1993, the controversy returned when new appointments were made by Chrétien for the 1997 election. This time, much of the fuss centred around the selection of four female candidates. Feminists wondered why there hadn't been more criticism when male candidates were appointed, but others claimed that it was demeaning to the women to imply that they were not capable of winning the nomination on their own.

◆ Something to Think About

How much say should the party leader have in the selection of candidates? What do you see as the pros and cons of giving a party leader the authority to select a limited number of candidates (let's say no more than 20) for the party? On what grounds could exercise of this power be most justified?

Election Costs and Financing

As noted above, money—or the lack thereof—can be a factor limiting the availability of candidates. This issue is directly linked to that of party endorsement, since becoming a party candidate gives one access to additional sources of funding. Over the years, however, there have been concerns about where parties receive the increasingly large amounts of

---

[13]*Ibid.*

funding required to mount election campaigns and how such funding might influence the decisions made by parties and their members.

Much of the increase in costs coincided with the growing use of television advertising. Media costs from all sources became a very significant portion of total election costs. For example, in 1979 the Liberal media advertising campaign (TV, radio and newspapers) was estimated at $2.25 million, the PCs at $2.5 million, and the NDP at $1.2 million. These figures represented 71%, 62%, and 61%, respectively, of the three parties' total campaign expenditures. The 1988 PC advertising campaign was reported at $4.7 million, with the Liberals spending $3.8 million and the NDP $3.1 million. These expenses as a percentage of total campaign spending by each party were 59%, 56% and 44%, respectively.[14]

By the 1993 election campaign, it was estimated that:

- The national parties spent $45 million (comprising $10.6 million each by the Liberals, Conservatives, and NDP—their limit under the election financing legislation—$6 million by Reform, $4 million by the Bloc, and $2 million by the National Party).
- Candidates spent $50 million in the 295 ridings across Canada.
- Some $30 million was spent on pre-election spending and indirect expenses (notably polling), much of it by the then cash-rich Conservative Party.
- *More than half* of the expenditures were on advertising, about 70% of it for television ads.

By the time of the 1997 election, the maximum spending limit for parties sponsoring candidates in all 301 ridings was $11.3 million, and the spending limit for candidates in an individual riding ranged from over $50 000 to more than $70 000, depending mainly on the number of eligible voters in the riding.[15] Spending on the combined national and local campaigns approached $100 million, along with many millions of "unofficial" spending, on such matters as opinion polling and research.

---

[14]From the Report of the Chief Electoral Officer Respecting Election Expenses, 1988, as quoted in Jackson and Jackson, *op. cit.*, pp. 487-487.

[15]Details are available from Elections Canada Online at its web site *www.elections.ca*.

As the costs of campaigning escalated over the past several decades, we faced the prospect of candidates having to be wealthy or having to rely heavily on others for donations. Neither alternative is particularly healthy for a democratic system. There were growing concerns about sources of funding and what "strings" might come with the money being provided. Up until major reforms in 1974, the applicable legislation did not result in full disclosure, and when the public doesn't know, it fears the worst!

What was known was the two old-line parties (Liberals and PCs) had traditionally relied very heavily on big business for their campaign donations. Both parties utilized a "Finance Committee" composed of leading business people, and they focused their fund raising efforts on Toronto, Montreal and Vancouver—where the head offices of most corporations were located. They relied upon very large contributions ($50 000 was not unusual) from a relatively small number of donors—mostly corporations and wealthy individuals. The NDP was also beholden to an economic interest to an unhealthy degree, since it relied for much of its money on donations from unions.

Election Financing Legislation

The federal Election Expenses Act of 1974 (and associated legislative reforms) provided for the following rules governing election financing:

- A requirement that parties register (with the Chief Electoral Officer of Canada) to be eligible for the benefits available under the Act. [An Ontario court judge ruled, in March 1999, that it was unconstitutional to require a party to nominate a minimum of 50 candidates to remain registered, but this ruling is binding only on political parties within Ontario and may be the subject of appeal.]
- A requirement that registered parties designate those agents who are authorized to receive and spend money on their behalf.
- A dollar limit (based on a formula related to the number of voters in the ridings being contested) on the amount of election expenditures by a party.
- A dollar limit (based on a similar formula related to the number of voters in the particular riding) on the amount of election expenditures by a candidate.

- A requirement for audited financial reports—annually by a party and after each election by individual candidates.
- A requirement that the names of donors who give more than a total of $100 must be disclosed.
- Candidates receive a partial reimbursement of their expenditures, if they receive 15% or more of the popular vote (and if they have complied with all of the requirements of this legislation).
- Donations are made tax-deductible, to attract a broader base of support.
- There are limits to the period of advertising, from 29 days to 1 day before an election.
- Six and one-half hours of free TV advertising time are divided among the registered parties, according to a formula. The time had been apportioned on the basis of each party's popular vote and number of seats won in the previous election, but the Reform Party successfully challenged this formula in court—arguing that it obviously favoured the incumbent and long-established parties and disadvantaged newer and smaller parties.

These reforms did deal with the main concerns regarding election financing. A ceiling on spending by parties and candidates addressed the issue of ever-increasing costs and expenditures. Subsidizing the election

> These reforms did address concerns about election costs, reliance on big business, and disclosure.

costs for candidates made the contests less a rich person's game. The need for greater disclosure was met by the requirements concerning audited financial statements and names of donors. The provision for tax-deductible donations helped initially to broaden the support base of the parties, but in recent years there has been a return to reliance on large donors. Consider the following statistics:

Party	Donors in 1974	Donors in 1980
NDP	27 910	62 428
PC Party	6423	32 720
Liberal Party	9882	17 670

Not surprisingly, the NDP continued to have the largest number of individual donors, but it is striking to note the fivefold increase in Conservative donors in the first six years following the new legislation. The Liberals were much slower to make the transition contemplated by the new legislation—partly, it has been suggested, because during his long years as leader Trudeau largely neglected head office and "housekeeping" types of activity. This neglect was certainly one of the factors contributing to the financial problems which plagued the Liberal Party up until its election victory in 1993.

In spite of this promising beginning, the number of individual donors to parties began to wane by the mid-1980s, and fund-raisers renewed their emphasis on major corporate contributions as the essential ingredient in a well-financed campaign. In 1995, for example, the Liberals raised $5 million from 39 000 individuals and $7 million from 7000 companies, while the Conservatives raised $5.4 million evenly split between 2000 companies and 15 000 individuals.[16]

Other problems arose from loopholes in the election financing legislation. A particular concern is that spending limits in the legislation apply only to *election* expenses, not *campaign* expenses, like volunteers' expenses or polling research. Much of what the parties raise and spend for months in advance of an election call is campaign-specific but uncounted. This abuse can be expected to continue and to intensify, now that the federal election period has been reduced from 47 days to 36 days. The limits also don't apply to annual, ongoing expenditures. So, parties can transfer expenditures to this category if they are in danger of exceeding their election spending limits.

Issue of "Third Party" Spending

One of the continuing problems and concerns relates to so-called **third party spending**. This potentially confusing term does *not* refer to spending by political parties but by various interest groups which may wish to support or oppose various issues during an election campaign. Since the legislative reforms discussed above are quite strict in limiting parties and candidates as to how much they could spend and when, they

---

[16]Figures from Ross Howard, "Parties set to spend $100 million," *Globe and Mail*, April 14, 1997.

also initially restricted (indeed outlawed) spending by these so-called third parties. There was a legitimate concern about the possible influence of "political action groups" which have been very prominent in the United States.

However, a court challenge led by the National Citizens' Coalition led to the ruling that such restrictions violated the Charter. Freed from any legislative controls, business groups spent between $2 million and $10 million during the 1988 election campaign, promoting the free trade agreement (and, therefore, promoting the PCs, the only party which supported this agreement). We don't have a more precise measure of how much was spent because there are no requirements on these groups to file audited financial reports. They aren't even prevented from advertising on election day—unlike the political parties.

The politicians tried again, in April 1993, passing a law (Bill C-114 or the "Gag Law" as its opponents quickly dubbed it) which made it an offense for anyone except political parties to purchase more than $1000 in advertising during an election campaign. Once again, a court challenge was mounted, with opponents arguing that this law repressed individual rights and impinged upon democracy by allowing political elites to control the flow of ideas during an election campaign. Once again, the courts rejected the attempt to restrict advertising—on the basis of the Charter.

As a result, we have a system under which there are strict limits on how much money can be spent by candidates and parties, and no limits on what anyone else can spend during the same election. An example of the inequities that can arise occurred when Sheila Copps resigned over the GST issue and ran in a by-election in Hamilton East in mid-1996. The National Citizens' Coalition and several anti-GST groups spent thousands of dollars campaigning against Copps, thereby augmenting the funds spent by her opponents.

> We have strict limits on spending for parties and candidates, but no limits on anyone else.

On the other hand, third party spending restrictions could lead to extreme limitations or abuses, such as we have witnessed with the charges which were laid under Québec's referendum law against non-

Québecers who helped to organize the huge unity rally in Montréal during the fall 1995 sovereignty referendum. While we may deplore unfettered spending by big business, it seems at least as unacceptable to have laws which could prevent Canadians from trying to save their country. In October 1997, the Supreme Court ruled that the spending limits under Québec's referendum law of $600 per private citizen or organization was too low and a violation of the Charter's guarantee of free expression. The Court went on to offer the unsolicited opinion that the rejection (by the Alberta Court of Appeal) of the federal government's bill limiting third party spending to $1000 was wrong.

◆ Something to Think About

How do we reconcile the notion of individual freedom of expression with the concern that those with unlimited funds should not be allowed unrestricted opportunities to sway public opinion?

How could legislation of this sort be drafted in a way which would avoid a successful Charter challenge? Is the basis for a compromise on this important issue found in the Charter provision that the basic rights and freedoms within it are "subject to such reasonable limits prescribed by law as can be demonstrably justified in a free and democratic society."

A third attempt at legislating spending limits is found in Bill C-2, before the House at the time of writing. Instead of a limit of $1000 in spending by individuals and groups, the new bill will permit $3000 per riding and $150 000 nationwide.[17] Opponents of limits on third party spending argue that Canadians should be free to vote according to the first flashy ad campaign they see or the last, whether it is produced by a registered party or a special interest group. They reject the argument that one-sided spending (as might happen without legislated limits) would dictate an election outcome, and point out that the Yes side spent over $12 million promoting approval of the Charlottetown Accord, only to lose to the No side which spent less than $1 million.

---

[17]See Lorne Gunter, "End Campaign Spending Limits. Let the People Judge," *Policy Options*, Montreal, Institute for Research on Public Policy, September 1999, pp. 58-61, on which the discussion in this section is based.

They further argue that efforts to limit third party spending are really designed to maintain the electoral advantage held by incumbents.

Provincial and Municipal Election Financing

Maintaining that advantage is also alleged to be the motive behind recent changes (Bill 36, passed in June 1998) to Ontario's election financing rules, according to critics.[18] The limit on party spending during a campaign has been raised from 40 cents to 60 cents a voter, or up to $4 million from $2.7 million. Polling and travel expenses, which have usually cost the parties about $500 000 each, are now exempt from this ceiling. Together, these measures allow parties to spend an additional $1.8 million on the province-wide campaign, an increase of 66% which clearly favours the cash-rich Conservatives. The limit on spending by candidates has also been raised, bringing the average riding maximum from $52 000 to $62 000. The election campaign has been shortened from 37 days to 28 days, another move which favours incumbents with their higher name recognition.

Municipal arrangements understandably vary somewhat from province to province but still exhibit some common themes. Several provinces require or allow provision for financial deposits. For example, section 29 of the Local Authorities Elections Act in Alberta allows a municipality to require a financial deposit of $100 or $500, the amount depending on whether its population is under or over 100 000—but only Edmonton has used this provision.[19] Candidates for municipal office in Nova Scotia must pay a deposit of $200, unless council has specified a lesser amount or eliminated the deposit altogether.[20] Recent changes in Ontario under the Better Local Government Act, passed in mid-December 1996, authorize the Minister of Municipal Affairs to establish by regulation the amount of refundable financial deposit ($100) which must be paid by candidates.

---

[18]See Ian Urquhart, "Tories deal themselves election aces," *Toronto Star*, June 13, 1998, on which this discussion is based.

[19]Masson, *op. cit.*, p. 308.

[20]Kell Antoft (ed.), *A Guide to Local Government in Nova Scotia*, 3rd Edition, Halifax, Dalhousie University, 1992, p. 4.

These financial deposits are usually justified on the grounds of discouraging frivolous candidates. For that purpose, the deposits may or may not be successful, but they can deter serious candidates who are without financial means. As Masson argues, "at a time when property qualifications for holding office and voting have become almost an anachronism, the erection of financial barriers to prevent 'undesirables' from running for public office is at the very least inappropriate."[21] Requiring a candidate's nomination papers to be signed by a significant number of fellow electors would appear to be a better way to ensure that candidates are serious, and yet the recent changes introduced in Ontario have removed the requirement for 10 signatures which had been in existence.

Other requirements deal with such matters as limits on the amount of money which one donor can give to a candidate, requirements for candidates to file financial statements, and provisions for the disposal of surplus funds following an election campaign. For specific details, you should consult the legislation in your particular province.

Techniques of Direct Democracy

Even more direct ways of participating in the affairs of government are possible using features of what is usually termed "**direct democracy**," a concept which gained renewed interest in recent years. The key features involved are the referendum, initiative and recall.[22]

Use of a **referendum** involves submitting a policy question or proposed law to the electorate for approval or rejection. The referendum can be binding or it can be consultative only, to provide guidance to decision makers. The latter type of exercise is usually called a plebiscite in Canada. Canada has not made widespread use of this device at the national level, where only three plebiscites have been held, but there have been about 60 held at the provincial level, and several thousand at

---

[21]Masson, *op. cit.*, p. 309.

[22]The discussion which follows is largely based on the articles by Boyer and Charlton in Charlton and Barker, *op. cit.*, pp. 304-335.

the municipal level.[23] Notable votes include the one on conscrip
1942, the fixed link connection between PEI and the mainland in
the Charlottetown Accord in 1992, the creation of a new separate
territory in the Eastern Arctic that same year, and the cliff-hanger vote
on Québec separation in 1995.[24]

The **initiative**, which is common in many American states, allows
citizens to propose new laws which are then submitted to voters for
approval. Support, in the form of a specified number of signatures from
the electorate, is required before a proposal can be placed on the ballot.
This process essentially allows the public to initiate a referendum
exercise on their own, without having to rely on government putting a
question to the voters.

The **recall** is the most dramatic of the three instruments of direct
democracy. It allows the public to remove from office an elected representative whose performance is felt to be unsatisfactory. If a petition
is filed with sufficient signatures, a vote has to be held on whether or
not the individual can continue in office.

Much of the interest in these
forms of direct democracy arises
from public disillusionment with our
existing governing institutions. The
House of Commons is regarded as
far from representative of "typical"
Canadians, as discussed in Chapter 5.

> Disillusionment with
> government institutions
> and politicians underlies
> much of the interest in
> direct democracy.

The mainstream political parties offer little in the way of distinctive
policies or clear choices. Members of Parliament largely ignore the
wishes of the electorate because of the requirement to follow the party
line in voting. An added concern, which fuelled the populist movement
in Western Canada in the 1920s and 1930s, was a feeling that the
national government was overly preoccupied with the economic interests of Central Canada, to the neglect of the interests of farmers and

---

[23]Patrick Boyer, "Direct Democracy: The Referendum, Plebiscite, Initiative
and Recall," in Paul Fox and Graham White (eds.), *Politics Canada*, 8th Edition,
Whitby, McGraw-Hill Ryerson Limited, 1995, p. 375.

[24]All cited in Boyer and Charlton, *op. cit.*, pp. 308 and 310.

workers and outlying regions. An agrarian-based protest party known as the Progressives won 65 seats in the federal election of 1921, placing it second in the standings. Provincially, the United Farmers won power in Alberta in 1919 and the Social Credit party was victorious in 1935, both on platforms which emphasized direct democracy. Once in office, however, both parties functioned much like any other parliamentary government.[25] In a fascinating parallel, another western-based party pledging more democratic, accountable operations swept into Ottawa in 1993 with 52 seats, just two shy of second place. That party, of course, is Reform, which in many ways is a reincarnation of the Social Credit party; just as its leader is the son of the former Social Credit leader, Ernest Manning.

♦ Something to Think About

Do we need more elements of "direct democracy" in Canada's political system?

Would selective use of the referendum, the initiative, and even the recall, encourage greater citizen participation in the affairs of government and add greater legitimacy to the decisions which are made?

Proponents of direct democracy claim that the public becomes educated and informed because a referendum process involves "the politics of engagement."[26] Under traditional governing arrangements, Canadians have no real say in the decisions that are made, so why should they make the effort to become informed and involved. "Why study for an exam if nobody is going to ask you the questions?"[27] In contrast, when Islanders were given an opportunity to vote on the fixed link issue, the ensuing debate made residents active and much better informed participants in this important issue affecting the future of Prince Edward Island.

---

[25] *Ibid.*, p. 334.

[26] A term used by Boyer, *ibid.*, p. 309.

[27] *Ibid.*, p. 310.

Direct Democracy in Rossland, BC

The positive benefits of direct democracy seem to be evident in the experiences of Rossland, BC.[28] Concerned about the growing rift between citizens and their governments in the aftermath of the collapse of the Meech Lake Accord in 1990, the Rossland council gave its citizens three avenues to participate more directly in city government. First, there would have to be a referendum for any change to be made to the new constitution by-law of Rossland. Second, either council or the citizens (provided that 20% of them signed a petition) could subject a council decision to public confirmation by initiating a referendum within 30 days of the third reading of a by-law. Third, members of the public (again with 20% backing) could initiate a referendum to force council to take action on an issue.

The most important aspect of the Rossland approach is not the number of referendums (there had only been 13 as of the end of 1998, along with one plebiscite) or their outcome, but the changed atmosphere in the community. Instead of just complaining about council action or inaction, more people are discussing policy issues. Because they have been given some say in municipal decisions, they feel a greater responsibility to be informed and to exercise their new power thoughtfully. They are also gaining a sense of ownership of city policy.

According to André Carrel, Rossland's chief administrative officer, the real value of the referendum is when it is provided as part of a series of changes which demonstrate a commitment to openness, consultation, and public participation on the part of council. Holding an occasional referendum will accomplish little in the absence of such changes. In Carrel's words, "a referendum thrown to an angry and frustrated citizenry, like a bone to a hungry dog, is not a democratic act."[29]

The limited experience in Rossland is far from conclusive. Nor does it necessarily follow that what may work in a small Western Canadian municipality could be successfully transplanted to larger cities, much less used on a province-wide or Canadian basis. Indeed, evidence from

---

[28]The summary which follows is based on Tindal and Tindal, *op. cit.*, pp. 342-344.

[29]André Carrel, "Municipal Government Leadership," presentation at Capilano College, March 14, 1997, p. 6.

the referendum experience of other jurisdictions raises doubts about how much the voter becomes involved and empowered through this exercise. In countries such as Switzerland and the United States where direct democracy is a common feature, voter turnout is disappointingly low. It has averaged only 35% for referendums and initiatives in Switzerland in recent years.[30] American studies indicate that referendums have little drawing power in getting out voters when held in conjunction with elections and even less success with voter turnout when they are held separately.

Whatever the turnout, some observers express doubt that referendums provide a vehicle which stimulates greater participation on the part of the general public. Issues get placed on the ballot only if they receive the required number of signatures. In places like California, the task of obtaining these signatures has increasingly been turned over to professional firms who pay petitioners for each signature, with those signing often having little understanding of what they are signing. As a result, over time the petition process has come to be dominated by special interest groups who can afford the expensive petition gathering process.[31] This domination has been furthered by the decision of the United States Supreme Court that quashed restrictions on campaign spending by interest groups. As discussed earlier in this chapter, the same position has been taken by the courts in Canada as well, leaving interest groups without limits on their spending. As a result, there is reason to expect that referendums will be dominated by the educated and the wealthy, the same groups that have long dominated our other democratic institutions and processes as well.

An intriguing variation on the referendum is the deliberative opinion poll,[32] in which randomly chosen respondents in a national sample gather over a period of several days for intense discussion with

---

[30]Boyer and Charlton, *op. cit.*, p. 323.

[31]These observations are drawn from Mark Charlton, "The Limits of Direct Democracy," in Mark Charlton and Paul Barker (eds.), *Crosscurrents: Contemporary Political Issues*, 3rd Edition, Scarborough, Nelson, 1998, pp. 417-418.

[32]See Heather MacIvor, "A Deliberative Opinion Poll for Canada," Montreal, IRRP, *Policy Options,* November 1999, pp. 16-17.

experts on selected issues. The strength of this approach is that it provides not only a greater quantity of public input into policy making but also improved quality through education and deliberation.

Canada's experience with recall has been even more limited and even less positive in terms of the benefits of this tool. In spite of the popularity of the recall in a number of American states, especially in the west and mid-west, it never took hold in Canada. Members of the United Farmers of Alberta favoured recall, but after gaining power in Alberta in 1921, they soon decided that this tool was no longer really needed. Recall was then adopted by the Social Credit Party, which promised during the 1935 election campaign in Alberta that it would legislate this tool.

Recalling the Recall[33]

Social Credit won that election and Premier William Aberhart moved quickly to fulfil his promise by passing the Legislative Assembly (Recall) Act in April 1936. The first, and only, action under this legislation was launched in 1937—against Premier Aberhart himself. His response was to have the legislature repeal the recall legislation retroactive to the day it had originally received royal assent, thus voiding any action taken under it.

Recall began to receive new attention with the arrival of the Reform Party, which advocated various forms of direct democracy. While it failed to gain many adherents at the national level, Reform's advocacy of recall was to have an impact on the province of British Columbia. The Social Credit Party was in power in that province in the second half of the 1980s, but had faced mounting controversy which culminated in the resignation of its leader, Bill Vander Zalm. His successor, Rita Johnson, borrowing from Reform, introduced a referendum in which 80% of British Columbia voters expressed support for a recall law. Social Credit was defeated shortly after (in 1991), leaving it to the NDP government to follow through on the legislation. This they did with

---

[33]The description which follows is based on Boyer in Fox and White, *op. cit.*, pp. 379-380.

apparent reluctance, setting a fairly high threshold which required 40% of the voters registered in the last election to sign a petition for recall within a 60 day time frame.

A number of petitions have been filed under the recall legislation, but there have been difficulties in obtaining a sufficient number of valid signatures within the limited time period provided and allegations that some ineligible persons signed deliberately to invalidate the exercise. One of the problems is that the recall legislation provides no specified grounds for recalling a politician. At least some of the recall efforts in British Columbia seemed more directed to unseating enough NDP members to bring down the government than they were to addressing unsatisfactory performances by individual members of the legislature. As the government saw it, "many of the public proponents of recall turn out to represent special interest groups and failed politicians who plan to use recall to refight the last campaign."[34]

Mintz makes a similar point when he states that "rather than an action initiated by concerned citizens, recall petitions are likely to be instruments of well-financed and well-organized special interest groups with a particular axe to grind."[35] He also contends that recall is inconsistent with Canada's parliamentary system of government, in which it is the Cabinet—not individual members—that is responsible for developing and implementing policies. In fact, individual members, bound by party discipline, are "sitting targets for local resentment,"[36] and may be forced to take the fall for something over which they had very little choice. If a government holds only a slim majority, successful recalls could result in its defeat (as appeared to the strategy being attempted in British Columbia). But, as Mintz points out, this means that a small minority of the provincial population, those voting in recall ridings, would determine the fate of a government which had been elected by the entire population.

---

[34] According to a confidential government document quoted in Jennifer Hunter, "Power to the people," *Maclean's*, February 2, 1998.

[35] Eric Mintz, "Recalling Governments," *Policy Options*, May 1998, p. 44.

[36] Peter McCormick, "The Pros and Cons of the Recall," in Fox and White, *op. cit.*, p. 392.

Hare's concerns about direct democracy is that in making MPs more individually accountable, it has the effect of reducing the discipline of parties and leaving parliament—like the United States Congress—at the mercy of special interests. "Enforced by rights of recall, 301 constituencies would be empowered at the expense of one nation."[37]

On the other hand, McCormick argues that the recall provides a way for voter choice to mean something and for public opinion to have an impact, not just when a government chooses to have an election but

> The recall can be seen as more respectful of elected members than other tools of direct democracy.

when the voters feel strongly enough about an issue to press the matter. He also makes the case that the recall actually is more respectful of elected representatives than the other tools of direct democracy. The referendum and the initiative essentially ignore the elected representatives, "doing an end run around them by forcing issues and resolving questions in ways that make elected assemblies irrevelant."[38] In contrast, the recall provides a means for citizens to call elected representatives to account, to require them to explain why they behaved in a certain way. If the petition is unsuccessful, then dissatisfaction with the member is not widespread. If the petition succeeds, but the member is returned in the ensuing election, a new mandate has been given by voters who have presumably become persuaded of the merits of the member. Either way, the recall expands the dialogue between citizens and representatives, "while ensuring that the latter has ample incentive to pay attention."[39]

The Inter*medi*aries

Public interest and involvement in government is affected, positively or negatively, by the media coverage provided. Few Canadians have direct

---

[37]John Edward Hare, "Making Parliament National: A Burkean Reverie," *Policy Options*, Montreal, IRRP, October 1998, p. 71.

[38]McCormick, *op. cit.*, p. 393.

[39]*Ibid.*

contact with their governments, and much of the contact which does arise is at the municipal level, simply because of its physical proximity to local residents. Instead, our information about, and impressions of, government come mainly from media sources, just as those sources influence government impressions of us and our views and concerns.

Conflicting Views of the Media

The role of the media in liberal democracies like Canada is usually presented in a very positive light.[40] The media are viewed as a "fourth branch of government," meeting the needs of citizens by presenting the information required for informed participation and by providing a forum for debate on issues of public interest. As part of this process, they help governments by communicating information about public services and government accomplishments, while also providing opportunities for opposition parties to criticize and to suggest alternatives. In a colourful analogy, the media supposedly act as watchdogs, sniffing out abuses of power and barking out an alarm.

An alternative view is that the media is part of, and serves, the dominant ideology in society, providing a justification for the economic and political status quo and thereby serving the interests of the rich and powerful.[41] According to this view, the mass media promotes consumerism, which supports the economic system, and the myth of "middle-classness," which offers the promise that society's advantages are equally available to all. Since those who control the mass media form a significant part of Canada's economic elite, it is argued that they have a stake in perpetuating the existing power structure.

Who are the mass media which prompt these contrasting views, what roles do they play, and how concerned should we be about them?[42] The mass media are a multi-billion dollar industry, whose busi-

---

[40]The discussion which follows is based on Frederick J. Fletcher and Daphne Gottlieb Taras, "The Mass Media: Private Ownership, Public Responsibilities," in Michael S. Whittington and Glen Williams (eds.), *Canadian Politics in the 1990s*, 4th Edition, Scarborough, Nelson, 1995, p. 295.

[41]This discussion is based on *ibid.*, pp. 295-296.

[42]The exploration of these matters is largely based on *ibid.*, pp. 292-298.

ness is to attract audiences to sell to advertisers. This objective affects the coverage they provide in several ways. Immediate, personal and very tangible subjects attract audiences better than a discussion of complex or long term issues. The line between news and entertainment becomes increasingly blurred and, generally speaking, entertaining us is more profitable than informing us. Partisanship or strong ideological slants of any sort are unlikely, whatever the leanings of media owners, because of a desire not to alienate segments of the potential audience.

The Electronic Media

It is useful to distinguish between the electronic media (especially television) and the print media (especially newspapers). The potential impact of television is evident from the fact

> More time is spent viewing TV than anything but working and sleeping.

that television viewing takes up more of the average Canadian's time than anything but work and sleep, and that nearly half of our population say that they stay informed by watching television news.[43] Because it is a visual medium, television must seek out the colourful, dramatic, emotional, or entertaining pictures. Things like riots, demonstrations, and political conventions usually make much better television than the daily routine of politics. According to Dyck, "television meets the needs of the average citizen with a short attention span who is looking for visual stimulation and does not wish to invest much effort in understanding our political system."[44] The preoccupation with the visual leads television news to focus on the leaders of the parties, "their charm under fire, their 'telegenic' attributes such as warmth and sincerity, and their delivery of campaign speeches."[45] This emphasis contributes to the cult of personality surrounding our parties, and to the relative neglect of local members and party policies.

---

[43]*Ibid.*, p. 292.

[44]Dyck, *op. cit.*, p. 127.

[45]Fletcher and Tara, *op. cit.*, p. 295.

Canada's electronic media is distinctive in comprising both public and private systems, operating side-by-side. The CBC was set up as a crown corporation in 1932 as a way of ensuring that Canadian programming reached our widely scattered population and as protection against the inundation of American broadcasting. The choice at the time has been described as "the state or the United States." A television service joined the radio network in the 1950s. Canada's cultural sovereignty remains a hot topic to this day, and has become more vulnerable, as discussed in Chapter 10, since the negotiation of free trade agreements with the United States and Mexico.

In the context of this chapter, the main issue is that a publicly owned broadcasting system can raise questions about independence and freedom from government censorship—given that the CBC receives the bulk of its operating revenue from the government and has its Chair appointed by the government. For example, late 1998 saw the beginning of a major controversy concerning the alleged bias of CBC reporter Terry Milewski in his coverage of the inquiry into the extent of government involvement in the RCMP clampdown on protestors at the APEC (Asian Pacific Economic Cooperation) summit in Vancouver.

Was Terry Contrary?

The Prime Minister's Office (PMO) based its complaint, at least in part, on e-mail between Milewski and one of the student protestors at the summit. In response, the CBC withdrew Milewski from coverage of the APEC story and he was suspended for three days following a CBC internal investigation. He was later suspended for a further 15 days, as a result of a commentary article he wrote in the *Globe and Mail* on November 10. After a five month investigation, the CBC Ombudsman reported on March 23, 1999, dismissing all charges of bias against Milewski and finding the PMO's complaint not justified. However gratifying this verdict, the fact remains that the PMO managed to make Milewski part of the story and put an end to his coverage, which was seen as damaging to the government.[46]

---

[46]Details on the Milewski affair can be found in *The National Online*, at web site *http://tv.cbc.ca/national/pgminfo/apec*.

The Print Media

Turning to the print media, and specifically newspapers, they are capable of providing much more in depth coverage than television. Some thorough and insightful coverage of public issues is to be found. But since newspapers are privately owned and exist to maximize their profits, they have an understandable tendency to sensationalize their coverage. Bad news is news, while good news isn't. As a result, you will never see a headline proclaiming that "the Department of Public Works ran efficiently for the past six months." But administrative foul-ups, over-spending, inefficiencies, or conflict between departments—all of these matters will command attention.

It is appreciated that a primary role of a free press in a democracy is to keep government under scrutiny and to expose inefficiency and wrongdoing as a means of keeping governments accountable. But it must be recognized that consistently negative and critical media coverage contributes to the poor impression of government held by many Canadians. Westell, among others, feels that the press has become too critical and adversarial. He argues that the Canadian parliamentary system has an institutionalized opposition and does not need an adversarial press. "The central business of the press is to facilitate communications between the institutions which do the business of a democratic society and the public which are supposed to oversee them."[47]

Another issue about newspapers has to do with the pattern of ownership. Whatever limited concern there might be about public ownership of the CBC is dwarfed by the concern felt by many about the extent to which newspapers are owned by a few large private corporations, which are themselves part of larger economic entities. When the Senate Committee on the Mass Media called for legislation to limit concentration in 1970, 45% of newspapers were controlled by just three

---

[47]Anthony Westell, "The Press: Adversary or Channel of Communication?" in Harold D. Clarke et al. (eds.), *Parliament, Policy and Representation*, Toronto, Methuen, 1980, p. 49, as quoted in Fletcher and Tara, *op. cit.*, p. 307.

> Concentration of owner-
> ship has gone from 45% in
> 1970, to 57% in 1980, to
> 76% today.

corporations, and this figure had risen to 57% by the time the Kent Commission made a similar recommendation 10 years later.[48] Concentration is even greater today, with Conrad Black controlling 60 of Canada's 105 general interest daily newspapers, the Sun Media Corp. 11, and Thompson 9, for 76% control by just three chains.[49]

Chain ownership can bring the benefits of shared resources, including national and foreign coverage well beyond what smaller, locally-owned dailies could afford. But it can also lead to homogenization of coverage and insensitivity to local concerns.[50] There is also more opportunity to influence public opinion through a common editorial stance. In addition, the broader economic power wielded by the newspaper owners as large business interests carries its own threats. For example, the Irving family is often accused of failing to give appropriate coverage to events that might be detrimental to its business interests in New Brunswick.[51] It is noteworthy that when Canadians were polled on how they would realign power in Canadian society, it was the media (along with big business) whose power they most wanted to reduce.[52]

Parliamentary Press Gallery

When it comes to political reporting, the largest and most important group is found in the parliamentary press gallery in Ottawa. There are about 400 members of the gallery, most from the electronic media. According to Fletcher and Tara, the gallery often operates with some-

---

[48]Figures from Maude Barlow, "Press Inc.," *Canadian Forum*, June 1997, p. 11.

[49]These figures are from the Canadian Newspaper Association, as found on September 25, 1999 at its web site *www.cna-acj.ca*.

[50]These points are made by Fletcher and Tara, *op. cit.*, p. 305.

[51]*Ibid.*

[52]Frank L. Graves, "Rethinking Government," in Leslie A. Pal (ed.), *How Ottawa Spends 1999-2000*, Toronto, Oxford University Press, 1999, p. 52.

thing approaching a "herd instinct," with the major stories of the day generally identified collectively and given a common interpretation.[53] In addition, much government activity goes unreported because of the media concentration on Question Period and government announcements (with opposition reactions thereto). This focus is understandable, claims Westell,[54] since Question Period is "almost a perfect media event. Public personalities come into conflict over current controversies, providing in one neat package the basic ingredients of a news story."

Another factor affecting political reporting is the almost incestuous relationship which develops between reporters and the reported. Since politicians want publicity for themselves and their programs, and reporters want information and quotes for their stories, a state of mutual interdependence develops. Allan Fotheringham claims that "the narrowest line in journalism is the line between exploiting your sources (without ever destroying them) and being captured by them."[55]

Public Opinion Polls

Media coverage is influenced by the results of public opinion polls which purport to show the issues of concern to Canadians. Professional polling organizations (such as Gallup, Environics, Decima and Angus Reid) use small, representative samples of the population to extrapolate public views which are held to be highly accurate—within 4%, 19 times out of 20, in the case of election surveys. Not all pollsters or polls are that scientific, however, and results obtained on a pretty shaky foundation can be used to push particular points of view. Whether accurate or not, polling results are always of great interest to politicians. Since the media now hire or own polling firms themselves, survey results become major news items in their own right.[56]

---

[53]Fletcher and Tara, *op. cit.*, p. 307, on which this section is largely based.

[54]Anthony Westell, "Reporting the Nation's Business," in Stuart Adam (ed.), *Journalism, Communication and the Law*, Scarborough, Prentice-Hall Canada Inc., 1976, p. 63, as quoted in *ibid.*, p. 307.

[55]Quoted in Dyck, *op. cit.*, p. 129.

[56]*Ibid.*, p. 133.

A particularly controversial issue has been the publication of public opinion polls in the midst of election campaigns. They may not create the bandwagon effect feared by critics, but such polls may have a positive or negative impact on party morale and may deflect media coverage to items highlighted by the polls. Their very appearance tends to direct attention to the "horse-race" aspect of the contest, with the result that more media coverage is concerned with who is ahead than with a comprehensive analysis of party policies.[57]

The Canada Elections Act was amended to ban public opinion polls in the final three days of an election campaign, but this legislation was then challenged, successfully, in 1998 by Southam and Thompson as a violation of freedom of the press. The government has responded by proposing new amendments (not passed as of late 1999) that would impose a ban on poll results within the last 48 hours of a campaign.

Concluding Observations

This chapter is far from a thorough examination of the many facets of public participation. But it does demonstrate that Canadians have a number of ways in which they can participate in the activities of their governments. In some respects, the more avenues there are for public participation, the more open and democratic the governing system may appear to be. This conclusion presupposes, however, that Canadians participate widely through all or most of these avenues. Instead, recent years have seen some evidence that a growing number of Canadians are "turning off" and "tuning out" their traditional avenues for democratic expression, centred on the election process and the operations of parliament. Many are joining pressure groups so that they can push for the particular issues that most concern them, and many others are demanding an even more direct say in decision making through the direct democracy tools discussed above.

The Canadian democracy is based on the principle of representative government. It is a system in which we elect individuals to repre-

---

[57] *Ibid.*

sent us and make decisions on our behalf. In almost all instances, these individuals are also members of political parties. If there are imperfections in this representative and party system—and there most certainly are—then they should be directly addressed and resolved. To the extent that Canadians give up on the parliamentary system and find ways of working around it (such as through the tools of direct democracy), they ignore the central core of our democratic system.

It may well be appropriate to use referendums on very infrequent occasions when fundamental issues are at stake. Amendments to the constitution would fall into this category, and the 1992 vote on the Charlottetown Accord may have established a precedent in this regard. It is certainly appropriate for citizens to become involved with interest groups and to use whatever other means they can to express their views and concerns. These avenues, however, should be seen as a supplement to, not an alternative for, the traditional methods of participation centred on elections and political parties.

This chapter also illustrates the significant influence wielded by the media in our lives and with respect to our perception of matters political. We need a free media as one of the underpinnings of democracy. But we also need to recognize that the mass media is dominated by a few large corporations which are part of the economic elite and that the bulk of the coverage provided by the media is supportive of the status quo, including the existing distribution (however fair or unfair) of power and influence. Just because we read something, or see something on television, doesn't make it gospel. We need to form our own judgments on political matters, not accept unquestioningly "the party line."

Whatever you do, don't stay on the sidelines, complaining about government or ignoring it. The only way to have "government of the people, by the people, for the people," is through "the people" becoming active participants.

The Last Word

Definition of Terms and Concepts

Direct Democracy:
A series of techniques to allow the public to participate much more directly in the activities of government, as in the use of the initiative, recall and referendum.

Franchise:
The right to vote in public elections. Also known as suffrage. Canada is said to have universal suffrage because the right to vote is so widely held.

Initiative:
A technique which allows citizens to propose new laws that must be submitted to the voters for approval, if they can get a specified proportion of voters to sign a petition in this regard.

Mass Media:
Consists of print media (newspapers and magazines) and electronic media (radio, television and films).

Recall:
A process under which voters can file a petition demanding a vote on an elected representative's continued tenure in office.

Referendum:
A process under which a policy question or proposed law is submitted to the electorate for approval or rejection. This process is also referred to as a plebiscite, although that term as used in Canada usually refers to referendums which are not binding and are only intended to provide guidance to decision makers.

Riding Association:
> The local party organization found in each riding or constituency which, among other things, selects the candidate for each election.

Third Party Spending:
> This does **not** refer to spending by political parties but by others, usually groups and associations which seek to advance their point of view during an election campaign. Largely because of successful Charter challenges, there is no limit on spending by these outside parties.

Points to Ponder

1. What do you think of the list of eight socio-economic "barriers" to candidacy? Do you think that it limits those who might offer themselves as candidates? Would these factors influence you in your choice of a candidate?

2. Some have suggested that if "third party" spending during election campaigns can't be limited, then neither should spending by parties and political candidates be limited? What is your view? Does election spending, particularly for television ads, influence your vote?

3. What do you see as the respective merits of direct democracy versus representative democracy, and why?

4. Select a few major news events and trace how they are covered in a number of different media. Is the coverage consistent and, if not, what kinds of variations are there. [This exercise may help to make you more aware of the need not to accept everything in the media without question.]

For Further Reading

See Mark Charlton and Paul Barker (eds.), *Crosscurrents: Contemporary Political Issues,* 2nd Edition, Scarborough, Nelson, 1994, for a good examination of the possible influence of business groups (Issue 17) and the pros and cons of direct democracy (Issue 16.) The 3rd Edition of this text (1998) also examines the pros and cons of referendums (Issue 18).

Paul Fox and Graham White (eds.), *Politics: Canada,* 8th Edition, Whitby, McGraw-Hill Ryerson Inc., 1995, has a number of pertinent articles in a section dealing with elections.

Robert Jackson and Doreen Jackson, *Canadian Government in Transition,* 2nd Edition, Scarborough, Prentice-Hall Canada, Inc., 1999, Chapter 11, provides a good treatment of both elections and the media, and these topics are also explored in more detail in *Politics in Canada,* 3rd Edition, 1994, Chapters 11 and 12, by the same authors and publisher.

Rank Dyck, *Canadian Politics,* Scarborough, Nelson, 1998, offers a good coverage of both the mass media (Chapter 7) and elections (Chapter 8).

The mass media is also well covered in the contribution by Fletcher and Taras in Michael Whittington and Glen Williams (eds.), *Canadian Politics in the 1990s,* 4th Edition, Scarborough, Nelson, 1995, Chapter 15.

Useful internet sources include *www.elections.ca* for Elections Canada Online and *www.cna-acj.ca* for the Canadian Newspaper Association. In addition, website *ajr.newslink.org* lists close to 5000 newspapers which are on line.

Chapter 5

Federal and Provincial Governments: A Closer Look

Objectives and Highlights

♦ To explain the roles and operations of the Executive Branch, the House of Commons and the Senate.

♦ To assess the demands on MPs by examining their various roles.

Every four years or so, Canadians have an opportunity to elect members to the House of Commons (and to the legislative assembly in their province). How significant is this democratic exercise, and how important are the roles played by these elected representatives?

This chapter examines the organization and functioning of the parliamentary system of government found at the senior levels. It discusses the reasons why the public service, the Cabinet and the Prime Minister have all gained in power and influence throughout the 20th century. It explores the nature and effectiveness of the representative, lawmaking and watchdog roles of the House of Commons, and it explains the key roles the Senate was expected to play and why its importance and legitimacy have declined over the years.

Our parliamentary system is certainly not without its problems and weaknesses. But it also has the potential to enforce a healthy degree of accountability—of the executive branch to the elected members and of the elected members to the public. By examining these links, this chapter helps you to understand how your government works and how you can most effectively participate in it.

Introduction

Both the federal and provincial governments are organized on the parliamentary model. According to this model, Parliament is supreme and Prime Ministers or Premiers and their Cabinets only govern as long as they are supported by a majority of the elected members in the House of Commons or the Provincial Legislative Assemblies. From at least the beginning of the 20th century, however, power began shifting from the legislative branch to the executive branch. By the middle of this century the only question for debate was *where* in that branch the power was concentrated: in the Cabinet or in the senior civil service.

Beginning in the late 1960s, a number of reforms were introduced to strengthen the legislative branch and to restore a greater balance in the executive-legislative relationship. These reforms have done little, however, to stop the increasing concentration of power within the executive branch and, more specifically, within the office of the Prime Minister. Yet any changes which can strengthen the legislative branch are extremely important to you. Since your main direct involvement is to elect a government every four years or so (assuming that you vote), the rest of the time you depend upon the elected members in the legislative branch (especially the opposition members) to keep an eye on the government for you between elections. How well they exercise that role has a lot to do with how well you are governed.

These shifting patterns in the focus of power in our governmental system will become apparent in this chapter, as we take a closer look at the governing machinery and how it operates. While the main focus will be on the national government, the provinces operate in essentially the same manner.

The Cabinet and its Growing Dominance

Historically, the Cabinet was a group of advisors to the Monarch (or the Governor in the case of the colony of Canada), without any real power of its own. Its official title was, and is, the **Privy Council**—reflecting its role as 'private' advisors.

The full Privy Council consists of all past and present Cabinet members, past and present chief justices of the Supreme Court, past and present Speakers of the Senate and Commons, and other distinguished persons whom the government wishes to honour. Once appointed to the Privy Council, a person is entitled to be referred to as "The Honourable," a title which is kept for life. (A Prime Minister receives the title of "Right Honourable.") The full Privy Council meets only in very exceptional circumstances, such as the ascension to the throne of a new monarch. Our focus in this section is on the active part of the Privy Council—that is, the Cabinet of the government currently in power.

With the introduction of the principle of responsible government in the 1840s, it became established that the Governor of the Colony (the forerunner of the Governor General) could only appoint as advisors people who would be supported by a majority of the elected members to the colonial assembly (and since Confederation in 1867, to the provincial and federal legislatures).

To this day, the Governor General officially appoints the members of the Privy Council. With the rise of disciplined political parties, however, support from the Assembly has become translated into support from the political party which controls the majority of seats in the Assembly. This, in turn, means that a Governor General really has no choice but to call upon the leader of the party which wins the most seats in an election to form a government. The leader of that winning party becomes the Prime Minister and decides which of his or her colleagues will be appointed to serve in the Cabinet. In practice, then, it is the Prime Minister who decides on the appointments to the Cabinet, even though they are officially and legally made by the Governor General.

The federal election in the fall of 1993 was fought with Kim Campbell as Prime Minister and the Progressive Conservative party in power in Ottawa. The election results reduced the governing Conservatives to two seats and gave the Liberal party 178 of the 295 seats in the House of Commons. Officially, it was the Governor General's responsibility to appoint the new government. In practice, the voters had left no doubt about the choice—as is appropriate for a democracy.

Choosing the Cabinet Members

On what basis does a Prime Minister select those who will be appointed by the Governor General to serve in the Cabinet? The recruitment process followed for most positions might suggest a search for the best qualified people among all Canadian adults. Instead, however, the talent pool to be drawn upon is dramatically more limited. One of the customs or conventions of our system of government is that those appointed to the Cabinet must have a seat in the House of Commons (or must secure such a seat within a short time of their appointment). The latter situation arose, for example, when Prime Minister Chrétien decided to strengthen his Cabinet representation from Québec following the very close vote on separation in late 1995. He appointed a trade consultant and foreign policy expert named Pierre Pettigrew and a university professor named Stéphane Dion. Both of these appointees then had to win election to the House of Commons (which they did) in order to retain their Cabinet positions.

Other Factors

There are also several other factors that a Prime Minister must consider when forming a Cabinet, including:

1. Geographic balance, since all areas of Canada expect representation in this important body.
2. Appropriate diversity, since Cabinets are expected to reflect the population of Canada by including women (in sufficient numbers), Francophones, new Canadians and other segments of society.
3. Prior government experience, since Cabinet members will assume many challenging responsibilities.
4. Background of education and experience appropriate for assuming a Cabinet post and heading a government department.
5. Past relationship with the Prime Minister, since, "all things being equal," Prime Ministers will tend to select those who have been long-standing acquaintances or supporters over those who may have supported their rivals within the party.

The personal connection was evident in several of the decisions made by Prime Minister Chrétien in assembling his first Cabinet after his election victory in 1997. Loyalist Sergio Marchi was rewarded with a move to the Trade portfolio, David Collenette's friendship with the Prime Minister got him back into the Cabinet (after an earlier incident had forced his resignation), and while Sheila Copps was given the relatively minor post of Heritage Minister, it was widely felt that she only remained in the Cabinet at all because of her long and close association with Chrétien.[1] The fate of those not considered to be loyal enough is illustrated by the cabinet choices of Premier Mike Harris following his reelection in Ontario in June 1999. He reappointed some marginal performers and promoted some inexperienced backbenchers while passing over five Conservatives with considerable government experience. The common thread among these five appears to be that they were outspoken individuals and perhaps too independent-minded for the Premier's liking.[2]

Reasons for Cabinet Dominance

The growing domination of the Cabinet in the 20th century came about because of several factors, notably:

- The fact that the Cabinet is usually backed by a majority of members in the House of Commons from the same political party;

- The growing volume and complexity of government activities in the 20th century, and the corresponding "knowledge gap" in the House of Commons, where opposition members had little in the way of staff or expertise to help in carrying out their watchdog role; and

- The change in the nature of the lawmaking process. Statutes or Acts must be passed by Parliament (comprising both the Commons and the Senate). However, statute laws have become increasingly general in nature. They no longer attempt to encompass the total law on a subject. This change has occurred mainly because Parliament (and its members) lack the time and the technical knowledge to elaborate

---

[1]For speculation and analysis about the Chrétien Cabinet see Robert Fife, "Making of cabinet an intriguing tale," *Ottawa Sun*, June 13, 1997, and Giles Gherson, "Baby boomers will remake Liberalism," *Ottawa Citizen*, June 16, 1997.

[2]This is the assessment of Ian Urquhart, "And backbench life for Harris' independents," *Toronto Star*, June 21, 1999.

the law in all of the detail required. Moreover, often the government is introducing law into new areas of economic or social activity, and needs the flexibility to adapt the law quickly as conditions change.

As a result, most statutes passed over the past several decades set out the general purpose of the law and delegate the authority to some part of the executive branch to elaborate the law in detail over time. The growth in this **administrative law** (also known as delegated legislation or subordinate legislation) has meant a reduction in the power and importance of Parliament and a further expansion of the power of the Cabinet (and civil service, who actually make the detailed laws). Consider the following example, which actually relates to a provincial law but will be familiar to most people.

Getting a "Lift" out of Lawmaking

Take a look at the wall in front of you in the next elevator in which you ride. You will see a notice which indicates that the elevator has been licensed to carry a certain number of people. It tells you that the elevator has been inspected by government officials to ensure its safe operation.

Try to imagine what it was like the first time a government tried to pass a law dealing with elevator safety. This is a very technical subject, concerned with things like thickness of cable, tensile strength, pneumatics and hydraulics. It does not lend itself to debate among political parties; nor is there a discernable difference between the Liberals, Conservatives, NDP or any other party concerning hydraulics!

As a result, the Elevator Safety Act itself is a brief and general statute, mainly establishing that there will be elevator safety standards and providing a mechanism for enforcing them. The Act then delegates to the executive branch the authority to establish the actual safety standards. These standards are equally the law of the land, arguably the most important part of the law. But they were not passed by the legislative branch in a statute. They were enacted later, gradually over time, by the executive branch. This kind of arrangement is logical for dealing with such technical matters. But as it is repeated over a wide range of government activities, you can see the effect it has on shifting power from the legislative branch to the executive branch.

The Increasing Power of the Prime Minister

As much as the Cabinet has gained in power and influence over the 20th century, it has been surpassed by the increasing concentration of power in the position of Prime Minister (and Provincial Premier). This development illustrates well the contrast between law and practice which is often found in the operations of the Canadian system of government. There is virtually no mention of the position of Prime Minister in the constitution of Canada; yet the occupant of that office is the undisputed leader and his or her dominance is reflected in the way governments are personalized, as in the Chrétien Government, the Mulroney Government, the Klein Government in Alberta or the Harris Government in Ontario.

Part of the Prime Minister's power, of course, comes from the fact that he[3] alone determines who will be chosen to sit in the Cabinet, what portfolios they will hold, and how long they will stay. There are some constraints on these choices, however, since powerful regional Ministers will expect, and will have to be given, Cabinet positions. The Prime Minister also chairs the Cabinet meetings and can exert influence over the decisions which are made—although he must obviously "pick his spots" and not try to force his view on every issue. Nor does he have time to get involved in every issue, making a selective or strategic approach necessary.

Much of the Prime Minister's power comes from being the head of a political party, especially when that party holds a majority of the seats in the House of Commons. There are a

> Being the leader of a majority party augments the power of the PM.

number of positive and negative inducements which ensure that members vote the party line. Party discipline is especially strong with respect to members of the governing party, since any defection by them could potentially bring down the government. Members are supposed to have an opportunity to put pressure on the government and Prime Minister in closed **caucus** meetings, but indications are that these are

---

[3]To simplify references, the pronoun "he" will be used throughout this section.

not very effective for the purpose. Indeed, veteran Liberal member Warren Allmand claims that the caucus has lost influence over the years and that its impotence is evident from the fact that the Cabinet now meets the day before caucus meetings instead of the day after, thus presenting the caucus with a fait accompli.[4] An ultimate weapon, to be used very sparingly, that a Prime Minister has to keep rebellious **backbenchers** in line, is to threaten to dissolve Parliament and bring on an election.[5] Going back to the electorate is a risky and expensive proposition for members, and a judicious use of this threat can be effective.

The Prime Minister, either on his own or acting officially as part of the Governor-in-Council,[6] also has extensive appointment powers which add to his power and influence. In addition to the selection of Cabinet Ministers, already mentioned, the Prime Minister appoints Senators, Supreme Court judges, ambassadors and a variety of other government positions. When Jean Chrétien came to power in 1993, for example, there were more than 2000 positions on the appointment list to be filled by his office.[7] As of March 31, 1998, after a little over four years in office, Chrétien's government had made 2,758 appointments, 19% of them to full time positions.[8] Many of those appointed—by whatever party is in power—are partisans, and having final say over the appointments gives a Prime Minister or Premier considerable leverage.

---

[4]Quoted in Donald J. Savoie, *Governing from the Centre*, Toronto, University of Toronto Press, 1999, p. 93.

[5]As discussed elsewhere in the Guide, dissolution is actually carried out by the Governor General on a request from the Prime Minister but, except in very unusual circumstances, this request will automatically be granted.

[6]Since the Cabinet per se is not mentioned in the constitution of Canada, when it wishes to speak legally it does so as the Privy Council in conjunction with the Governor General, or what is known as the Governor-in-Council. In practice, appointments made by this body are the choice of, or at least have the blessing of, the Prime Minister.

[7]Robert Jackson and Doreen Jackson, *Canadian Government in Transition*, Scarborough, Prentice-Hall Canada Inc., 1996, p. 128.

[8]Derek Ferguson, "Ottawa's passion for patronage," *Toronto Star*, April 5, 1998.

The Importance of Image

Above all else, however, a Prime Minister has great power if he is "a winner," if the party feels that he is the key to victory, if individual candidates believe that they owe their seats to the Prime Minister's personal popularity, that they have gone to Ottawa "on his coattails." In the age of television, "winnability" is largely determined by the image one is able to project and this enhances the value of party leaders who can be packaged and marketed effectively.

This is not a new development. Over 40 years ago, John Diefenbaker scored a stunning upset victory for the Progressive Conservatives after they had spent a generation in the political wilderness, then won again by a landslide the following year (1958). Many PC candidates rode to Ottawa on Diefenbaker's coattails that year, and they remained fiercely loyal to "The Chief" long after he had been deposed as party leader. The famous Nixon-Kennedy television debate was held just over 40 years ago (1959), as a result of which the underdog but much more photogenic Kennedy went on to defeat his rival. Robert Stanfield lost three election campaigns to Pierre Trudeau between 1968 and 1974, hampered by an unflattering public image, especially when contrasted with that of Trudeau. Whatever the substantive policy issues, what Canadians "saw" was the image of Stanfield fumbling the football at a pre-game ceremony for the Grey Cup game versus Trudeau sliding down bannisters, racing around in a sports car and dating Barbra Streisand. It doesn't matter whether either image accurately portrayed the individuals involved. Perception is reality, and nowhere more than in politics. Mulroney clearly demolished a rusty John Turner during the television debates preceding the 1984 election, while a better coached and better prepared John Turner solidly outperformed Mulroney in the 1988 debates. Kim Campbell was chosen by the Progressive Conservative Party to replace Brian Mulroney and the party's popularity rose impressively for a few months on the strength of little more than her lively image and irreverent style. Liberal leader Dalton McGuinty didn't sparkle in the television debate during Ontario's 1999 election campaign, and this reinforced the "weak leader" image with which the Conservative Party successfully saddled him.

The point of all these examples is that when Prime Ministers (or Premiers) have a very popular public image, and especially when they are clearly more popular than their party, they have great influence. The party knows that it can win with them, but it is not sure that it can win without them. The Liberal party is still doing well in the polls, but it scores well below the approval rating which Jean Chrétien continues to enjoy and which clearly augments his power. On the other hand, Prime Ministers who are less popular than their party may find themselves in a weak position, as in the case of Joe Clark at the end of the 1970s. The Conservatives seemed to feel that they had won the 1979 election *in spite of* Clark, not because of him, and the pressure continued to build until he resigned as leader and was replaced by Mulroney. Ironically, once deposed, Clark's public image steadily improved and he became the most respected member of the Mulroney Government.

The Prime Minister and the President

The popular image of the office of the President of the United States is that it is all-powerful. The incumbent exercises various powers, including Commander-in-Chief of the Armed Forces. He operates independently of Congress, can veto bills passed by Congress (although the veto can be over-ridden by a two-thirds majority in both Houses of Congress), and can negotiate treaties with foreign countries (although they must be approved by the Senate). Perhaps above all, the President holds office for a fixed, four year term—whether or not he is supported by Congress (which he often is not). In contrast, Canadian Prime Ministers have virtually no specific powers of their own and must answer at all times to the House of Commons, ultimately by seeking a new mandate in an election if the Commons withholds its support.

♦ **Something to Think About**

The reality of the Prime Minister–President comparison is rather different. The position of Prime Minister can be at least as powerful and some observers wonder if there are adequate safeguards to protect against abuse of power by a Prime Minister.

A Canadian Prime Minister backed by a majority government has a very impressive power base, especially when compared to an American President facing a Congress dominated by members of the opposite political party.[9] Actually, Presidents may have enough trouble when facing a Congress comprised of a majority of members of their own party! Voting patterns are not nearly as disciplined in the United States, partly because there is no such thing as "defeating a government" since the President is in office for a fixed four year term. Members of Congress often act and vote very independently, forcing Presidents to give careful attention to building support within their own party.

As already discussed, the media focus on the style and personality of the party leader can add greatly to the power and influence of a Prime Minister with a popular public image. The result has been the development of what has been termed "leadership politics." Veteran Conservative Dalton Camp observed that "elements of the imperial prime ministership crept in" during the Mulroney era, as evidenced by the ever-expanding entourage of aides, guards, courtiers and equipment that accompanied the Prime Minister on his travels.[10] Denis Smith concludes that "as long as Canada has party pollsters to guide the leaders, its own television networks to display them, and parliamentary elections to legitimize them, nothing much is likely to change in the dominance of the Prime Minister." He argues that the Prime Minister enjoys the powers of the President without the constraints imposed by an independent Congress.[11]

Joseph Wearing disagrees with this assessment,[12] and suggests that if there are problems or concerns, they arise from the ineffectiveness of such bodies as political parties, Parliament, the electorate, and the media in monitoring the exercise of Prime Ministerial power. He argues that

---

[9]The ensuing discussion is based on Denis Smith, "Is the Prime Minister Too Powerful? — Yes" and Joseph Wearing, "Is the Prime Minister Too Powerful? — No," in Mark Charlton and Paul Barker, *Crosscurrents: Contemporary Political Issues*, 2nd Edition, Scarborough, Nelson Canada, 1994, pp. 154-166.

[10]Quoted in Smith, *op. cit.*, p. 156.

[11]*Ibid.*, p. 158.

[12]Wearing, *op. cit.*, p. 162.

Prime Ministers need to rely on strong regional ministers and other leading members of their Cabinet, many of whom have important power bases in their own right. Members of the President's Cabinet have no such power base and are more easily replaced. Prime Ministers are also held to a greater accountability (precisely because they enjoy a solid block of support in Parliament) than Presidents, who can always blame an obstructionist Congress for their difficulties.

The Civil Service

As noted in Chapter 2, the day-to-day work of governing is carried out by full time employees known as civil servants or public servants. The majority of these employees work for departments headed by Cabinet Ministers. Others work for various boards and commissions such as the Atomic Energy Commission, the CBC and the Bank of Canada. They are still part of the executive branch of the government of Canada. These bodies are the counterpart of the ABCs which are prevalent within local government, except that the federal (and provincial) governments are free to create, alter or abolish their boards as they see fit. In contrast, local boards such as school boards have a mandated existence and are beyond the control of municipal councils.

With the increasing complexity of government activities in the 20th century, the full time experts in the civil service became more and more influential as advisors to the temporary amateur politicians supposedly in charge of the departments. The growing influence of the civil service was compounded by the long period of one party domination in Ottawa. A whole generation of civil servants worked only with Liberal politicians (who governed between 1935 and 1957) and a very close relationship developed. That closeness was shattered by the election of the Progressive Conservatives under Diefenbaker in 1957. It did not reappear with the return of the Liberals in 1963, largely because they had only minority governments during Pearson's two terms of office in the 1960s. As a result, they were more sensitive to the views of their members of Parliament (in fact, all members of Parliament) not just to the whispered asides of senior civil servants.

A majority Liberal government reappeared in 1968, but the new leader was Pierre Trudeau, and life would never again be the same for the civil service! Trudeau liked to question established ways of doing things, and doubted that the regular civil service would be very imaginative or creative in suggesting alternative approaches. His solution was to expand greatly the roles of two long-standing support offices— the Prime Minister's Office (*PMO*) and the Privy Council or Cabinet Office (*PCO*)—especially with respect to their policy advisory role. By so doing, Trudeau deliberately created alternative sources of policy advice from that of the regular civil service. If this new system gave the Cabinet a variety of viewpoints, it presumably assisted in the decision-making process. If, as its numerous critics charged, it only substituted a new PMO monopoly on policy advice for that of the old civil service monopoly, then it was not an improvement at all.[13]

The Strength of the Central Agencies

While many adjustments have been made over the years since, the changes introduced by Trudeau continue to prevail, in the form of strong central agencies, comprising not only the PCO and PMO but also the Treasury Board and the Department of Finance. But according to Savoie,[14] the preeminence of these agencies has not, as originally envisaged, strengthened the Cabinet. Instead, the influence of the Cabinet and individual ministers has been weakened, while the power of the Prime Minister and his senior advisors has grown. It is interesting to note, however, that the central agencies have not gained ground by successfully coordinating the diverse activities of government. While that might seem a logical, if elusive, goal, it is not their focus. Their role has been variously and colourfully described as keeping a lid on things that aren't priorities with the Prime Minister, falling on hand grenades before they explode, and making "a mush of things."[15]

---

[13]This was certainly the view of Walter Stewart in his critical and lively discussion of the "supergroup" then wielding power in Canada. See *Shrug: Trudeau in Power*, Toronto, New Press, 1971, Chapter 11.

[14]Savoie, *op. cit.*, p. 338.

[15]*Ibid.*, pp. 317-318 and 326.

These tactics are motivated by the fact that "the centre of government has no stomach for bold tries and bold failures."[16] This timidity may be regrettable but it is also understandable given the adversarial nature of the parliamentary system and the increasingly aggressive activities of the media. Above all, governments—and Prime Ministers—don't like to be caught off guard and forced into damage control. As a result, a major preoccupation of the central agencies is avoiding surprises. In the words of Tom Axworthy, former principal secretary to Prime Minister Trudeau: "Mistakes avoided are just as important as bills passed."[17] This reality is unlikely to change, and unless it does, the monitoring role of the central agencies will remain.

The Civil Service Under Attack

The civil service has not only declined in influence over the past several decades; it has also declined in public perception, in status, and in numbers. The widespread anti-government and pro-private sector views which have increasingly gained ground left public servants highly vulnerable. Critics claimed that they were poorly motivated, inefficient, and overpaid for what they contributed. For governments determined to cut costs and balance budgets, making do with fewer public servants seemed the obvious answer. Between 1993 and 1997, the federal government lost 55 000 employees, 20% of its staff complement. The average age of a federal civil servant is 47, and only 6% of the public service is under 30. This imbalance is unlikely to improve quickly, since polls indicate that only 6% of Canadians aged 18 to 35 consider politics a "desirable profession."[18]

Walter Stewart deplores the downsizing environment which has encouraged many of the best and brightest to take their golden handshake or to move to other careers. He charges that the bureaucracy is getting smaller, older and dumber day by day, and that eventually the

---

[16]*Ibid.*, p. 326.

[17]Quoted in *ibid.*, p. 316.

[18]These figures are all from Carol Goar, "Beleaguered civil service sets sights on recovery," *Toronto Star*, August 23, 1997.

complaints about its inefficiency will become a self-fulfilling prophecy.[19] He points out that despite the huge increase in government activity over the past 30 years, the proportion of federal public servants has significantly decreased, from one public servant to 90 Canadians to one per 109 Canadians. He also points out that public service wages have been frozen since 1991 and that the average salary of a full time unionized federal public servant is about $24 000 a year.[20] Modest wage increases in the last couple years of the 1990s have done little to alter this picture, which is certainly not consistent with the overpaid image promoted by critics.

This pattern of wage freezes and staff reductions has also been evident in most provincial administrations over the past decade. For example, between 1991 and 1995, the number of civil servants per 1000 provincial residents declined by 14% in Alberta, 10% in PEI, 9% in Ontario, and 7% in Nova Scotia.[21] Since the election of Mike Harris in 1995, Ontario has reduced its public service by 16 500. Professional civil servants had their salaries cut and then frozen between 1991 and 1997.[22] Predictably, the result has been a growing concern about burnout, about overworked public servants who feel that their efforts are not appreciated by their government or the general public.

Salvation or Sell-Out:
The "New Public Management" Reforms

In Canada, but even more so in countries like Britain, Australia and New Zealand, major changes in the operating context and operational philosophy of the public service have been introduced over the past couple of decades. Known as "the new public management," these changes have stimulated lively debate as to whether they are a means for

---

[19]Walter Stewart, *Dismantling the State*, Toronto, Stoddart, p. 25.

[20]*Ibid.*, p. 28.

[21]Bruce Little, "Despite cuts, Alberta still isn't leanest," *Globe and Mail*, December 9, 1996.

[22]J. Richard Finlay, "Hard times in the public service," *Financial Post*, September 10, 1998.

the public service to regain legitimacy or a further undermining of the public service.

Those who endorse the new public management claim that it incorporates such features as:

- providing high quality services that citizens value.
- increasing the autonomy of public managers so that they can operate with more of the freedom and flexibility found in the private sector. This greater autonomy is achieved by moving service delivery (as distinct from policy) responsibilities from the regular departmental structure to separate operating agencies.
- measuring and rewarding organizations and individuals on the basis of whether or not they meet demanding targets.
- appreciating the virtues of competition and keeping an open mind on which public purposes should be performed by the private sector rather than the public sector.[23]

> NPM presumes that private administration is superior, according to its critics.

Critics of the new public management[24] claim that its philosophy is rooted in the conviction that private sector management is superior to public administration. The solution, therefore, is to transfer government activities to the private sector through privatization and contracting out. Since that obviously can't be done for every government activity, the next best thing is to transfer business practices to government operations. But, claim the critics, private sector management practices are not easily transferred to government. If public management is lethargic, cautious, expensive, unresponsive, or any of the other criticisms levelled against it, these shortcomings have more to do with Parliament and politicians than with public servants.

Whatever the merits of these respective arguments, the fact is that the new public management has brought significant change in a number

---

[23]This summary of NPM features is based on Sandford Borins, "The new public management is here to stay," *Canadian Public Administration*, Spring 1995, pp. 122-132.

[24]The discussion which follows is based on Donald J. Savoie, "What is wrong with the new public management?" in *ibid.*, pp. 112-121.

of parliamentary democracies. For example, the British "Next Steps" program called for the establishment of separate agencies to carry out the operational functions of government within a policy and resources framework set by departments. These agencies were given significant financial and managerial freedom, but were held accountable through the limited period contracts given to their chief executives, for performance against specified targets covering financial results, efficiency, throughput, and quality. From its inception in 1988, this program had fostered the creation of 109 separate agencies covering close to two-thirds of the public service by the end of 1995.[25]

By contrast, the pace in Canada has been much slower. The federal government announced in December 1989 that special operating agencies (SOAs) would be established to provide increased management flexibility in return for agreed-on levels of performance and results. But the SOAs were given less autonomy than their British counterparts and by the time of the Liberal election in 1993 (which shifted the emphasis to a new customer service program), these SOAs covered only 3% of the federal public service. According to Savoie, the only feature of the new public management which has been much in evidence in Ottawa has been that of turning over government assets and activities to the private sector and these steps "have more to do with the need to raise cash and reduce spending than a desire to pursue the new public management agenda."[26]

At both the federal and provincial level, however, there has been a greatly increased emphasis on results, and it has become commonplace for departments to publish annual business plans on the basis of which their performance is supposedly measured. A similar approach is also receiving increasing attention at the municipal level.

On the surface, it would seem praiseworthy indeed if government is now becoming preoccupied with serving the customer and ensuring

---

[25]Leslie Seidle, *Rethinking the Delivery of Public Services to Citizens*, Montreal, Institute for Research on Public Policy, 1995, p. 34. See Seidle for a description of the experiences of Britain, Australia, and New Zealand. Another useful reference is Peter Aucoin, *The New Public Management in Canada in Comparative Perspective*, Montreal, Institute for Research on Public Policy, 1995.

[26]Savoie, *Governing from the Centre*, p. 316.

the wisest possible use of the tax dollar. That should have been the focus all along, you may be tempted to claim. Nonetheless, there is reason for concern if the new public management reforms become too focused on making government operate more like a business. It is fine for government to be cost-conscious and concerned with efficiency. It is good to emphasize productivity and to make comparisons with the private sector where appropriate. It makes sense to be entrepreneurial and alert to opportunities for revenue generation.

> Governments can't be reduced to a series of business units judged solely by their bottom line.

But governments cannot be reduced to a series of business units which are judged solely on their profit and loss statements. Governments quite properly provide services which don't, can't, and shouldn't operate at break-even, much less make a profit. They provide such services precisely because they are not revenue generators and thus would never be provided by the private sector. These public goods are paid from the tax dollars which citizens provide collectively. They respond to community needs, needs which cannot be addressed (and won't be) if everything has to measure up financially, and to meet the test of the market place.

Another concern with the new public management is its emphasis on people as customers. While good customer service is desirable in government as elsewhere, it in no way defines the total relationship between a government and its citizens. Customers have rights, such as the right to easy access, to choices and to quick handling of complaints, but citizens "have both rights and responsibilities to be active in setting the agenda of ... government and in debating policy options."[27] Whatever its benefits, the focus on customer service may restrict the public to a largely reactive role. As Seidle points out, such terms as customer or client do not capture the nature and complexity of the interaction that occurs when a government official serves someone who is, among other things, "a taxpayer, a recipient of certain monetary benefits from the state, a voter and possibly a member of a political party and/or one

---

[27]Paul G. Thomas, "Diagnosing the Health of Civic Democracy: 25 Years of Citizen Involvement With City Hall," in Nancy Klos (ed.), *The State of Unicity—25 Years Later*, Winnipeg, Institute of Urban Studies, 1998, p. 50.

or more voluntary organizations with an interest in public policy, and who carries expectations that extend beyond a particular contact with a particular public servant at a particular time."[28]

What About the Governor General?

So far, discussion has centred on three parts of the executive branch, the Cabinet, the Prime Minister and the civil service. The story has been essentially the same for all three—increasing power and influence throughout most of the 20th century. But what about the other part of the executive branch, the position of Governor General? According to the constitution, the Queen is the Head of State for Canada and the Governor General acts as her representative in Canada. Here again, however, there is quite a contrast between law and practice; although the position of Governor General has not become obsolete or without value, as some Canadians seem to think.

Historically, Governors General were appointed from outside of Canada, presumably to ensure the necessary detachment for performing their duties. Beginning in 1952, however, the first Canadian Governor General was appointed, in the person of Vincent Massey. The current Governor General is Adrienne Clarkson, a well-known Canadian broadcaster. She was appointed effective October 7, 1999, replacing Roméo Leblanc, appointed in February 1995, who asked to be relieved of his duties before the end of his term. The official term of office is six years, but appointees usually serve five.

The Governor General has many official duties, in Canada and abroad.[29] They include representing Canada at "non-political" international events, such as the opening of a world's fair or the coronation of a monarch. Other duties involve receiving dignitaries, heads of state and other important persons and awarding civilian or military medals recognizing the merits of citizens who have distinguished themselves.

---

[28]Seidle, *op. cit.*, p. 9.

[29]The summary which follows is based on John Fraser, *The House of Commons at Work*, Ottawa, House of Commons, 1993, pp. 8-9.

In addition, the Governor General provides a state presence at a variety of artistic, scientific and sports events, and makes many appointments. As discussed earlier, these appointments are on the advice of the Prime Minister and, indeed, the Prime Minister could carry out the other social and ceremonial duties of the Governor General—as the President or other Head of State has to do in countries which are republics. But the Prime Minister's workload is already substantial and, in any event, the Governor General is seen as a more neutral, non-partisan figure, better suited to representing all Canadians. There has been a concern that this important distinction was blurring, since such recent Governors General as Roméo Leblanc, Ramon Hnatyshyn, and Jeanne Sauvé were active in the Liberal or Progressive Conservative parties at the time of their appointments. In that respect, the recent appointment of Adrienne Clarkson, an individual whose many talents do not include partisan political experience, is seen by many as a very positive development.

In addition to social and ceremonial duties, the Governor General also has a limited number of discretionary powers which are the remnants of the prerogative power of the Crown, reflecting the notion that the Queen/Governor General is to act as the guardian of the constitution and protector of the public interest. Chief among these are the Governor General's responsibility to ensure that we always have a Prime Minister in office and a government in power and to receive and deal with any requests from Prime Ministers for **dissolution** of Parliament and the calling of an election. Usually the situation is straightforward and the Governor General's choice is obvious. But not always!

- In October 1925 Mackenzie King's Liberal Government was defeated in an election, falling to only 101 seats, compared to 116 for the Conservatives. Yet King didn't resign, persuaded the Governor General that he should be allowed to meet the House of Commons and attempt to govern, and did so for six months. When King then asked the Governor General to call another election, Lord Byng refused and turned to the Conservatives to form a new government when King resigned in anger.

- The 1972 election was a cliff-hanger, with the lead changing hands several times during election night. The Liberal Government headed by Pierre Trudeau lost a large number of seats but still ended up with two more than the Conservatives. While there was some question of who had won or lost, Trudeau never considered stepping down. After serving for a year and a half, he lost a vote in the House, obtained dissolution, and won a majority.

◆ Something to Think About

In 1979 Joe Clark formed a minority government. How long would he have to govern before he would be entitled to call another election? Would the Governor General have any say about this timing?

As it happened, Joe Clark's government lasted nine months, after which his request for an election was granted. But instead of a precise time frame, Canadians essentially leave this kind of "loose end" to be resolved by the Governor General if necessary. It may be argued that the Governor General can only come up with a decision which would have the support of the main political parties and, ultimately, of the Canadian people. That is quite true, and Governors General certainly prefer not to be placed in situations where the choices are not clear and where they may have to exercise some discretion. The fact remains that if Canada did not have a Governor General, we would need to set down some rules to deal with situations like how long a term of office needs to be before a party in power is entitled to seek reelection. We would also have to appoint someone to act as the "Grand National Host," since it would still be necessary to entertain foreign dignitaries. The office of Governor General handles these duties well, building as it does on centuries of tradition and pageantry. Rather than being an historical anachronism, the position continues to be of practical value.

Governor General Without the Monarchy?

As Canada enters a new century, there have been suggestions that its ties with the British monarchy should be severed, at least at the end of the reign of Queen Elizabeth if not before. Industry Minister John Manley mused about this possibility in late 1997, and apparently some senior officials in the PMO had promoted this step as a millennium project. Interest was also stimulated by the November 1999 vote in

Australia on a proposal to abolish the Monarchy. It was defeated, but perhaps more because of disagreement over how a replacement President would be chosen than because of support for the Monarchy.

Predictably, this issue has generated emotional debate. Some see abolition of the Monarchy as but one more step in the systematic elimination of the traditions of English Canada in a misguided attempt to placate French Canadian nationalism. Others claim that Canada is now a middle power, whose skill "at pioneering the concept of peacekeeping, of fostering a land-mines convention, and spearheading an international war crimes tribunal is not strengthened by perceptions of continued vassalage to a foreign power."[30]

Significantly, most discussion of abolishing the Monarchy presumes the continued existence of a Governor General. It is only the link between the Governor General and the Monarchy which would be severed. The intention is that the Governor General would continue to function exactly as he does today, but no longer as the personal representative of the British Monarch. Details are sketchy about the new model, but it appears that direct election of the Governor General would be introduced, perhaps for a seven year term. Any such change is unlikely, however, since the approval of all 10 provinces would be needed to end the Queen's role as head of state. Nor does it seem sensible to open the constitution and revisit "the nightmare of Meech and Charlottetown,"[31] just so that we can replace the Monarch with an elected or appointed Canadian head of state.

The House of Commons

If Canada has a democratic, accountable system of government, it must be centred on the House of Commons; this is the only body that we elect. As previously discussed, the House of Commons is composed of

---

[30]David Olive, "Severing the colonial connection," *National Post*, December 30, 1998.

[31]Reg Whitaker, "The Monarchy: Gone With the Wind?" *Policy Options*, Montreal, Institute of Research on Public Policy, May 1999, p. 12.

301 members, elected from 301 geographic areas (known as ridings or **constituencies**) into which Canada is divided. The composition of the House and the boundaries of individual ridings are reviewed after each census (compiled every 10 years),

> The House of Commons is the only body we elect in our system of government.

so that adjustments can be made to reflect the changing population patterns. In fact, the number of members increased to 301 from 295 at the time of the 1997 federal election. The geographic allocation of ridings is outlined in the table which follows. It illustrates the domination of the Commons by the two very populous provinces of Central Canada, which together hold 60% of the seats.

Province/Territory	# of Commons Seats
Alberta	26
British Columbia	34
Manitoba	14
New Brunswick	10
Newfoundland	7
Northwest Territories and Nunavut	2 (1 each)
Nova Scotia	11
Ontario	103
Prince Edward Island	4
Québec	75
Saskatchewan	14
Yukon	1
Total	301

The Layout of the House

The House is set up with two halves and a wide central aisle. This division reflects the fact that members are elected on party lines and that the House is organized into a 'Government' and one or more 'Opposition' parties. The aisle is slightly more than two sword lengths wide —a very practical consideration from a time in Britain when members wore their swords and scabbards in Parliament. Even if members drew their swords in the heat of debate, they could not reach each other across the aisle. In today's Parliaments, members content themselves with making cutting remarks instead.

The Speaker

At the front of the House sits the Speaker's chair on a raised platform. The **Speaker** has an extremely important role to play in presiding over the deliberations of Parliament and enforcing the rules of procedure. He or she is expected to be neutral and to ensure that the rights of all members are respected and protected. The Speaker is to enforce the rules in such a way as to allow the opposition members to pursue their watchdog role while also allowing the government to fulfil its mandate by governing. Achieving this delicate balance is no easy task, especially in a House filled with partisan debate and remarks more emotional than considered.

Until the mid-1980s, the Speaker was chosen by the Prime Minister, usually after consultation (as a courtesy) with the leader of the Opposition. Tradition called for each Speaker, upon being chosen, to be led very reluctantly to the front of the House, with the Prime Minister and opposition leader literally dragging the person along by each arm. This ritual was more than just an expression of modesty on the part of the new Speaker, more than a reluctance to assume the serious responsibilities of the position. Instead, it reflected the historical experience of early Speakers in Britain. When the "House of Commoners" met back in the days when the King ruled supreme, it would appoint someone to carry grievances to the King and to act as Speaker on behalf of the concerns of the common folk. The King was not amused with these interferences with his divine right to rule. His response was to have

early Speakers beheaded. Thus, the
Speakers of today have an historical
reason for feigning modesty. They
don't want to lose their heads over
their jobs!

> Early Speakers were afraid
> of "losing their heads"
> over their jobs.

Reforms introduced in the mid-1980s provide for the election of the
Speaker from the House of Commons. Conservative MP John Fraser
was chosen as the first elected Speaker in September 1986 after a mara-
thon session with many candidates. The current speaker is Liberal
Gilbert Parent, elected in January 1994, and reelected for the new
Parliament which began following the 1997 federal election. Given their
numerical strength, it is likely that a candidate from the governing party
will be successful in gaining election. Nonetheless, this change is seen
as reinforcing the notion of the Speaker as an independent officer of the
House, rather than a hand-picked choice of the Prime Minister.

The side of the House to the right of the Speaker holds the members of the governing party, with the Prime Minister and members of
the Cabinet along the front row (and the second row as needed). The
remaining members of the governing party sit further behind on the
backbenches—giving rise to their popular name as "backbenchers."

On the other side of the House are the opposition parties. If the
Government has a large enough majority, their members may spill over
onto the opposite side as well. Directly across from the Prime Minister
sits the leader of the **Official Opposition**. Around this leader sit other
senior members of the Official Opposition, those who would likely
form a Cabinet if their party were to win the next election. These senior
opposition members are usually assigned specific Cabinet Ministers and
departments to monitor and criticize as part of their watchdog role. It
is common to refer to this "cabinet-in-waiting" as a **Shadow Cabinet**.

The Parliamentary Schedule

A "Parliament" lasts from one election until the next. The current
Parliament is the 36th since Confederation and it began following the
federal election in 1997. A Parliament ends with dissolution (requested
by the PM and usually granted automatically by the Governor General)
which leads to an election.

Within a Parliament there will be several sessions, depending largely on the wishes of the government of the day. A session of Parliament begins with all members of both Houses gathering in the Senate to hear the Governor General read the **Speech from the Throne**. While this once was really a speech from the Throne or ruling Monarch, today it is a speech from the government setting out its plans and proposed legislation for that session. It ends with what is termed **prorogation**. All legislation not passed when the House is prorogued is dead, and must be reintroduced from the beginning.

There is much "pomp and ceremony" associated with the operations of Parliament, most of it representing historical traditions which remain important and are recognized and reinforced through the continuation of the ceremonial features. A good example is provided by the Mace, which is carried on the shoulder of the Sergeant-at-Arms when the Speaker travels from place to place. Without the Mace in the House, proceedings cannot begin. In the Middle Ages, the Mace was the weapon of the Sergeant-at-Arms, who was the bodyguard of the King. For another intriguing example, read on.[32]

"Black Rod" Comes Calling

A quaint, but historically significant, part in the opening of Parliament is played by the "Gentleman Usher of the Black Rod," surely one of the most curiously named personages to be found within a government. After the Governor General has taken a seat on the Throne in the Senate, Black Rod proceeds to the House of Commons to ask its members to come to the Senate to hear the Speech from the Throne. The door of the Commons is slammed in his face as he draws near. Three knocks with his ebony staff bring the question, "Who is there?" Upon replying "Black Rod," he is admitted to the House, extends his invitation, and then departs. The members of the House follow him, led by the Speaker.

This rather quaint position was thrust into the public spotlight in late 1997, when it was filled for the first time by a woman, and renamed

---

[32]This example is summarized from John Ricker and John Saywell, *How Are We Governed?*, Toronto, Clarke, Irwin and Company Limited, 1980, pp. 76-77.

Usher of the Senate. The Canadian Taxpayers Federation and others decried the annual salary of $75 000 for what was seen as an archaic institution. But while the process described above may seem strange or silly, it reflects an underlying fact of great significance. It draws attention to the independence of the House of Commons from the Monarch, a distinction members have made a point of emphasizing ever since Charles I entered the Commons in Great Britain to arrest some of its members. In fact, when members return to the Commons after hearing the Speech from the Throne, they emphasize their independence by deliberately introducing a subject of their own choosing for debate, rather than proceeding with any of the matters outlined in the Throne Speech. Moreover, the position of Black Rod, or Usher of the Senate as the position is now called, involves a good deal of other work, including being responsible for the Senate's information systems, maintenance, postal, messenger and trade services and acting as the Senate police officer if unruly Senators have to be ejected.[33]

Reforms introduced in 1983 provided a regular schedule for sittings of Parliament and for vacation breaks in the fall, winter and spring terms. Changes were also made to the hours of the House. Previously, MPs used to be in meetings with constituents, committees or caucus in the mornings and then in the Commons from 2 until 10:30 or more at night—a brutal schedule which almost ensured exhaustion and frequent absenteeism from the House. The new arrangements provided for the Commons to sit from 11 a.m. until 6:30 most days. Further changes introduced in 1991 lengthened the Christmas and summer recess periods and provided for an adjournment of the House every fifth week.

◆ Something to Think About

As you read this schedule, your first reaction is likely to be one of annoyance about all this "free" time that members of Parliament have. How can this be justified, you want to know.

---

[33]Buzz Bourdon, "Usher of the Black Rod says she's nervous, but ready," *Ottawa Citizen*, October 7, 1999.

Much depends on how that time is used. Canadians have often complained that their members lose touch with their roots, get too caught up in events in Ottawa, develop a "Central-Canadian" bias, or otherwise fail to represent properly those who sent them to Ottawa in the first place. Well, if you want your MP to be available in your riding, to stay in touch with local needs and concerns, you have to give him or her an opportunity to be there! This is a vast country and visits back to the riding represent a very long trip for many members. The main reason for providing for an adjournment every fifth week was to make it easier for members to stay in touch with their ridings.

The Roles of the House of Commons

As outlined in Chapter 2, the Commons has three main roles which will be examined a little more fully in this chapter: **(1)** representative role, **(2)** legislative role, and **(3)** watchdog role.

1. Representative Role

In theory, the 301 members of the Commons represent the views and concerns of the 30 million residents of Canada. In practice, there are several factors which make the Commons less than representative of the Canadian people. Chief among these are:

a)   *With the exception of a very rare independent member, almost all MPs are members of political parties.*

Party discipline restricts the ability of MPs to represent the views of their constituents, especially in the case of government backbenchers —who are constantly threatened that any desertion on their part could bring down the government and force an election. Dissident members, sometimes called "mavericks," may face party sanctions for their lack of complete loyalty, including not being appointed to committees of their choice, not being supported by the party in fund-raising efforts, or not being approved as a candidate for the party in the next election.

Some examples from the past decade illustrate the impact of this discipline. When Progressive Conservatives Alex Kindy and David Kilgour broke ranks and voted against their own party on the legislation introducing the GST, Mulroney expelled them from the party. In 1995,

Warren Allmand, a long time Liberal member and former Cabinet Minister was strongly critical of what he saw as the Chrétien government's abandonment of social programs in its preoccupation with the deficit and debt. His comments led to his removal as Chair of a Commons committee. In the spring of 1996, John Nunziata voted against his party because of its failure to live up to its promise to scrap the GST. For this act of rebellion he was expelled from the party caucus. He ran again in 1997, as an independent, and it is in this lonely category that he sits in the current House. Popular Newfoundland MP George Baker chaired the Commons fisheries committee and was quite outspoken about government mismanagement in the collapse of the fishing industry on the East Coast. His position as chair was not renewed by the government in September 1998 (although in mid-1999 he did make it into the Cabinet as part of a mini-shuffle).

b)   The composition of the Commons does not reflect the make-up of the population of Canada.

If it did, it would have 148 female MPs, half would be under 35, under 10% would have university degrees, and the largest single group would be unskilled workers and homemakers.[34] Instead, the Commons is overwhelmingly male, middle-aged, and drawn from a privileged socio-economic background. The number of women in the Commons increased marginally (from 53 to 58) as a result of the 1997 election. Just over 76% of MPs have taken university courses in one form or another. The largest single group is made up of lawyers, usually about one-quarter of all MPs.

◆ Something to Think About

Is it reasonable to assume that MPs from a privileged background are unable to represent effectively Canadians from "other walks of life?"

To put it another way, if we could somehow produce a Commons which reflected accurately a cross-section of all Canadians, would all of their views be represented more effectively?

---

[34]W. L. White, R. H. Wagenberg and R. C. Nelson, *Canadian Politics and Government*, 6th Edition, Toronto, Harcourt Brace, 1995, p. 202.

The short answer is "not necessarily." One should not assume that an MP from a privileged background is incapable of speaking out force-fully for the rights of the less fortunate. Nor should one assume that a "have-not" MP would be an eloquent and effective speaker on behalf of those he or she represents. Nonetheless, the *perception* is that the Commons isn't representative of ordinary Canadians and, as has been said before, perception is reality.

c)   The electoral system causes serious distortions between the percentage of popular vote and the percentage of seats won.

This happens because a candidate doesn't have to win 50% plus one to be elected, just more votes than any other candidate—a system often termed "first-past-the-post." With several candidates contesting each riding, rarely does the winning candidate have 50%.

To illustrate, consider the Mulroney landslide victory in 1984. The Progressive Conservatives won 75% of the seats with 50% of the vote. The Liberals won 14% of seats on 28% of the vote, and the NDP won 11% of the seats with 19% of the vote. If the number of seats had reflected the popular vote received, the standings would have been Conservatives 141, Liberals 79, NDP 54, and all others 8. An even more dramatic example, the 1993 federal election, is summarized below.

Federal Election Results, 1993

Party	% of Vote	% of Seats	# of Seats
Liberal	41	60	178
Reform	19	18	52
Conservative	16	1	2
Bloc	14	18	54
NDP	7	3	9

With only 41% of the vote, the Liberals won a substantial majority. They gained 60% of the seats in the Commons even though almost exactly that percentage of Canadian voters in the election did not support them. Perhaps even more dramatic was the positive result for the Bloc. Even though it was fourth in percentage of popular vote, with seats in only one province, the Bloc won the second largest number of seats in the Commons and became the Official Opposition. In contrast, the Progressive Conservative Party was nearly wiped out in the House of Commons, even though it retained significant support among the voters. With the Bloc votes concentrated in Québec and the Reform votes concentrated in the West, the Conservatives were squeezed out in their two traditional strongholds.

The 1997 federal election results also produced serious distortions. The Liberals managed to win a little over half the seats (155 out of 301) with only 38% of the popular vote. Incredibly, the Liberals won 101 of these seats from Ontario (out of 103 seats available), on the basis of only 49% of the vote. The PCs increased their popular vote by less than 3% across Canada, but their number of seats increased from two to 20. The inequities in the electoral system are evident from the fact that it took 32 000 votes to elect one Liberal in 1997, 68 000 to elect a member of the NDP, and over 120 000 to elect a Progressive Conservative.[35]

The regional nature of Canada's political parties is exaggerated by the distortions produced by our electoral system. To illustrate:

- the Liberals captured 25% of the vote in Western Canada, where they are perceived as having virtually no support because of the few seats they won.
- the Reform party continues to be shut out in Ontario, but it did receive 19% of the votes cast in that province.

◆ Something to Think About

Should Canada introduce a system of **proportional representation**? In other words, should there be some formula which assigns political parties a number of seats that constitutes about the same percentage of total seats in the House as each party's votes are a percentage of all votes cast? Such a system is used in countries like Denmark, Ireland and Israel, and Australia uses it for Senate elections.

---

[35]Miriam Lapp, "End First-Past-the-Post," Montreal, IRRP, *Policy Options*, November 1999, p. 20.

While the results under PR might be "fairer," they would rarely produce a majority government.[36] Only a few times in the 20th century has a winning party won more than half of the popular vote in a federal election. As more parties contest elections, such results are likely to be even less in evidence. So a PR system would presumably mean frequent minority governments for Canada. How much of a drawback this is, of course, depends upon one's view of the merits of minority governments. Moreover, it is possible to minimize this problem by adopting a mixed system (such as found in New Zealand, Germany and Sweden), in which half (or some larger portion) of the members are elected from constituencies as they are now and the remainder are drawn from party lists according to the parties' share of the popular vote.[37] One drawback of this arrangement is that it produces two classes of elected member, one chosen directly by the voters and one via lists developed by the political parties. Proponents of the scheme argue that these lists facilitate the advancement of women and minorities, but experience suggests that parties can top their lists with long time party stalwarts who are tired or unwilling to tempt fate in a constituency election.[38]

d)   Rural areas are over-represented on the basis of their populations.

This imbalance is unavoidable, given their small, scattered populations. Although the ideal arrangement is to have each MP representing roughly the same number of people, rural ridings would be much too large to cover if they were to encompass as many people as are found in compact urban areas. The result is that an MP from a city riding may represent 90 000 people, while an MP from a rural riding represents only 75 000. Every effort is made to ensure that population

---

[36]For details on PR systems, see Paul Fox, "Should Canada Adopt Proportional Representation?" in Paul Fox and Graham White (eds.), *Politics: Canada*, 7th Edition, Whitby, McGraw-Hill Ryerson Limited, 1991, pp. 343-350. For arguments for and against this system, see John Hiemstra, "Getting What You Vote For" and Paul Barker, "Voting for Trouble" in Charlton and Barker, *op. cit.*, pp. 280-301.

[37]Andrew Coyne, "First-past-the-post electoral system is broken," *Kingston Whig Standard*, October 17, 1996.

[38]Jeffrey Simpson, "Are Canadians ready to pay the price of minority government," *Globe and Mail*, June 19, 1997.

variations are not wider than 25%. Excessive discrepancies are vulnerable to a Charter challenge, as has already occurred with respect to some ridings in Saskatchewan. The Supreme Court did not find it unconstitutional that rural voters were given more weight in a legislature than urban voters. But it is clear from the ruling that electoral boundaries are subject to judicial review and that section 3 of the Charter protects "effective representation," which includes the notion of voter parity.[39]

2. Lawmaking Role

Most legislation results from government initiatives designed to carry out its election promises or otherwise fulfill the agenda of the party in power. However, legislation can result from *three* different kinds of bill. As will become clear from the brief summary below, these can be distinguished on the basis of their sponsor, their scope and their fate.

1 Government Bill

It is sponsored by the Government, and introduced by the appropriate Minister. For example, a bill dealing with farming would be introduced by the Minister of Agriculture. Government bills are national in scope and they almost always pass. In the unlikely event that a Government bill is defeated, the result is usually interpreted as a loss of confidence and the Cabinet finds itself under strong pressure to resign or to seek a new mandate from the Canadian people by calling an election.

2 Private Members' Bill

This type of bill is equally national in scope, but has quite a different fate. It is sponsored by any private member (that is, anyone not in the Cabinet). Private members' bills are usually introduced by an opposition backbencher as a way of criticizing deficiencies in government legislation, with the result that the government—which controls the agenda—does not make time for them to be passed. Procedural reforms ensure discussion of a few private members' bills on a weekly basis, but their chances of passage remain slim.

---

[39]The *Reference re Provincial Electoral Boundaries* case is discussed in Andrew Sancton, "Canada as a highly urbanized nation: new implications for government," *Canadian Public Administration*, Fall 1992.

An early "success" under these reforms was the passage of Bill C-204, the Non-Smoker's Health Act, in June of 1988. What is popularly known as the anti-smoking legislation was introduced as a private members' bill, randomly selected for further study, given second reading after five hours debate, reviewed and amended by a legislative committee, and finally passed by the House after a further two hours of debate provided under the new rules.[40] An important piece of legislation, affecting the health of all Canadians, this bill was initiated by a back-bench MP, Lynn McDonald of the NDP. Unfortunately, these examples are all too rare. In the Liberal Government's first term in the 1990s (1993-1997) only nine of 410 private members' bills were passed.[41]

One of those which did not was a highly publicized bill by Liberal backbencher Roger Galloway, designed to put an end to the practice of negative option billing by cable companies, in which customers were given and charged for new television channels and had to notify the companies if they did not want them.[42]

Billing Bill Blocked By Bloc

Widespread consumer anger at this tactic prompted Galloway to sponsor the bill, which initially passed through the Commons in just three weeks in September 1996. It then bogged down in the Senate for six months, allegedly because of intense pressure from cable companies who feared that they would be unable to market new specialty channels coming on stream if the bill passed. The Senate finally passed the bill, but with amendments, which mean that it had to return to the Commons to be approved again. A filibuster by the Bloc kept it from going to a vote, and it died when the summer 1997 election was called. The Bloc claimed that the bill would limit the market for new French language specialty channels due to appear that fall.

---

[40]This summary is based on Nora Lever, "What's Happened Under The New Rules," *Canadian Parliamentary Review*, Ottawa, Autumn 1988, pp. 14-16.

[41]Sheldon Alberts, "New rules will give more power to backbenchers," *National Post*, November 28, 1998.

[42]The summary which follows is based on information in Chris Cobb, "Senate stalling TV bill, MP says," *Ottawa Citizen*, March 12, 1997 and Chris Cobb, "Bloc kills bid to stop hated cable billing," *Ottawa Citizen*, April 23, 1997.

Rule changes introduced in late 1998 now give private members' bills a somewhat better chance of being passed. Governments will no longer be able to kill private members' bills simply by proroguing Parliament and calling a new session. In addition, backbench MPs will also be able to force debate of private members' bills if they can get the signatures of 100 members, including at least 10 from two different parties.[43]

3   Private Bill

Sponsored by a Senator, this bill is very limited in scope or jurisdiction and almost always passes. Examples would include a company charter or a bill authorizing the use of a professional designation by a particular organization. These bills are introduced first, and receive their main examination, in the Senate.

The Bill Passing Process

How does a bill pass through Parliament, and what is meant by the various "readings" which are given to a bill? For the purpose of this very brief summary of the process, let us assume that we are dealing with a Government bill, which has been introduced into the House of Commons.

Step 1 First Reading

The bill is introduced by the appropriate Minister and copies are distributed to all members. There isn't any debate or vote. The significance of this stage is that the bill is now officially before Parliament.

Step 2 Second Reading

After what may be a considerable interval, the bill returns for second reading. This involves what may be extensive debate and then a vote on the general principle(s) of the bill. If the bill is defeated at this stage, it is dead—and so might be the government, for reasons already discussed. If the bill passes this stage (as it almost invariably does), then its principle cannot be changed thereafter, only its details. This restriction limits the scope of the amendments which may be made at committee stage. However, changes to the

[43]This summary is based on Alberts, *op. cit.*

rules of the House in February 1994 set out procedures by which a bill can be referred to committee for detailed study *before* second reading, thus allowing for a wider scope of amendments.

Step 3 Committee Stage

The bill is referred to the appropriate Commons committee for detailed examination, clause-by-clause. These committees are composed of members of Parliament, in proportion to party standing in the House. Through the use of these committees, members are able to specialize in examining the same kinds of legislation over and over, rather than the whole House trying to be experts on everything by attempting detailed examination of every bill.

Step 4 Report Stage

The bill is reported back from committee to the full House. This stage is both debatable and amendable, in case the Commons wants to undo any changes made in committee. (Most of the time, however, the Commons defers to the expertise of those who have given the bill detailed examination in committee.)

Step 5 Third Reading

This stage is largely a formality. The bill has already been approved in principle at second reading and examined in detail at committee and report stage. But there is provision for debate and a vote.

Step 6 Senate Approval

The bill then goes through essentially the same process in the Senate, although Senators give most of their attention to refining the details of the bill in committee. If the bill is defeated in the Senate (an extraordinarily rare occurrence), it is dead. The Government's life is not affected, however, since the Cabinet is responsible only to the Commons, not the Senate. If the bill is amended in the Senate, then it must return to the Commons and be passed again in its amended form. In other words, the same piece of legislation must pass through both Houses of Parliament. Further reference to the Senate's role in lawmaking is found later in this chapter.

Step 7 Royal Assent

This must be given by the Governor General. It is considered an automatic or rubber stamping duty of the Governor General, but until royal assent is given, a bill does not become a law.

3. Watchdog Role

The third major role of the Commons that we are examining is the watchdog role. Unlike the previous two, it is almost entirely carried out by the opposition members of the Commons—not by the whole House. The opposition members are supposed to keep an eye on the government for Canadians, between elections. Through their close scrutiny, criticisms and suggestions, they are to ensure better legislation and wiser use of funds.

The watchdog role is important in at least two key respects. Through this role, the opposition parties act to protect our interests between elections. If we are to have responsible government, if the Cabinet (and civil service) really are to be held responsible to the legislative branch, there must be an effective watchdog role. Second, and perhaps paradoxically, a strong opposition is also good for the "government," that is, for the party in power. Without an effective opposition, the governing party inevitably becomes complacent and arrogant, thereby sowing the seeds for its own potential downfall at the next election. Pushed by an effective opposition, the governing party is forced to extend itself, to perform better. There is much to the old saying that a good opposition produces a good government.

What are the various tools available to the opposition parties to carry out their watchdog role? Leading the list in familiarity is daily **Question Period**, especially since its highlights

> The opposition parties have various means to enforce the watchdog role.

have been a prominent feature on television in recent years. The saying that "familiarity breeds contempt," may well apply in this case, however, since the behaviour of members during Question Period has done little to enhance the image of our parliamentarians. Much of the time seems to be taken up with angry exchanges or good-natured banter, usually accompanied by desk-thumping and cries of "hear, hear" or "shame, shame"—depending on which side of the House is speaking or responding.

Question Period is held at the beginning of each day's sitting of Parliament, during which members can ask questions of any member of the Cabinet, including the Prime Minister. The questions are spontaneous, meaning that the government does not know in advance who may be asked what. This is the key redeeming feature of Question Period. Since the government sets the agenda (the "Orders of the Day"), it is usually in control. The opposition parties are largely restricted to reacting to what the Government presents. Not so during Question Period! The government doesn't know what to expect. It can be (and often is) caught off guard. Even though most of the time in Question Period may be wasted on trivial or childish exchanges, it is arguably well worth preserving because of its ability to trip up the government with well-timed, unexpected questions.

Any detailed examination of the other watchdog tools is beyond the scope of this Guide, but a brief summary of the main ones is found in *Appendix A* for those who are interested in learning more about them. Over the years, there have been a number of reforms which have strengthened the watchdog role—changes such as the provision of research funds for parties to close somewhat the "knowledge gap" in the House of Commons as compared to the expertise available to assist the governing party. Even the backbenchers of the governing party are not always as meek and obedient as their public demeanour would suggest. Behind the closed doors of weekly caucus meetings, they have an opportunity to raise concerns and to pressure the government to respond to these concerns—although, as noted earlier in this chapter, caucus appears to have become less influential.

The Senate

As mentioned in Chapter 2, Senators are appointed not elected. They are appointed by the Governor General (officially), but on the advice of the Prime Minister—who actually makes the choices. Senators must be at least 30 years old, and must have real estate worth $4000 net. These rather strange requirements date from the origins of the Senate, when it was expected to be made up of people of property and maturity, appointees who would bring a "sober second thought" to decisions of the elected House of Commons. A further requirement is that the Senators must reside in the province or territory for which they are appointed.

Clearing a Surprising Hurdle

Outdated and foolish as the $4000 property qualification may sound, it almost prevented the September 1997 appointment of Sister Peggy Butts. Having taken a vow of poverty 40 years before, the first Roman Catholic nun to serve in the Canadian Senate did not have the required $4000. The matter was resolved when the government and her Montreal-based order arranged the transfer of a parcel of scrub land in the Antigonish area into her name.[44]

Originally, there were to be 24 Senators each from Ontario, Québec, the Maritime Provinces (10 each for Nova Scotia and New Brunswick and four for PEI) and the West (six for each of the four Western Provinces). When Newfoundland joined Confederation in 1949, it was given six Senators. Two more were added to represent the Yukon and Northwest Territories, for a total of 104. With the creation of the new territory of Nunavut in April 1999, one more Senator has been added, bringing the new total to 105.

The original idea was that the Senate would represent and protect the interests of each of the regions in the Parliament of Canada. Each region would have the same number of Senators to counter-balance the dominance that some regions held in the House of Commons, based on representation by population. However, as Western Canada has grown in population and economic importance over the past few decades, there has been growing dissatisfaction with the fact that the West is still limited to 24 Senators while Atlantic Canada (thanks to Newfoundland's late arrival) has 30 Senators. This imbalance underlies much of the push for Senate reform which has emanated from Western Canada in recent years.

Considerable attention was given to the composition and responsibilities of the Senate during the discussions leading up to the formation of the new country of Canada. It was expected to represent and protect provincial interests and it was given virtually equal law-making powers to those of the House of Commons. The only exception to this state-

---

[44]Edward Greenspon, "Vow of poverty almost thwarts Senator," *Globe and Mail*, September 24, 1997.

ment was the fact that legislation providing for the expenditure of public money or the imposition of taxes must be introduced in the House of Commons, even though it must still be passed by the Senate to become law.

Senate Decline

Given the important responsibilities with which it started, why has the Senate declined so much in influence and public perception? First of all, because the Senators are appointed and not elected, they were doomed to play a less and less influential role as the concept of a democratically elected and accountable government gained ground. They lack the legitimacy to block or overturn measures approved by the elected Commons; yet, if they simply rubber-stamp those measures they appear unnecessary.

Second, under the principle of responsible government, the Cabinet is responsible only to the House of Commons. A vote in the Senate can never defeat a government. As a result, all of the drama of our government system (and the media coverage) focuses on the House of Commons.

Even with these limitations, the Senate might have continued to play a useful role but for the shameful abuse of the appointing power by every Prime Minister since Confederation—a third and, arguably, the most significant cause of Senate decline. Rather than appointing leading Canadians from all walks of life, Prime Ministers have appointed party faithful, filling the Senate with (mostly) old politicians being rewarded for past service. As a result, the Senate has been dominated by appointees of whatever party formed the government for a period of years.

The Senate was overwhelmingly Conservative in the 19th century, thanks to that party being in power so long (under Macdonald and his four successors). The Liberals dominated much of the 20th century and after 22 consecutive years in power (from 1935 to 1957) they had almost completely filled the Senate with Liberals (78 to only five Conservatives) by the end of the King/St. Laurent era. Diefenbaker redressed the balance somewhat during his time in office and Mulroney got the Conservatives back to a slight majority during his eight years in power. Not long after taking office, however, Chrétien had regained a slim majority position, which he has gradually strengthened during the 1990s. With the odd exception, such as the appointment of former Conservative MP Doug Roche in September 1998, Chrétien has continued the tradition of appointing Liberal stalwarts and friends.

While many individual Senators have a wealth of experience and take their work very seriously, the overall image of the Senate is that of a retirement home for elderly partisans. The Senate's yearly schedule isn't especially onerous and yet a number of Senators have very spotty attendance records (about a quarter of them miss 40% or more of the sittings)[45] and are perceived as doing little to earn their $64 000 annual salary and $10 100 tax-free expense allowance. Senators who miss more than 21 sitting days in a session are docked $120 per day of absence. But absences can be excused (and usually are) on the grounds of illness or performance of duties.

Canada's "Senator from Mexico"

The truancy of Senators became a lively public issue in 1997, when the media began to focus on the attendance record of Andrew Thompson, who had made an appearance only 12 times throughout the 1990s. He cited ill health as the reason for his absence and for the fact that he and his wife resided in Mexico for four months each winter. The resulting public anger was enough to generate a long-overdue response, and the Senate voted in February 1998 to suspend Thompson without pay for the rest of the current session of Parliament. Ironically, only half of the Senators were present for the vote! However, well before the end of this session of Parliament—in December 1999—Thompson turned 75, the age of mandatory retirement. But he is still eligible for a pension of almost $50 000 a year.

Whatever goodwill the Senate might have gained from finally taking a stand with respect to Andrew Thompson was quickly dissipated by its actions in June 1998 in endorsing a $181 a day tax-free allowance for those Senators who show up for work.[46] Perhaps it was felt that this

---

[45]"Absence makes the claim grow weaker," Editorial, *Globe and Mail*, December 17, 1997.

[46]"Sneaky senators," Editorial, *Toronto Star*, June 23, 1998.

positive inducement would improve attendance. It could hardly be justified on the grounds offered by some Senators that they found it too expensive to come to Ottawa, or were forced to stay in "meagre accommodation." Unfortunately, the episode simply confirmed the jaundiced view of many Canadians that the Senators were out of touch, insensitive to public opinion, and far more costly than they were worth.

Still Life in the Senate?

Notwithstanding its image as a do-nothing body, the Senate has shown a willingness over the past couple of decades to exert its considerable authority. During the Mulroney years, the Senate took a more active and confrontational role than usual on several occasions. With Liberals in the majority, the Senate attempted to block several government initiatives including the Canada-U.S. Free Trade Agreement and the imposition of the Goods and Services Tax (GST). The former issue was resolved by the 1988 election campaign, which reelected the Conservatives on a free trade platform. The GST deadlock was resolved when Prime Minister Mulroney appointed eight additional Senators in December 1990, under a section of the constitution that allowed such action in exceptional circumstances involving a serious conflict between the Senate and the House of Commons. This expanded Senate was temporary, however, since the constitution provides that the number must return to "normal" for each region and for the Senate as a whole before the government appoints any additional Senators.

The Senate has continued its more active and aggressive role since the Liberals assumed office in October 1993, as the following examples illustrate.

- In late 1995, Conservatives in the Senate threatened to derail Liberal Justice Minister Allan Rock's controversial gun control legislation by making major amendments to it. Ultimately, however, the legislation did pass through the Senate without incident.
- In June 1996, the Senate defeated a bill which was intended to limit compensation to developers affected by the Chrétien Government's cancellation of the Pearson airport privatization deal. The plan had been approved by the Conservatives in the dying days of the 1993 election campaign and cancelled by the Liberals shortly after their

victory. The defeat of the bill left the courts to decide the amount of compensation to which those involved in the cancellation of the airport deal were entitled.

- The end of November 1996, saw another Liberal bill defeated in the Senate, this time with 35 Liberal Senators among those who voted it down. The bill involves a constitutional amendment to end the church-run education system in Newfoundland, a matter which has generated considerable controversy.[47]

While these events serve to remind Canadians that the Senate exists, they don't necessarily generate any increase in support for it. Depending on the public view on an issue, any Senate opposition to actions of the government of the day may be seen as an undemocratic intervention. As long as it remains an appointed body, the Senate lacks legitimacy in the eyes of many Canadians. Without legitimacy, it is hard for it to exert its views over those of the elected House of Commons. If it can't exercise an independent judgment on public affairs, why have it?

Senate Reform

There have been many suggestions for reform of the Senate over the years. One of the most persistent suggestions in recent years has been for a **"Triple E" Senate**—elected, equal and effective. According to proponents of this reform:

- *Election* is needed to give the Senate legitimacy and credibility, so that it can exert its powers without criticism.
- *Equality* is needed, precisely because some provinces are so much larger and more dominant than others. For constitutional purposes, a province is a province. This is something the United States has always recognized, with its provision for equal numbers of Senators from all states—Rhode Island and California included.
- *Effectiveness* would follow from the first two features.

The Triple E Senate has been strongly pushed by the Western Provinces, but any such significant change does not appear imminent. While almost everyone agrees that the West really should have more

---

[47]Susan Delacourt, "Senate vote returns Nfld. school plan to MPs' agenda," *Globe and Mail*, November 28, 1996.

Senate seats, Québec (especially) and the Atlantic Provinces won't consent to any substantial reduction in their proportions of Senate seats. Since the approval of 2/3 of the provinces with at least 50% of Canada's population is needed for such reform, it seems unlikely.

In the meantime, the Senate carries on, performing much useful work in examining legislation and in conducting research and making recommendations on policy matters, but saddled by a negative public image which it seems to lack the fortitude to address effectively.

Summary:
Do MPs Earn Their Salary?

Given all of this background, we are now in a position to summarize the main roles of a member of Parliament, that much-maligned individual who is supposedly overpaid and underworked. These roles are:

1. Representing the interests, views and concerns of constituents.

2. Acting as an "ombudsman" or complaints investigator on behalf of constituents who have particular problems in their dealings with the government. This may be seen as an extension of the representative role, but it deserves separate billing. With the complexity of government today, the MP is a vital point of contact for citizens who have a problem (getting a passport, tracing a missing pension cheque, determining eligibility for some program) but don't know where to turn.

3. Acting as a "business agent" for the riding. This is also in some respects an extension of the representative role, but again one deserving of separate mention. While the specifics vary somewhat with the economic circumstances of each riding, members of parliament are expected to make a contribution to the economic well-being of the riding. They are judged partly on how successful they are in attracting government grants, government buildings, the relocation of government offices, the start-up of new businesses, and any other initiatives which help to provide economic growth and employment in the riding. If carried to an extreme, this is little more

than "pork-barrel politics." But it is an activity which MPs ignore at their peril, especially if their riding is suffering economically.

4. Acting on behalf of the party, not only in the actions taken in the House of Commons but in giving speeches, attending meetings and undertaking any other work which advances the cause of the party.

5. Being a member of the party caucus and attending its regular meetings. This is related to the fourth role, but deserves special mention as well. The effectiveness of any party, whether in government or in opposition, depends partly on how well developed its strategies are. Much of this work is done in caucus meetings, where individual MPs can make an important contribution.

6. Being a "parliamentarian," participating in Commons debates, taking an active part in Question Period and otherwise carrying out the responsibilities associated with being a member of Parliament.

7. Serving on standing (and occasionally special) committees of the Commons, working on the examination of departmental estimates and on the specifics of legislation.

8. Undertaking research on particular topics, whether as preparation for speeches, as background for reviewing legislation or departmental estimates, or as the basis for introducing a private members' bill.

This is by no means an exhaustive list—although it can easily be an exhausting one! It also deals only with the duties of a "backbench" MP. Members who are also appointed to the Cabinet have another full list of duties relating to work on Cabinet Committees, discussion of proposed legislation, strategy sessions on behalf of the party and overall responsibility for the operation of the particular departments for which they are Ministers. Members who take their responsibilities seriously have an enormous workload, one that can all too easily take its toll on their health or their family life.

A Day in the Life of an MP

At 9 a.m. on December 22, 1998, MP Maria Minna has already begun a day-long series of meetings with constituents in her Beaches-East York riding. Among those who visit that day are:

- A woman cut off welfare and desperate about what to do.
- A German immigrant upset because his 19 year old brother has been denied a visa for a visit to Canada over Christmas.
- A 21 year old university student who did volunteer work in her office in past summers. Minna has asked him to help her run a federally funded youth employment program.
- A former children's heart surgeon who left his practice to found Smartrisk, an organization devoted to reducing accidental injuries, and who wants to talk about setting up a Canada-wide data bank on injuries.
- A representative from the Canadian-Ukranian Immigrant Aid.
- A constituent with work problems.
- Someone working on ways to measure children's readiness to learn.

Minna has three staff in her constituency office, who get 30 to 50 new cases a week. While constituents complain that they don't get enough attention, efforts to increase office budgets for MPs meet with public resistance. For her, Christmas is the busiest time of the year. It involves a mad scramble of Christmas tree-lighting ceremonies, speeches, meetings on community issues, and meetings in her office with constituents tied up in red tape.[48]

What are MPs paid for their work? In 1991, they got a 3.8% pay raise, bringing their basic pay to $64 000 and their tax-free expense allowance to $21 300. That remuneration was frozen for seven years, as politicians accepted the same kind of restraint being experienced by public servants and private sector employees. In early 1998, a three member panel recommended that the tax-free allowance be eliminated and the salary of MPs be increased to $106 000 a year. It also proposed to double the housing allowance for members, from $6000 to $12 000. Even though the old arrangements provided the equivalent of $106 000 or a little more (because of the tax-free portion), it was widely felt that

---

[48]This summary is based on Rosemary Speirs, "Just another busy day in the life of an MP," *Toronto Star*, December 24, 1998.

the public would not stomach what appeared to be a whopping increase. Instead, legislation was passed in June 1998 authorizing a pay increase of 2% on the base salary of $64 000 as of January 1, 1998, and a further 2% each January 1 thereafter, for the duration of the 36th Parliament. The housing allowance was increased to $12 000, as recommended, but the tax-free expense allowance was left unchanged.

MPs also receive what many Canadians have regarded as an overly generous pension—available after five full years of service. What tends to be overlooked in the criticism of the pension is that members contribute 10% of their salaries toward it, and that many do not win the two elections which are needed to qualify for the pension. It is striking that 200 federal politicians retired or were defeated in the 1993 general election[49]—although that was an admittedly larger turnover than usual.

Not long after its election victory in 1993, the Liberal Government introduced some pension reforms and outlawed "**double-dipping**," an expression which describes a situation in which an MP retires, receives a pension, and then takes a government job and a second pay cheque. The government also reduced a few of the "perks" enjoyed by MPs by removing free shoe shines and reducing the subsidies on meals in the parliamentary dining room.[50]

◆ Something to Think About

As in any group of 300 people, parliamentarians include some "bad apples." Those who want to be critical can always find members of parliament who don't appear to earn their salary.

But what you have to ask yourself is whether you want to base the remuneration of MPs on the lowest common denominator, or whether you want to pay at a level which will attract the best qualified and most talented people within our society. As it stands now, most of those regarded as community leaders can make more money and have a more stable home life by avoiding elected office. Is this the way to improve government?

---

[49]Robert Jackson and Doreen Jackson, *Canadian Government in Transition*, Scarborough, Prenctice-Hall Canada Inc., 1996, p. 152.

[50]*Ibid.*

Parliamentary Government at the Provincial Level

As previously mentioned, the governing machinery at the provincial level is the same, except that there is a Lieutenant Governor instead of a Governor General, there is a Legislative Assembly instead of a House of Commons, and there isn't any upper chamber like the Senate. The operating principles are the same, as are the challenges relating to the dominance of the executive branch and the need to strengthen the watchdog role of the opposition parties.[51]

For example, Fred Schindeler's landmark study of Ontario at the end of the 1960s concluded that the Legislative Assembly had become nothing more than "an ineffective appendage employed to make noises of approval or discontent."[52] While there have been some reforms which redressed the balance somewhat, concerns about executive domination came to the fore in the second half of the 1990s, after the election of the Conservative Government of Mike Harris. The new government's attempt to secure quick passage, in December 1995, of an omnibus bill (Bill 26) covering amendments to some 47 statutes, provided a dramatic example of why we need watchdogs with teeth. When the opposition resorted to various delaying tactics in an attempt to block controversial legislation like the bill creating the "megacity" of Toronto, the government responded, in August 1997, with a number of rule changes designed to limit opposition delays and facilitate passage of legislation. The government has also made extensive use of **closure** to move its heavy legislative program through the Assembly. For example, in the 51 sitting days from the summer recess to the Christmas break in 1997, the government passed 30 bills—an average of a new law every two sitting days.[53]

---

[51] For a recent examination of government structures and operations in various provinces, see Christopher Dunn (ed.), *Provinces: Canadian Provincial Politics*, Peterborough, Broadview Press, 1996.

[52] F. F. Schindeler, *Responsible Government in Ontario*, Toronto, University of Toronto Press, 1969, p. 261.

[53] Ian Urquhart, "Closure has disarmed opposition," *Toronto Star*, December 18, 1997.

Concluding Observations

This lengthy chapter has barely scratched the surface of this complex topic, but it is hoped that it provides you with sufficient information to improve your understanding of the machinery of government at the senior levels and how it operates. A major issue at both levels has been the growth in the size and complexity of government and the resultant difficulties faced by the opposition parties in carrying out their watchdog role on our behalf.

The government-opposition relationship is one largely defined in House rules which are technical and complex, and which rarely engage the interest of the public. There was virtually no public reaction, for example, when the Harris Government tightened the rules to limit debate in the summer of 1997. Indeed, given the general antipathy toward politicians in today's society, it is also possible that many in Ontario at the time felt that the changes were beneficial because they would reduce "politicking" and allow governments to get on with their programs. This view is consistent with the widespread feeling today that governments must become more efficient, that they must act more like a business. But governments are not supposed to act like business— which makes "quick decisions behind closed doors, for private profit."[54] Governments in a democratic society need to consult widely, they need to consider the views of those who will be affected by the decisions they make, they even need to give due consideration to the objections and concerns of opposition parties, who also have a mandate from the electorate. The result may be a governing process which is slower and more convoluted than some would prefer, but efforts at streamlining which also weaken democracy are even less preferable.

---

[54]David Osborne and Ted Gaebler, *Reinventing Government*, New York, Penguin Books, 1993, p. 22.

Appendix A
Watchdog Techniques

As discussed earlier in the chapter, these are the techniques available to the opposition parties to question, criticize and hold accountable the government for its actions. Chief among these techniques are:

1 *Oral Question Period,* discussed earlier, which can be foolish and embarrassing, but which also keeps the government on its toes because of the spontaneity of the questions.

2 *Written questions,* which can be useful in obtaining information from the government, but only after an interval—which may be extensive—and without any of the drama associated with Oral Question Period.

3 *Debate on the Speech from the Throne* (now limited to six days), during which members (especially from the opposition parties) respond to the government's proposals for action during a session of Parliament.

4 *Debate on the Budget* (now limited to four days), during which members (again especially from the opposition) respond to the Budget statement from the Minister of Finance.

5 *Specific motions of non-confidence.* These are introduced as part of the debate on the Throne Speech and on the Budget, and may also be introduced at other times when the opposition is seeking to defeat a government. There is little chance that such motions will pass if there is a majority government, but debate on these motions can help to focus on alleged government shortcomings.

6 *"Opposition days"* (now 20), provided at intervals during each session of Parliament. On these days, the opposition parties choose the topics for debate.

7 *Private members' bills* which, as discussed above, can be used by opposition members to draw attention to alleged deficiencies in the government's legislative program.

8 *The lawmaking process,* especially at second reading and at committee stage, where members get an opportunity to debate both the principle and then the detail of proposed legislation.

9 *The estimates process* (also known as "the power of the purse strings"), which involves parliamentary approval each year of the expenditures which will be incurred by the government.

There is often confusion about the estimates process and the budget process. In federal government parlance, estimates refers only to estimated *expenditures* for the coming fiscal year. These must be presented to the House by the end of February each year, are referred to the appropriate standing committees for detailed examination and must be reported back to the House by the end of May for final approval by the end of June.

A budget is a broader document containing not only the planned expenditures, but the methods of financing them, the net financial position of the government anticipated for the coming fiscal year, and various economic measures relating to issues facing the economy at the time. Budgets usually appear in February or March and are as much a political and economic document as a financial statement.

The Last Word

Definition of Terms and Concepts

Administrative Law:
(Also known as subordinate or delegated legislation.)
This is law made by the administration (that is, the executive branch of government) in contrast to statute law which is made by Parliament (or the provincial and territorial legislatures). Most statutes passed over the last 50 years or so authorize the executive branch to spell out the law in detail over time. It is this detailed law which is often referred to as administrative law.

Backbenchers:
Members of Parliament who are not in the Cabinet or the "Shadow-Cabinet," and are so-named because they occupy the backbenches in the House of Commons.

Caucus:
Closed meeting of party members in which strategies are discussed. In the case of the governing party, a primary purpose of the caucus meeting is to give backbench members a chance to voice any concerns about proposed government legislation before they are called upon to support it in public. Opposition party caucus meetings focus on how best to expose shortcomings in the government's performance.

Closure:
A procedural device used by the government to force an end to discussion and voting on a particular stage of a bill.

Constituency: (Also known as riding.)
Geographic area into which Canada is divided for electing members to the federal House of Commons and provincial legislatures.

Dissolution of Parliament: (See also Proroguing of Parliament.)
This ends the life of a Parliament and is followed by an election. It differs from prorogation or proroguing of the House, in which a session of Parliament ends, but is followed by a new session and a new Speech from the Throne.

Double-Dipping:
Term to describe ex-politicians (and public servants) who retire on a pension and then take another paying job with the government.

Official Opposition:
Title usually given to the party with the second largest number of elected members, who act as a watchdog and offer themselves as an alternative government.

PCO (Privy Council Office)
Not to be confused with the Privy Council or Cabinet, the PCO consists of staff who provide secretarial and research support to the Cabinet. These staff are civil servants on secondment (temporary reassignment) from regular departmental duties.

PMO (Prime Minister's Office)
This consists of staff who support the Prime Minister in carrying out his or her responsibilities, not only as head of the government but as leader of a political party. Its work parallels that of the PCO, except that it is more partisan and political. Its staff are mostly "outsiders" selected for their expertise and creativity with respect to policy making.

Prerogative Power:
Remnants of discretionary power once exercised by the Crown.

Privy Council:
Essentially the legal name for the Cabinet, although it consists of all those who were ever appointed to any Cabinet, as well as a few honourary appointees. When the Cabinet of the day wishes to act legally, it does so in the name of the Governor in Council, which means the Governor General and the Privy Council (the active part of it represented by the current Cabinet).

Proportional Representation:
System of election in which provisions are made to ensure that the number of seats awarded to a party is proportional to the percentage of popular vote it received in the election.

Prorogation of Parliament:　(See also Dissolution of Parliament.)
When Parliament is prorogued, it marks the end of that session, which had begun with the introduction of a Speech from the Throne a year or

more earlier. [There is no set time for a session of Parliament. The government decides when it has achieved the major portion of its legislative objectives and when it is time to announce new priorities through a new Speech from the Throne.]

Question Period:
Period at the beginning of each day's sitting of Parliament for spontaneous questions to be put to members of the Cabinet.

Shadow Cabinet:
Group of leading members of the official opposition who act as a kind of "government-in-waiting."

Speaker:
Presiding officer in the House of Commons (and the Senate) who enforces the rules of debate.

Speech from the Throne:
Statement of government's plans for the coming session of Parliament, read by the Governor General (or Monarch) on behalf of the Government.

"Triple E" Senate:
Name for Senate reform proposal which calls for a Senate which would be elected, equal and effective.

Points to Ponder

1. Did you realize how limited is the "pool" from which Prime Ministers can choose members of the Cabinet? Do you find the various constraints on Cabinet selection appropriate?

2. What do you think about the merits of proportional representation? Did you realize how little relationship there could be between the percentage of popular vote for a party and the percentage of seats won by that party?

3. Have you reconsidered your view of the value of members of Parliament and whether or not they earn their salary? Are you at least willing

to agree that good members, who take their varied roles seriously, have a demanding workload?

4. Should members of Parliament be free to represent the views of their constituents rather than being obliged to vote the party line? If you say yes, how will you hold any party accountable for its performance if its members are free to vote as they wish? Imagine Parliament as an enlarged version of a municipal council. Have you had much success trying to hold municipal councillors accountable?

5. It is clear that the Senate has flexed its political muscles rather more often in the past 15 years or so. Do you see value in having this upper chamber of Parliament to take a second look at legislation passed by the Commons? If the Senate is to remain, how would you amend it to make it more effective?

For Further Reading

There are many good texts providing detailed information on the structure and operations of government at the senior levels. For example, you could consult such works as:

Christopher Dunn (ed.), *Provinces: Canadian Provincial Politics*, Peterborough, Broadview Press, 1996.

Paul Fox and Graham White, *Politics: Canada*, 8th Edition, Whitby, McGraw-Hill Ryerson Limited, 1995, which includes sections on the Cabinet, Civil Service, House of Commons, and Senate.

John Fraser, *The House of Commons At Work*, Montréal, Les Éditions de la Chenelière inc., 1993, provides a very detailed look at the House of Commons.

James John Guy, *How We Are Governed*, Toronto, Harcourt Brace & Company Canada, 1995, covers the basics of government, including chapters on the provincial and municipal levels.

Robert Jackson and Doreen Jackson, *Politics in Canada*, 3rd Edition, Scarborough, Prentice-Hall Canada Inc., 1994, Chapters 7 and 8 especially.

See also Chapters 6, 7 and 8 of *Canadian Government in Transition,* 2nd Edition, 1999, from the same authors and publisher.

Graham White, *The Ontario Legislature*, Toronto, University of Toronto Press, 1989, is a good source of information on the operations of the Ontario Government, including the "watchdog" reforms introduced there over the past couple of decades.

A wealth of information is also available on the Internet for the federal and provincial/territorial governments at *www.intergov.gc.ca.*

Chapter 6

Local Governments: A Closer Look

Objectives and Highlights

◆ To describe categories of municipality and other local governing bodies.

◆ To examine municipal roles and responsibilities.

◆ To evaluate the merits of current amalgamation initiatives.

The level of government most taken for granted is also the level which would be most quickly missed were it to disappear. It is the services, facilities and regulations provided by local governments that largely shape the quality of our day-to-day lives. The existence of a large number of local governments provides decentralization, convenient access for public participation, differing responses to the varying needs of different localities, and opportunities for creativity and innovation. All of these strengths have been exhibited, to a greater or lesser extent, by Canada's municipalities.

Reform efforts underway in a number of provinces place at risk the "localness" of local government. Provincial policy makers are preoccupied with the creation of larger units of administration (whether for municipalities or local boards like school boards) which they feel will better handle the provision of services. They are not just ignoring the representative and political role of municipal governments but are, in provinces like Ontario, actively citing the elimination of local councillors as a positive benefit of the amalgamation process.

This chapter will attempt to give you an appreciation of the nature of local governments, how they govern, what they do, and why you should care about their survival.

Introduction

If Canadians know something about government, it is likely to be about their federal or provincial government. The senior levels receive most of the media attention and are considered to be involved in the more important and more "glamorous" activities. Local governments are apt to be dismissed as minor players. They are just people from the community, fussing over roads and sewers and other mundane topics.

> Local government may be the most important level, in its impact on our day-to-day lives.

Look again! Far from being insignificant, local governments may just be the most important level of government, especially in terms of the impact on our day-to-day lives. That paradox is but one of many which one encounters in any study of local government. Others are:

- Local governments include many of our oldest governing institutions, with many municipalities incorporated well before Confederation in 1867 brought us our national and provincial governments. *Yet* they also include many of our newest governments, since they continue to be established in response to population growth and to go through restructuring and reform initiatives.

- They are the level of government closest to the people, and are hailed by some as the foundations of democracy. *Yet* they can be secretive, remote and bureaucratic and are frequently criticized for serving the interests of the property development industry more than those of the general public.

- They are the weakest level of government, having no guaranteed right to exist in the constitution—unlike the national and provincial levels. *Yet* they may assume growing importance as the 21st century unfolds. The federal and provincial governments are preoccupied with their deficit and debt problems. As discussed elsewhere in this Guide, part of their solution is to "pass the buck" (and more responsibilities) to the next level down. As the senior levels retrench, local governments are being called upon to fill the gap that is being created.

What are the local governments that face these future challenges and opportunities? As previewed in Chapter 2, they exist in great numbers and wide variety. Canada has one national government, ten provincial governments and three territorial governments. But it has over 4000 municipalities and probably close to that many agencies, boards and commissions which also form part of what we know as local government. Our first task, therefore, is to provide a brief overview and some definitions. We begin with municipalities, since they are what most people think of when there is a reference to local government.

Municipalities

Municipalities are elected local governments. They have a defined geographic area and are distinguished from other local governments in having the power to levy taxes on the inhabitants and landowners within their boundaries. They are also corporations, limited to the powers given to them by the body which incorporates them, that is, the government of the province. These powers are exercised on behalf of all residents of the municipality by a council elected by those residents. This arrangement is somewhat similar to that found with a private corporation where the powers are exercised by a Board of Directors on behalf of the shareholders.

Depending on where you live in Canada, you may find yourself under a number of possible municipal government arrangements.

i) You may be governed by two levels of municipal government. This occurs when your local (**lower tier**) municipality is part of a **two tier** system, in which you receive some of your municipal services from the **upper tier** county, region or district municipality.

ii) You may be within a **single tier** municipality, which is not part of any two tier system, and from which you receive all of your municipal services.

iii) You may not be within a municipality at all. Much of the area of Canada (although only a small proportion of its population) is what is known as "unorganized territory." This means that it is not within any incorporated municipality. This is true, for example, of much of

Northern Ontario, the vast majority of British Columbia and large stretches of the Northern territories. Inhabitants within unorganized territory may receive local services from a nearby municipality, from a provincial or territorial government, from a local board, or from various types of community organization.

Classifications of Municipality

Provincial legislation provides mainly for two broad categories of municipality, urban and rural, and may distinguish several types within each category. Nova Scotia, for example, has cities, towns and rural municipalities, while Manitoba provides for cities, towns, villages and rural municipalities. In the case of Alberta, cities, towns, villages and summer villages are considered urban municipalities, and municipal districts, counties, improvement districts and special areas are designated as rural municipalities.[1]

Ontario has one of the most elaborate municipal structures, originally designed for the mid-19th century, when urban and rural differences were quite pronounced. There is a rural municipality known as a township, three types of urban municipality known as villages, towns and cities, and an upper tier municipality known as a county or region. Counties date from the original Municipal Act of 1849 and provide a limited range of services on behalf of all townships, villages and towns within their geographic area. Cities do not form part of the county system—a reflection of the fact that they were quite distinct from surrounding rural areas when this structure was first created. In contrast, cities do come under the jurisdiction of regional municipalities, which also differ from counties in having more responsibilities. (The two structures are depicted in the chart on the next page.) A further difference is that county councils are "**indirectly elected**" in that they consist of members who were initially elected as reeves and deputy reeves of the lower tier township, village and town councils. While most regional councils started out with that kind of composition, an increasing number have moved to direct election of their members.

---

[1]Jack Masson with Edward Lesage Jr., *Alberta's Local Governments*, Edmonton, University of Alberta Press, 1994, p. 69.

Chart 1
County and Regional Two-Tier Systems

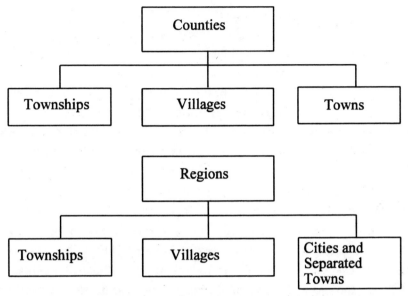

Ontario's municipal classifications also include separated towns, which are towns which have left the county system and essentially operate like cities. There are also specialized municipal units created for the small and scattered population found in Northern Ontario, notably improvement districts and local roads area boards and local services boards. The basic classifications are summarized in tabular form below.

Rural	Township	1000 to 25 000 population
Urban	Village Town City Separated Town	500 to 2000 2000 to 15 000 Over 15 000 Town not in county system
Upper Tier	County Regional	Townships, villages and towns are part of county system All municipalities, including cities, are part of regions

Local Boards and Commissions

While they are numerous and diverse enough, municipalities are not the only form of local government found in Canada. There are also a wide variety of special purpose bodies, often referred to as agencies, boards and commissions or **ABCs**. Their prevalence varies by province, with Ontario having the largest concentration of these bodies and providing the examples used in this section. Probably the best known example is that of school boards, which in Ontario—until changes introduced in 1998—spent more of the local tax dollars raised than municipalities did. Other bodies with which you are likely familiar are public utilities commissions, health units, conservation authorities, community centre boards, library boards and police services boards.

By their very nature, these boards operate outside of the municipal structure. They usually have only one or a very limited range of functions, as implied by the term "special purpose" body. Some boards finance at least part of their operations from **user charges**, such as the bus fares charged by a municipal transit system and the ice rental and concession charges of a community centre. While some boards operate within the boundaries of the municipality, many are intermunicipal in nature and take in two or more (often many more) municipalities.

A local government structure which includes many of these separate boards is often criticized for being fragmented and lacking in overall priority setting. Concerns are also raised about accountability, since most boards—with the notable exception of school boards and public utilities commissions— are not elected but appointed, and their sheer numbers make it easy to evade responsibility for problems that arise.

On the other hand, it is possible that more of these boards will be established in the future, as a vehicle for administering and coordinating new partnerships which are being promoted amongst municipalities and between municipalities and the private sector. In part, this reflects the growing recognition that municipalities can be **service arrangers** rather than necessarily direct service providers. This involves a council working with the local community to identify what services are needed and then making whatever arrangements are most cost-effective for the delivery of those services.[2] In response to the Ontario government's objective of streamlining municipal government, a number of areas (including Hamilton-Wentworth, Waterloo, and Ottawa-Carleton) have discussed the replacement of existing upper tier governments with some form of joint servicing board. This board would arrange for the delivery of a limited number of cross-boundary services over whatever combination of municipalities produce the greatest economies of scale. This flexible structure is essentially a variation of the regional district model which has operated in British Columbia for over 30 years. While a limited version of this type of joint board has been established in the Greater Toronto Area (GTA), it is not part of the restructuring model proposed in November 1999 for the Ottawa and Hamilton areas, and discussed later in this chapter.

How Are Municipalities Governed?

As noted in Chapter 2, the basic governing structure of municipalities is quite simple, compared to the senior levels of government with their separate executive and legislative branches. The basic municipal model simply consists of the council and the municipal staff—with the latter organized into a number of separate departments reflecting the major responsibilities of the municipality.

Unlike the situation at the senior levels of government, there isn't any group (similar to the Cabinet) responsible for taking a leadership role and answering to the full elected body for its performance; nor is their any group responsible for acting as a watchdog or alternative government. Instead, there is one governing body—the municipal council—within which everybody is responsible for everything, which also means that no one is really responsible for

> At the municipal level, everyone is responsible for everything, which also means that no one is really responsible for anything.

---

[2]This concept was popularized as the difference between steering (setting direction and determining needs) and rowing (providing services) in David Osborne and Ted Gaebler, *Reinventing Government*, New York, Penguin Books, 1993.

anything. While there are concerns about executive domination (by the Cabinet and the senior civil service) at the senior levels of government, municipalities have usually wrestled with a contrasting concern about the lack of strong leadership and effective coordination in both its political and administrative spheres. In response, a number of modifications to the municipal structure have been introduced or advocated over the years, four of which are briefly described below.

The CAO System

One modified structure increasingly found in municipalities is that of the **Chief Administrative Officer** (CAO) system. This involves the appointment of a senior official responsible for leading and coordinating the administrative activities of the municipality within the policy guidelines laid down by council. The simplest version of this model is depicted in Chart 2 below.

Chart 2
CAO System

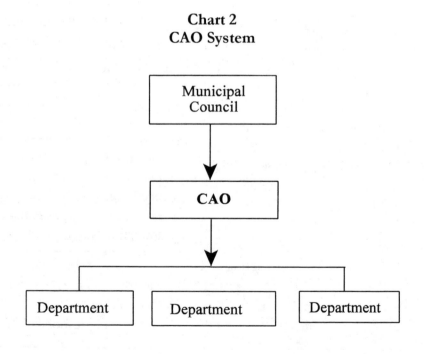

At its best, a CAO structure can significantly improve the coordination of municipal operations—both in terms of the development of municipal policies and the implementation of these policies. A smoothly functioning CAO system can allow councillors to concentrate on their primary roles of representing the public and determining priorities for action. At its worst, however, the CAO system can become very bureaucratic. Councillors may feel rather cut off from the day-to-day operations of the municipality since all staff report to council through, and receive directions from, the CAO. Department heads may become resentful, unless the CAO is skilled in developing a sense of teamwork and in demonstrating the benefits of working together. If the CAO becomes too prominent, there may be friction with the head of council or other councillors. To a considerable extent, the difficulties that can arise relate to the age-old problem of how to keep the expert (the CAO) "on tap, but not on top."

Executive Committee System

While CAOs may provide strong administrative leadership, other internal structures have been introduced in an attempt to provide stronger political leadership. Essentially, these involve the establishment of some form of **executive committee** of council. One of the most common versions of this system is to have an executive committee chaired by the head of council and comprising the chairs of the major standing committees of council. This arrangement, which is illustrated on the following page, is supposed to approximate the cabinet structure found at the senior levels—but it lacks the twin cohesive forces of collective responsibility and party solidarity.

The executive committee in this model is normally given responsibility for spending decisions and often for personnel, and there may be a further provision that reports of standing committees go through it to council. However, the effectiveness of these arrangements obviously depends on the personalities involved, their willingness to work together, and the ability of the head of council or other dominant members to forge a team approach. Unfortunately, such cooperative action is not always forthcoming, and executive committees have not been as successful in providing political leadership as CAO systems have in providing administrative leadership.

Chart 3
Executive Committee System

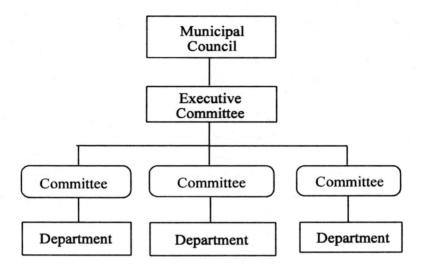

Political Parties: The Missing Link?

Those seeking stronger political leadership sometimes advocate the introduction of organized political parties at the local level—on the grounds that a council organized on party lines would better approximate the parliamentary model of the senior levels.[3] By this reasoning, which clearly is most applicable to the very large municipalities, the position of any executive committee and head of council would be strengthened by the backing of a solid block of party votes. Assuming that more than one party would contest the seats on council, there would be an official opposition group providing a "watchdog" function. These arrangements would provide a much clearer focus of accountability than is normally found on council. Other alleged benefits from introducing political parties include the fact that parties would subsidize the increasingly high cost of election campaigns and that party debate would stimulate more interest and increased voting.

---

[3]The following discussion of pros and cons is based on C. Richard Tindal and Susan Nobes Tindal, *Local Government in Canada*, 5th Edition, Scarborough, Nelson, 2000, pp. 281-284.

Opponents of political parties at the local level rebut a number of the alleged advantages. They point out that much would depend on the nature of the political parties involved.

> Would there be one party domination or a preoccupation with national issues?

Proponents assume a balanced situation with two or more parties which would alternate in power. If one party is very dominant and controls council over a period of years however, then there is undoubtedly more likelihood of insensitivity to public opinion and other abuses—traits exhibited by the provincial and federal governments in the same situation. Those opposed to local parties often point to the long period of domination in Montreal by Jean Drapeau and his Civic Party to illustrate their concerns.

Opponents of parties at the local level also wonder whether the parties which might become involved would be local parties focused on local issues, or just branches of the existing national parties. In the latter case, the concern is that the parties would likely neglect local issues and become essentially a grass roots organization for the senior level party. There is also the danger that local election results would reflect the popularity or unpopularity of the "parent" parties rather than the positions taken by the parties on local matters. This pattern has been noted in Britain, where many municipal council elections are contested by the national Labour and Conservative parties.

One of the main arguments against the introduction of parties is that they would bring division where none exists or should exist. "There is no political way to build a road," claim proponents of this viewpoint that reflects the lingering notion that local government activities are administrative not political in nature. Yet, if the actual construction of a road is a matter of engineering not politics, the decision on where to locate a particular road is certainly political. The decision on whether the traffic problem in question should be solved through building a road or providing an alternative form of public transportation is also clearly political. The decision on whether the scarce financial resources of the municipality should be used on transportation or some other pressing need is again political. Indeed, if the municipal council is concerned with establishing priorities in relation to conflicting public needs and demands, its role must be political. If the council is not to be charged with this task, one may well question the value of a separate level of local government.

> ... politics like sex, cannot be abolished. It can sometimes be repressed by denying people the opportunity to practice it, but it cannot be done away with because it is the nature of man to disagree and contend. The fact is that even in a society of altruists or angels there would be politics, for some would conceive the common good one way and some in another.[4]

It must be acknowledged, however, that parties tend to exaggerate differences and to criticize excessively for purely partisan purposes— traits all too evident in the actions of the parties operating at the senior levels of government. It is understandable that many do not want to see such a divisive, confrontational style dominate council discussions.

Ultimately, it doesn't really matter how soundly based are the arguments against the introduction of local political parties. If people *feel* that they are a bad idea, then they won't receive support, whatever might be their objective merits. To date, the vast majority of Canadians appear to see more drawbacks than advantages to party politics in local government. Yet in those municipalities with councils of 20 or more members, it is hard to think of a more effective way of providing a focus for concerted action than that provided by organized political parties.

Building Business Models

In recent years, a number of municipalities have restructured internally in ways consistent with the new public management movement occurring at the senior levels of government and described in the previous chapter.[5] Traditional departmental structures have been replaced by core business areas and, within these, by business units. The latter are designed to consolidate functions and processes that deliver specific products and/or services to local citizens. These activities are isolated into

---

[4]Edward C. Banfield and James Q. Wilson, *City Politics*, Cambridge, Harvard University Press, 1963, pp. 20-21.

[5]For a more complete discussion of this development, on which this section is based, see Tindal and Tindal, *op. cit.*, pp. 286-294.

separate units in the expectation that results will be easier to measure, productivity improvements easier to introduce, and accountability enhanced. Business plans are required, with a strong emphasis on ways of moving operations closer to break-even. **Alternative service delivery** (ASD) options are to be explored fully, including the possibility of privatizing municipal services. Performance measures (efficiency and effectiveness measures) are used to gauge improvements over time and to compare municipal performance with that of other institutions.

Even this brief summary indicates that fundamental changes in operating philosophy underlie these new business models. The municipality is recast as a service provider whose objective is to have satisfied customers through cost-effective delivery of the product. Instead of councillors wrestling with conflicting community concerns and values, we have the objective and scientific evidence of performance measurement on which to base decisions which are free of "politicking."

The problem with this approach, especially if carried to an extreme, is that it overlooks the fact that municipalities are governments, not businesses, and have other objectives besides narrow financial ones. They provide services which don't, can't,

> The danger is that political judgment of councillors is replaced by the judgment of the market place or the balance sheet.

and shouldn't ever break even— precisely because these services are not revenue generators and hence would never be provided by the private sector. Under these new business models, there is a real danger that the judgment of the market place and of the balance sheet will be substituted for the political judgment of elected councillors. However rational and scientific the former approach may appear to be, it represents a diminution of democracy. It parallels the dangers which are present at the senior levels of government, where market forces again—this time the forces of the global market place—are increasingly dictating how governments operate. In effect, we are being told that what we need is "more bang for the buck," rather than "more benefit from the ballot."[6]

---

[6]B. Guy Peters and Donald J. Savoie (eds.), *Governance in a Changing Environment*, Kingston, McGill-Queen's University Press, 1995, p. 75.

What Do Municipalities Do and Why Should We Care?

The most obvious purpose served by municipalities is that they provide a wide range of services and facilities which affect the quality of our day-to-day lives. The rather fanciful adventures of our student Frank N. Earnest, found in Chapter 2, illustrated this fact.

The importance of municipal services in the everyday life of Canadians cannot be overemphasized. To suggest that "the city council's services mean the difference between savagery and civilization" is scarcely an exaggeration—even though this observation was made 150 years ago![7] If anything, the observation rings more true today. Look around you. You drive on municipal roads, walk on municipal sidewalks and, increasingly, cycle on municipal bike paths. Any land you own can only be developed in conformity with planning policies and regulations established by your municipality. That land is serviced by municipal water and sewer lines or, in most rural areas, by a well and septic tank system inspected by local health officials. Your property is protected by a municipal fire department, perhaps made up of volunteers from the community. You enjoy recreational and library facilities provided by the municipality and attend cultural events in facilities provided or supported by the municipality. Your garbage is collected by the municipality—whether directly by municipal staff or indirectly through the hiring of a private contractor. Depending on your circumstances, you may make use of day care centres, homes for the aged, public housing, or public health programs—all provided or financially supported by municipalities. A few examples are expanded on below, to illustrate further the significance of local services and responsibilities.

Balanced Growth

How a community grows and develops is influenced by municipal planning and development policies and initiatives. Without growth, lack of

---

[7]By Sir Ernest Simon, about British local government, as quoted in K. G. Crawford, *Canadian Municipal Government*, Toronto, University of Toronto Press, 1954, p. 4.

employment opportunities close to home may send people—especially young people—farther afield, resulting in depopulation and a downward spiral. On the other hand, too much growth, encouraged "at any price," can also be harmful, both to local living conditions and to the environment. Since the tax base of a municipality is the assessed value of real property (land and buildings on land) within its boundaries, a municipal council has little choice but to pursue growth so as to increase its assessment and tax base. This inclination, together with the influence of the local property development industry and the close ties that it seems to have with many municipal councillors, can affect land use decisions.

Environmental Issues

It is hard to imagine a more critical responsibility than the provision of clean drinking water and this falls to municipalities, supported by varying degrees of provincial financial assistance. Municipalities are also responsible for protecting the water supply through properly maintained sewer lines and sewage treatment facilities. One of the biggest environmental challenges at the beginning of the 21st century is that of garbage disposal or, more specifically, finding new locations for landfill sites as existing ones continue to fill up—even with the widespread public support for the 3 Rs (reduce, reuse, recycle). Fierce opposition to the designation of such sites has been perhaps the most visible manifestation of the NIMBY (Not In My Back Yard) syndrome.

Safety In Our Neighbourhoods

Policing is another issue attracting considerable attention today. In spite of statistics which show a decline in crime, many Canadians have become concerned about safety and security in their homes and neighbourhoods. Some believe the answer lies in more police and tougher penalties for those convicted. Others find logic in the community policing initiatives of recent years, which feature much greater emphasis on identifying the underlying causes of crime and attempting to address them. The populations of Canada's largest cities now contain a great variety of nationalities, partly because of the immigration policies of the federal government. Police forces have been slow to reflect in their staff complements the diversity of the populations they serve and protect, leading to concerns about racial discrimination.

Policing services in municipalities may be provided by the Royal Canadian Mounted Police, provincial police forces in Ontario and Québec, or municipal police forces. Even in the latter case, however, the actual responsibility for policing is often vested in a separate board (in Ontario, for example, it is a police services board) to ensure that it is free from political interference. As a result, the accountability of police to local communities and their values is a matter of concern.

Social Programs

In provinces such as Ontario, municipalities play an important role with respect to many of the social programs that enhance the quality of life of local citizens. Public housing and community shelters are more and more essential as the homeless population grows, and this responsibility has increasingly been downloaded to municipalities by the senior levels of government. Public health programs benefit the entire population with their emphasis on prevention of disease. While health education programs are usually provided through separate local or regional health agencies, municipalities contribute financial support (50% in the case of Ontario). Municipalities are also directly involved in promoting healthy communities through their planning and servicing responsibilities. Indeed, as Chapter 9 notes, local governments were in the forefront of the public health movement, dealing with sanitation, sewage, and the treatment of drinking water. Municipal public works departments grew out of the public health movement, as did urban planning, parks, housing, and social service functions.[8] While most provinces have increasingly taken over social assistance programs, these have been downloaded in Ontario, leaving municipalities on the front line in implementing the shift from welfare to workfare in that province.

---

[8]Trevor Hancock, Bernard Pouliot, and Pierre Duplessis, "Public Health," in Richard Loreto and Trevor Price (eds.), *Urban Policy Issues*, Toronto, McClelland and Stewart Inc., 1990, p. 192.

Property Taxes and User Fees

Not surprisingly, one of the biggest issues facing municipal councils is the level of taxation placed upon property owners. While the public dislikes taxes in general, they have reasons for being particularly critical of the **property tax**. A number of the taxes levied by the senior levels of government are hidden. The personal income tax is made somewhat manageable in that it is normally deducted from one's pay cheque throughout the year. It is also presented as a fair tax because it is progressive—meaning that the tax one pays reflects one's ability to pay, since higher tax brackets apply to those with larger incomes.

In contrast, the municipal property tax is anything but hidden or inconspicuous. It is determined annually, as part of the municipality's budget deliberations each spring, and once established, the full amount owed on one's property is known—although more and more municipality's are softening that impact by providing for a number of installment payments. Instead of being progressive, the property tax is criticized for being regressive, meaning that it bears most heavily on those least able to pay, as in the example below.

How Fair Is This?

Consider two identically assessed homes paying taxes of $2000 each. For the owner with an annual income of $40 000, the tax burden is 5%. But for the second owner, retired on an income of $20 000, the burden is 10%.

Throughout much of the 20th century, property taxes could be kept under control because provincial grants to municipalities usually increased in line with inflation or to cover costs of new mandated municipal responsibilities. That situation has changed dramatically over the past couple of decades as a kind of fend-for-yourself federalism has evolved. Preoccupied with resolving their deficit and debt problems, the senior levels have cut grant payments and/or downloaded costs and responsibilities. As the lowest level in the intergovernmental system, this has left municipalities with nowhere to pass the buck. As a result, they have felt strong upward pressure on property taxes. To avoid this politically unpopular step, municipalities have increasingly turned to a variety of user fees as an alternative means of raising revenues.

Some user fees may serve a worthwhile purpose in encouraging conservation and good practices. Examples would include the use of metered water billings to cut water consumption or the use of "bag tags" and "tipping fees" at the landfill site to encourage the 3 Rs. In many other instances, however, the user fees are little more than a "revenue grab," a thinly disguised version of a tax. They are often advocated by those who believe that individual municipal operations should be as self-sufficient as possible, that they should run more like a business. The effect of this kind of approach is to shift the financing of municipal services from all taxpayers (through the property tax) to individual users (through the user fees they pay). While this sounds attractive on the surface, it is not a practical way of financing many municipal services. As already noted, governments often provide services which can not and should not operate at break-even and which are provided by government precisely because the private sector would not deliver them. The danger is that a user fee policy would leave important community services to be financed only or primarily by a portion of the population which could not do so on its own. It is argued that collective or public goods which benefit society at large should not be funded, to any large degree, from user fees.

What Fares Are Fair For Public Transit?

Consider the example of public transit. It is frequently criticized for running at a loss. The usual response by those in charge is to reduce service and increase fares. Those who don't need to rely on public transit presumably find this situation acceptable, but increasing fares too much puts the service beyond the reach of those who most need it.

Looked at more broadly, however, public transit could be considered a bargain. By reducing the reliance on the motor car, public transit reduces air pollution and helps to relieve congestion in downtown areas. Facilitating the flow of traffic provides positive economic benefits. It also saves money on "fender-benders," and associated police, court and insurance costs. A proper cost-benefit analysis might find that public transit actually does operate at break-even.

One of the concerns is how far municipalities will go with user fees. There have been reports of fire departments charging for using the "jaws of life" to extricate a non-resident (and, non-municipal taxpayer) from a car accident. Picture the scene. The spectacular crash, the sirens screaming to

Will that be cash, or charge?

the rescue, the tension as the jaws of life do their work, the smiles of relief from the assembled crowd, and then—as quickly as the victim can be revived— the time-honoured question: *"Will that be cash, or charge?"*

In another controversial example, the Ottawa Police Department, in 1997, introduced alarm permits for home-owners and businesses with alarm systems. Those with such systems received a notice to pay up or police would not respond, prompting one commentator to wonder how this approach differed from an old-fashioned protection racket.[9]

Focus on Services and Taxes Misplaced

In spite of the amount of attention claimed by issues related to services and taxes, these are not—or should not be seen as—the main role of municipal government.[10] Municipalities are not just a vehicle for service delivery. Their primary purpose, heretical as it may sound, is not to reduce taxes. Municipalities are a separate, elected level of government. As such, they have a representative and political role which is the primary reason for their existence. The real value of municipalities is that they provide a political mechanism through which a local community can express its collective concerns. At their best, they exist as an extension of the community, as the community governing itself. Municipalities have this potential because they are the government closest to

---

[9]Dave Brown, "Police alarm fee alarming," *Ottawa Citizen*, June 12, 1997.

[10]The discussion which follows is largely based on Tindal and Tindal, *op. cit.*, especially Chapter 1.

the people (certainly in the physical and geographic sense), most aware of local conditions, concerns and needs, and most responsive (usually) to such local knowledge.

Municipal Amalgamations On the Rise

Over the past few years, however, municipalities in a number of provinces (especially in Central and Eastern Canada) have faced strong pressure to **amalgamate** into larger units. Provincial governments have promoted this step on the grounds that many municipalities are too small to cope, especially as the senior levels reduce financial assistance and shift costs and functions downward in an effort to deal with their own deficit problems. Resulting amalgamations include:

- the Miramichi, Saint John, and Edmunston areas of New Brunswick
- the Cape Breton and Halifax areas of Nova Scotia
- the Charlottetown and Summerside areas of Prince Edward Island
- the St. John's and Northeast Avalon area of Newfoundland
- more than 200 municipalities in Ontario, including the creation of the much-publicized "megacity" of Toronto.

As this last example illustrates, it is in Ontario, since the election of the Conservatives under Mike Harris in 1995, that amalgamation has been pursued most aggressively. In December 1999, the province stated that it would create single enlarged municipalities in the Hamilton-Wentworth, Ottawa-Carleton, and Sudbury areas, and two enlarged municipalities covering the former counties of Haldimand and Norfolk. As a result of these and other initiatives, there will be fewer municipalities after the municipal elections of November 2000 than there were when Ontario became a province (with 539 municipalities) in 1867.

♦ Something to Think About

Do these amalgamations make sense to you? On the surface, it sounds logical that having fewer governments should mean less duplication and less cost. But even if that were the case, are you comfortable with *local* governments that become this large?

In some situations, amalgamation may indeed make sense. Municipal boundaries often reflect historical patterns that bear little relation to the population movement of today and may divide natural "communities of interest." Divided jurisdictions within one socio-economic area may inhibit desirable cooperation or may produce inequities in the sharing of costs for services which are accessed across municipal boundaries. One should be wary, however, of the two main benefits which have been promoted as the rationale for amalgamation in the province of Ontario—that it will save money and that it will reduce the number of municipalities and municipal politicians.

Saving Money?

The first argument flies in the face of the substantial body of evidence that amalgamations increase costs rather than reduce them.[11] Some important cautionary comments in this regard were provided by the recent Task Force on the GTA which noted that the benefits of amalgamation are often overstated. Whatever savings may be achieved from eliminating administrative duplication are often lost because of the upward pressure on wages and service standards that occurs when different wage and service structures are combined. The Task Force also pointed out that amalgamation means fewer municipalities against which to compare efficiency and performance and less pressure to keep costs down.[12] This absence of choice and competitive pressure is, of course, why we fear monopolies in the private sector. Experience has shown that they usually result in higher prices and lower quality. It is strange that we should advocate through municipal amalgamation the creation of the same monopoly situation we seek to avoid in the private sector.

There have been some media reports in Ontario that amalgamations have saved more than $200 million. What the Minister of Municipal

---

[11]Much of this evidence has been very effectively summarized and analyzed by Andrew Sancton, "Reducing Costs by Consolidating Municipalities: New Brunswick, Nova Scotia and Ontario," *Canadian Public Administration*, Fall 1996, which, contrary to its title, demonstrates that cost reductions do not occur.

[12]Report of the GTA Task Force, *Greater Toronto*, Toronto, Publications Ontario, January 1996, pp. 212-213.

Affairs actually stated (in a speech to the Association of Municipalities of Ontario on August 24, 1999) is that savings of this magnitude were *anticipated* at the maturity of the restructuring process (whenever that is). To the extent that savings are found in this latest round, it will likely be because the current era of fiscal restraint encourages the use of restructuring as an opportunity to establish an entirely new municipality which has no obligations to past employees— or to past collective agreements if they can be voided—and which can set up a leaner, cheaper operation. Substantial staff reductions have accompanied many of the amalgamations, mirroring the downsizing which has been pursued at the senior levels of government. However, initial savings from such downsizing can be largely offset by the severance packages which must be paid. Nor are the savings assured over the longer term, since it is often discovered that staff reductions have left the new municipality deficient, both in numbers and particular skills, leading to new hirings.

Quite apart from these considerations, we need to ask if cost reduction should be the primary objective of municipal restructuring. What about maintaining or enhancing the quality of local democracy? What about improving the delivery of services desired by local citizens. It can be argued that these should be the primary objectives of any restructuring. Any cost reductions would be a by-product or bonus.

Less Government?

> Amalgamation does not give us less government; it gives us bigger and more bureaucratic government.

The second widely cited argument in support of amalgamation is both dangerous and inherently anti-democratic. Proponents play on the widespread public disillusionment with government and politicians in praising the fewer municipalities and municipal politicians which will result. *Let us be very clear.* Amalgamation does not give us less government; it gives us bigger government, farther removed from the people it is meant to represent and to serve. It gives us more bureaucratic government, in which the personal touch which citizens enjoyed in small municipalities is replaced with the touch tone phone and the computerized list of numbers to push to listen to recorded messages while searching vainly for a live voice. It results in increased workloads for councillors, which often makes the job full time and thus unavailable to a wide cross-section of citizens. The fact that campaigning over larger areas is more expensive further reduces the pool of potential candidates.

You should ask yourself what benefits are gained when the number of municipal councillors in an area is reduced by half or two-thirds. What is beneficial about reducing the number of representatives who are elected by, and on behalf of, the local community? There isn't even any significant savings in taking this action, in part because of the very low salaries paid to councillors in most municipalities. Moreover, those salaries inevitably go up because of the increased workload associated with amalgamation. The Halifax example is instructive. The number of councillors governing the new regional municipality has been reduced from 60 to 23, but at a salary which has more than doubled.[13] Experience in Winnipeg also demonstrates that as the number of councillors has been reduced over the years, the salary for the councillors and Mayor has increased substantially and has, since 1992, extended to an allowance of $35 000 per councillor to hire political staff.[14]

Perhaps you aren't overly impressed with your particular municipal councillors, but they are all you have in support of local democracy—"a poor thing, but your own." Why would you expect that fewer councillors, further removed from your locale, would somehow provide enhanced representation? Whatever the faults of your municipality, it is *your* municipality. Don't give it up without careful consideration if you find yourself in the midst of an amalgamation exercise.

School Board Amalgamations Also

School boards or boards of education are similar to municipalities to the extent that—with limited exceptions— they are composed of elected

---

[13]Remarks by Gloria McCluskey (former Mayor of Dartmouth) on *Commentary*, CBC Radio, November 14, 1996.

[14]Jae Eadie (Deputy Mayor, City of Winnipeg) in *Municipal World*, November 1996, p. 25.

representatives (trustees) and have access to the real property tax field, through a levy on their member municipalities. Another similarity is that school boards have gone through restructuring and amalgamation, in fact earlier and to an even greater extent.[15] Consider these examples:

- In Alberta, for example, where the first major consolidations occurred, almost 4000 distinct school districts, each with its own school board, were amalgamated into just over 100 consolidated districts between 1935 and 1940.

- After a study in 1945, British Columbia regrouped its 650 school boards into 75.

- In Ontario, by 1950, 3465 small rural districts had been consolidated into 536 township boards. A further major restructuring at the end of the 1960s reduced the number of school boards in Ontario to 166, and Québec reforms in the 1970s regrouped some 1800 local school authorities into fewer than 200.

Many of the small school districts which merged had lacked an adequate financial base. Amalgamation was seen as a way of spreading education costs over a broader economic base and enhancing the quality of programs available.

However, the amalgamation process has intensified in the 1990s, and the particular form it has taken raises some serious questions about local control of education. New Brunswick reduced the number of school boards from 42 to 18 in 1992 and then eliminated the remaining boards in 1996, replacing them with provincial superintendents advised by 18 district councils. Alberta reduced the number of school boards from 181 to 57 in a two stage process which began in 1994. Twenty-two boards were amalgamated into six regional boards in Nova Scotia, along with one province-wide board for Acadian and Francophone education.[16] The Québec government recently replaced 159 religious boards with 72 linguistic boards and effective January 1, 1998, Ontario cut the

---

[15]The discussion which follows is based on Tindal and Tindal, *op. cit.*, pp. 119-121.

[16]The preceding examples are all from Ontario Ministry of Education and Training, Backgrounder, *Education Reform and Finance in Other Provinces*, 1997.

number of school boards in half, to 66, although it subsequently provided for an additional six district school boards for Northern Ontario to ensure adequate public access.

The latest Ontario reforms have produced very large areas for the administration of education. For example, the Upper Canada District School Board takes in eight counties in Eastern Ontario, an area twice the size of Prince Edward Island, bigger than three American states, bigger than Jamaica, and only slightly smaller than Northern Ireland.[17] Critics believe that the combination of vast school areas and a provincially imposed cap of $5000 for annual remuneration for trustees will discourage candidates from running for office and will make it difficult for those elected to do their jobs.

Trustees may also find that they have considerably less to do, since Ontario's Education Quality Improvement Act (Bill 160, the one that prompted a teacher's strike in 1997) centralizes many decision making powers in Queen's Park. Under Bill 160, the Cabinet can establish school boards, dissolve or amalgamate them, allot the number of board members, control their assets, even sell school buildings. Moreover, if the Minister of Education doesn't like the way a school board is managing its finances, the Minister can arrange through the Cabinet to take over the board.[18] On top of these changes, municipal finance legislation in Ontario (Bills 106 and 149) has removed from school boards any power to raise money from property taxation. The province now pays approximately half of the education costs previously borne by residential property taxpayers and sets the tax rate to be levied upon these taxpayers for the remainder, as well as the education tax rate to be paid by businesses.

Less Show, More Tell

The property tax changes may be a good example of the old saying "be careful what you wish for, because it may come true." For years,

---

[17]Kelly Egan, "Mega school board worries many," *Kingston Whig Standard*, February 17, 1998.

[18]This summary is based on Ellie Tesher, "The staggering control of power in Bill 160," *Toronto Star*, November 7, 1997.

municipalities and many of their residents have complained about what they saw as excessive spending by school boards—spending which required councils to pass on unpopular tax increases. Provincial control over education spending might seem a welcome development, especially with the Ontario government's plans to freeze education tax rates for several years. But there are good grounds for believing that one of the reasons that the Conservatives have asserted greater control over education is to reduce spending in this area as part of their fiscal restraint efforts. Ontario residents used to have the discretion, through their elected school boards, to give as high a priority to education as they are prepared to finance. They are now powerless. If they decide that education is underfunded, their only recourse is to appeal to Queen's Park. School boards no longer have any power to enrich education programs through access to the property tax field.

In today's Ontario, controversy over school closings rivals the upheaval being caused by the hospital closings which have also been triggered by fiscal restraint. For many smaller communities, such institutions are central to their local identity. As they are removed, and as municipalities are consolidated into ever-larger units, the sense of dislocation grows.

Education Being Privatized?

With their funding restricted, school boards are turning to other sources to meet their expenditure needs. Private advertising is now appearing on school buses and properties. Corporate giants like Pepsi gain monopoly access to school cafeterias in exchange for cash. There are growing concerns about corporate influence over schools and their curricula, especially in a province like Ontario whose Premier sees the role of education as one of training young people to compete in a global economy.

Private fund-raising ventures are also becoming more prevalent and large scale. Some boards have recently established foundations to formalize their fund-raising activities, much as many hospitals have been forced to do. The results of such efforts can be quite uneven, depending in part on the economic health of the school area and the incomes of parents. A dramatic example of this reality is found in the relative ease with which a group of Oakville parents raised $150 000 to buy computers for the two elementary schools attended by their children.[19] The generosity of the parents is commendable, and one can hardly fault them for wanting to support their children. Nonetheless, such a large private donation raised serious questions about equity and equal educational opportunities within the school board system. This example also illustrates an emerging pattern in Canada, in which services that we supposedly can't afford to provide through our governments are financed privately. The latter option is usually not any cheaper, it results in selective as opposed to universal availability, and it leads to the development of a two tier system—just as is happening in other areas such as health care.

Indeed, the Ontario government is suspected of favouring the establishment of charter schools, which made their first appearance in Alberta in 1994. Under the Alberta approach, students can go to any school they choose—charter, separate, or public—and the school gets funding for each one enrolled. Partial funding is even provided to private schools.[20] Proponents of this approach claim that it provides more choice and encourages improved performance through the competition in the education marketplace. Critics claim that charter schools are creating a two tier education system and are nothing more than publicly funded private schools. Some additional choice and the spur of competition may be useful. But any such changes must be carefully scrutinized for any adverse impact on the provision of free public education at the elementary and secondary level, at consistent standards to all students, by democratically elected local boards.

Concluding Observations

Municipalities have usually been the most neglected level of government in Canada—not only in terms of their limited resources and lack of constitutional recognition, but also with respect to the degree of apparent public interest in their activities. As this chapter has attempted

[19]Lynda Hurst, "Parents up the education ante," *Toronto Star*, May 4, 1997.

[20]Tanya Talaga, "C is for Choice," *Toronto Star*, June 19, 1999.

to show, however, municipalities play (or should play) a fundamental representative and political role, providing a vehicle through which local communities can identify and address their collective concerns. Municipalities and other local governing bodies also provide a wide range of services, facilities and regulations which help to define the nature of the local community and its quality of life.

How well municipalities will play their political and service delivery roles in the future is a matter of debate at present. As the lowest level in Canada's complex intergovernmental system, municipalities find themselves bearing the brunt of the downsizing and other debt and deficit reduction strategies being pursued by the senior levels of government. They continue to face heavy, even increasing, demands for services, while the resources available to them are sharply curtailed through cutbacks in provincial transfer payments. International pressures, many relating to the globalization of the economy, also place constraints on municipal actions. To cope with the challenges they face, municipalities are encouraged to embrace business practices which have the potential to reduce the role of the elected councillors and to reduce the status of citizens to customers. They are also being encouraged, in some provinces very forcefully, into amalgamations which may also undermine their representative role.

Now, as perhaps never before, it is essential that citizens give far more attention to that level of government they have too often taken for granted in the past. To ignore it, is to run the risk of losing it, and to end up with local governments which are no longer "local," either in terms of the area served or the capacity to make decisions which reflect local rather than provincial priorities.

The Last Word

Definition of Terms and Concepts

ABCs:

Agencies, boards and commissions—a term used to described the variety of separate bodies (such as school boards and utility commissions) which form part of the local government system.

Alternative Service Delivery (ASD):

Options could include providing a service directly, contracting it to another municipality, arranging for shared delivery with a number of municipalities, and contracting with the private sector.

Amalgamate:

To join together two or more complete municipalities to form only one. This contrasts with the process of annexation in which part of one municipality is joined to another, leaving the two separate municipalities, one now larger and one smaller.

CAO (Chief Administrative Officer):

Coordinating officer appointed by council to lead and direct the other employees of the municipality, to provide cohesive policy advice to council and to coordinate the implementation of council's decisions.

Executive Committee:

Senior coordinating committee of council, usually composed of the chairs of the various standing committees and headed by the Mayor. This committee is expected to provide leadership and executive direction, especially in relation to setting priorities and allocating finances.

Indirectly Elected:

Refers to situations in which members of a municipal council hold their position by virtue of their prior election to another governing body. For example, reeves and deputy reeves elected to Ontario township, village and town councils automatically become county council members.

Lower Tier: (See Two Tier system.)

Municipalities:
   Elected local governments which exercise assigned responsibilities, including the power to levy the property tax, within a defined geographic area.

Property Tax:
   Tax levied upon the assessed value of real property (land and buildings on land) found within a municipality.

Real Property: (See Property Tax.)

Service Arranger:
   Term to describe the fact that municipalities need not be direct service providers, but can deliver services through partnership arrangements with other public bodies or with the private sector.

Single Tier:
   Term to describe municipalities which are not part of a two tier system. Only Ontario, Québec and BC have two tier systems, and in Ontario single tier municipalities are still found in the North and in the case of cities separate from the county system.

Two Tier System:
   Municipal government systems which comprise a lower tier of cities, towns, townships and other municipalities, and an upper tier of counties, regions or districts.

Upper Tier: (See Two Tier system.)

User Fees or Charges:
   Charges levied on users of various municipal services, such as public transit or arenas, designed to recoup at least part of the cost of the service from individual users rather than taxpayers at large.

Points to Ponder

1. How old is your municipality? Was it incorporated before Canada became a country? Has it gone through any boundary changes or other restructuring in recent years?

2. Is your municipality part of a two tier system? If so, do you know which tier is responsible for what services?

3. Do you know what local boards operate in your area? Try preparing a list of these boards, along the lines of the *Guide to Government Directory* in Chapter 2.

4. Look at your last municipal tax bill. It will identify the portion of taxes related to municipal services and (if applicable) education and upper tier expenditures. Where is your property tax money going, and how satisfied are you with what you are getting in return?

5. What user fees are charged by your municipality? Does the amount of the fee seem reasonably related to the cost of the program or service you receive in return? How do you feel about municipalities raising revenues in the future more from user fees and less from the property tax?

For Further Reading

For a good introduction to various aspects of local government across Canada, see C. Richard Tindal and Susan Nobes Tindal, *Local Government in Canada*, 5th Edition, Scarborough, Nelson, 2000.

Other books with a general or Canada-wide perspective include James Lightbody (ed.), *Canadian Metropolitics*, Toronto, Copp Clark Ltd., 1995, Richard Loreto and Trevor Price (eds.), *Urban Policy Issues*, Toronto, McClelland & Stewart Inc., 1990, and Katherine Graham, Susan Phillips and Allan Maslove, *Urban Governance in Canada*, Toronto, Harcourt Brace & Company, 1998.

There are also a number of books which focus on the local government system in individual provinces. Examples include:

Kell Antoft (ed.), *A Guide to Local Government in Nova Scotia*, 3rd Edition, Halifax, Dalhousie University, 1992.

_____ and Jack Novack, *Grassroots Democracy: Local Government in the Maritimes*, Halifax, Centre for Public Management, Dalhousie University, 1998.

Robert Bish, *Local Government in British Columbia*, 2nd Edition, Victoria, University of Victoria, 1991.

Jack Masson (with Edward Lesage Jr.), *Alberta's Local Governments: Politics and Democracy*, Edmonton, University of Alberta Press, 1994.

Ontario Municipal Management Institute, *You and Your Local Government*, 3rd Edition, Whitby, 1993.

Various articles on local government developments, and information on legislative changes affecting the local level, are found in the magazine, *Municipal World*, St. Thomas, monthly.

Useful internet sources include:
- *www.intergov.gc.ca*, which has links to all three levels of government. Municipal addresses follow a standard format consisting of the type of municipality followed by its name, the provincial short form, and ca. For example, the address for Edmonton is *www.city.edmonton.ab.ca*, and that of Oakville, Ontario is *www.town.oakville.on.ca*.
- *www.munisource.org* is a site maintained by the Maritime Training and Development Board. It has direct links to over 2700 municipal sites in 26 countries and a "municipal forum bulletin board."
- *www.municipalworld.com* is the address for *Municipal World* magazine and includes a discussion forum and a series of links to other sites.
- Most of the municipal associations in the various provinces have their own web sites, including *www.fcm.ca* for the Federation of Canadian Municipalities, *www.ubcm.ca* for the Union of British Columbia Municipalities, and *www.amo.com* for the Association of Municipalities of Ontario.

Chapter 7

The Constitution, Charter and Courts

Objectives and Highlights

◆ To explain the continuing conflict surrounding Canada's constitution.

◆ To describe the significance and limitations of the Charter and its impact on the operations of government.

◆ To appreciate the special roles of the courts in our system of government.

For more than 100 years after Canada became a country, the central document of its constitution, the British North America Act, remained a statute passed by a foreign legislature (that of Britain). The constitution was finally brought home (or patriated) in 1982, only to have a new constitutional saga begin because of the refusal of the Québec government, then or since, to sign the agreement. This chapter provides a brief overview of Canada's continuing constitutional adventures.

Also examined is the Charter of Rights and Freedoms that was added to the constitution of Canada in 1982, and the impact that the Charter is having on intergovernmental relations and on the balance of power within our government system. Part of that impact, of course, has been to elevate the status and influence of the courts, which are called upon to interpret government actions in light of the Charter. Accordingly, the chapter includes a brief examination of the courts and the administration of justice, both of which also reflect the intergovernmental nature of Canada. Special attention is given to the Supreme Court of Canada and the important roles that it plays in our system of government.

Introduction: Once More into the Meech

Tennyson penned "once more into the breach" in his epic poem *The Charge of the Light Brigade*, but those soldiers doing battle in the Crimean War were scarcely more brave (or foolhardy?) than the Canadian politicians who have engaged in constitutional battles over the past half century. In our case, it has been "once more into the Meech," an adventure which has haunted us for more than a decade.

Meech Lake is a pleasant body of water near the Prime Minister's summer residence in the Gatineau Hills. It was at this location that a major amendment to the Canadian constitution was agreed upon in 1987, one which failed to receive approval from all 10 provincial legislatures within the three year time limit specified. The **Meech Lake Accord** was not the first unsuccessful attempt to amend the **constitution** of Canada, nor—as we will see—was it the last.

♦ Something to Think About

Why have Canadian politicians expended so much time and energy in a futile effort to amend the constitution of the country?

What is a constitution and why are we so concerned about ours? Why should individual Canadians care about a constitution, and how can it affect them?

What Is a Constitution?

A constitution is a legal document setting out the fundamental "rules of the game" concerning a governmental system and its operations. A country does not absolutely have to have a constitution in order to exist and to function. However, a country which is a federation (like Canada) needs some type of written document outlining how powers are divided between the national and intermediate governments.

The country of Canada was created by the British North America Act, an 1867 statute passed by the British Parliament. Important as that statute was to Canada, it aroused little interest among the British politicians. According to Donald Creighton, the mention of things "colonial" was enough to clear the House of Commons, and the statement of the

Colonial Secretary (in introducing the BNA Act) was lost in the noise of members departing "for the more intellectual atmosphere of the lobbies or neighbouring chophouses." The few members who remained could scarcely conceal their boredom. After the ordeal was over, "they turned with lively zeal and manifest relief to the great national problem of the tax on dogs."[1]

The BNA Act and its amendments over the years formed the central core of Canada's constitution. It provided for the machinery and operation of government at both the national and provincial levels, as well as for the distribution of governing powers between the two levels. But, as an Act of the British Parliament, the BNA Act could only be amended by Britain. As the decades went by, it became increasingly embarrassing for Canada to have to ask another country to pass legislation whenever it wanted to amend its own constitution!

The British Parliament would gladly have given up this task. In fact, it passed the Statute of Westminster in 1931, declaring that it would only legislate for Canada in response to a request from Canada. At that time, Canadians were urged to take over responsibility for any future amendments to the BNA Act. But as the decades went by, Canada's provincial and federal politicians were unable to agree on how they would bring home the constitution—and especially on what amending formula they would employ to change it as needed once it was brought home.

> Canadian politicians could not agree on how to bring home the constitution, or to amend it once here.

Unsuccessful initiatives in this regard were launched on several occasions over a period of 50 years. We came tantalizingly close to an agreement twice, with the Fulton-Favreau formula of 1964 and the Victoria Charter of 1971. The details of the long constitutional saga are well documented elsewhere, including in some of the readings cited at the end of this chapter.

---

[1]Donald Creighton, *Toward the Discovery of Canada*, Toronto, Macmillan, 1972, quoted in Jack McLeod (ed.), *The Oxford Book of Canadian Political Anecdotes*, Toronto, Oxford University Press, 1988, p. 23.

Where Were You in '82?

Patriation was finally achieved in 1982, following determined efforts by Pierre Trudeau, who had been reelected Prime Minister in 1980. A Constitution Act was passed by the Canadian Parliament. Incorporated within it was the BNA Act. An amending formula was included, which for most purposes requires the approval of the federal government and 2/3 of the provinces containing at least 50% of Canada's population. The provinces were given expanded powers over their natural resources, a response to the concerns of Western Canada and its reaction to the federal government's National Energy Program launched at the beginning of the 1980s. The other very significant addition was a **Charter of Rights and Freedoms**, discussed in a later section of this chapter.

Most of the initial attention given to the patriation process centred on the fact that one province—Québec—did not sign the agreement to bring home the constitution. Given the tremendous amount of time and effort which had been needed to reach agreement between the federal government and nine provinces, the decision was taken to proceed even without Québec. Since the Québec Government at that time was controlled by the Parti Québécois, headed by René Lévesque, it is reasonable to assume that it would not have signed *any* constitutional agreement, no matter how worded. Nonetheless, there were criticisms that Québec had been betrayed or humiliated by the decision to proceed without its approval.

This interpretation of events was advanced strongly by Brian Mulroney once he became Prime Minister. It became his objective to undo this betrayal of Québec and to reach agreement on new arrangements which would allow Québec to return to the constitutional family. Strictly speaking, of course, Québec had never left the constitutional family. It might have refused to sign the patriation agreement, but it remained part of Canada and under its constitution.

The Meech Lake Accord

The Meech Lake Accord was to be Brian Mulroney's great triumph in statesmanship. It incorporated the conditions which Québec felt were a necessary prerequisite to signing the constitution. These were:

1. The recognition of Québec as a distinct society.
2. Increased powers in immigration.
3. The appointment of three Supreme Court judges from the Québec bench.
4. Containment of the "federal spending power."[2]
5. A Québec veto on any future constitutional changes.

Agreement was reached on amendments to the constitution following a day-long meeting between the Prime Minister and the 10 provincial Premiers at Meech Lake in April 1987. The agreement was presented as a *fait accompli*, something which had to be accepted without change. Any rejection of Meech, warned Prime Minister Mulroney, would be a rejection of Québec. This was a very dangerous, high-risk strategy, as well as being an unfair characterization of the situation.

It is true that some of the opposition to Meech was based on anti-Québec or anti-French sentiment. But it is equally true that much of the opposition was based on very real

> A key issue was how the distinct society clause might affect the Charter.

concerns by Canadians about the kind of country they wanted and how that might be changed if Meech were passed. A central issue (*never* fully explained or resolved) was how the inclusion of the **distinct society** clause might affect the provisions of the Charter. Would the Supreme Court be obliged to weigh any Charter challenges against actions taken by a future Québec government in light of Meech's declaration that the role of the Québec government was to "preserve and promote the distinct identity of Québec?" Were important distinctions involved, or just sloppy draftsmanship, in the use of the phrase "distinct society" in some sections and "distinct identity" in others?" It didn't help public concern when the politicians involved issued totally contradictory and incompatible statements concerning the distinct society provisions—telling English Canadians that the provisions were just symbolic, a recognition that Québec was different, while telling French Canadians that the provisions were fundamental and of great significance in protecting their interests.

---

[2]As discussed in the next chapter, this is the power of the federal government to spend money in areas in which it doesn't necessarily have the power to legislate.

There were also concerns about whether or not the Charter rights of other groups might be adversely affected by Meech. Shortly after the agreement was first announced, a clause was added to ensure that nothing in the Accord would affect the clauses in the 1982 Constitution Act that dealt with multiculturalism or aboriginal peoples. That prompted a demand that women's rights be given similar protection through specific wording. Much of the opposition to Meech came from "the fears of feminist groups, aboriginals, visible minorities, social policy activists and the disabled, that Meech Lake threatened their existing status or future goals."[3] Groups like these were also reacting to the secrecy surrounding the Meech Lake deliberations in contrast to the open process which had led to the patriation of the constitution in 1982.

A major problem faced by the Meech Lake Accord was the fact that a three year period was stipulated, within which the federal government and all 10 provinces must ratify the agreement. Over such a long time period, a number of the key players changed because of elections in several provinces. When the time limit expired (in June 1990), approval had still not been received from two provinces. That's right! *Two* provinces failed to ratify Meech. The Conservatives found it convenient to lay all of the blame on the Liberal Premier of Newfoundland, Clyde Wells, a version of events which has been repeated to this day. The facts are, however, that after experiencing a number of delays at the hands of one of its MLAs, Elijah Harper, who expressed various concerns of native groups across Canada, the Manitoba Legislature adjourned on that final day of the three year time frame—without even beginning the public hearings at which some 3000 delegations were listed to speak.

The Charlottetown Accord

As long and fruitless as the Meech Lake experience was, it is far from our last foray into constitutional battles. Spurred on by Québec plans for a separation referendum in 1992, the federal government launched a new drive for constitutional reform culminating in the **Charlottetown Accord**. If the Meech Lake Accord had been seen by many as a "Qué-

---

[3]Alan C. Cairns, *Disruptions*, (edited by Douglas Williams), Toronto, McClelland and Stewart, 1991, p. 244.

bec round" of constitutional talks, the much more comprehensive (and complex) Charlottetown Accord had something for everyone. There was Senate reform for the West, aboriginal rights, native self-government—even a Canada clause to counterbalance the recognition of Québec's distinct society.

Charlottetown also differed from Meech in one other important respect. All Canadians would be involved in its ratification, in a vote scheduled for October 1992. As the time for the vote drew near, all political parties and much of the "intelligentsia" strongly supported the Charlottetown Accord. There was extensive advertising and a concerted national campaign to persuade Canadians of the wisdom of voting yes. Instead Canadians in six of the ten provinces voted no. One of the four provinces to vote yes was Ontario, but by the narrowest of margins.

By this time, most Canadians were suffering from constitutional fatigue. While some in Québec saw the twin defeats as further evidence that separation must be pursued, many Canadians (including many Québecers) were just tired of hearing about what seemed to be a pretty abstract subject, compared to their real concerns about jobs, health care, the environment and so on. Those still paying attention to this subject began to appreciate the following definitions:

Meechified: Overcome by constitutional debate. (stupefied)

Son of a Meech: Offspring of parties to constitutional debates.

To Meechorize: To mesmerize, reduce to semi-comatose state. (See meechified, above.)

Meech ado about nothing: Common view of the whole process.

The Current Constitutional Situation

Canada appeared to move "from Meech to the Breach" when almost 50% in Québec voted for separation in a provincial referendum held on October 30, 1995. The federal government appeared complacent when the referendum campaign began and caught off guard when Lucien Bouchard replaced Jacques Parizeau as the leader of the separatists and energized their efforts. The charismatic Bouchard then became leader of the Parti Québécois and Premier of Québec, and was reelected in

December 1998. However, the less than 43% of the popular vote his party received was widely considered to be a weak mandate for pursuing another referendum. Indeed, a number of public opinion polls in the late 1990s indicated that people in Québec were solidly against a referendum—even while supporting a party pledged to hold one.

A possible response to at least some of Québec's concerns was presented following a September 1997 meeting of provincial Premiers in Calgary—all premiers except Bouchard. In what quickly became known as the "**Calgary Accord**," the premiers agreed to a set of seven principles. Instead of a distinct society, Québec was described as having a "unique character," and this acknowledgement was balanced with a recognition that all provinces were diverse in their characteristics and equal in status. The wording of the accord was carefully crafted, perhaps to the point of being convoluted, in an attempt to placate the widely varying views on this issue. Prime Minister Chrétien met or spoke with most of the premiers prior to their Calgary conference[4] and wasted no time in declaring the principles of their accord acceptable to the federal government.

Plan "B" and the Supreme Court Reference

In the meantime, the federal government had been wrestling with the question of whether or not it ought to take a tougher line on the issue of Québec separation, by pursuing a so-called Plan "B." Such a plan would contend that if Canada is divisible, so is Québec, and it would include a court challenge to the right of Québec to separate. The latter course of action was commenced when the federal government asked the Supreme Court of Canada to answer three questions about the legality of Québec separation, namely:

1. Under the constitution of Canada, can Québec secede from Canada unilaterally?
2. Under international law, can Québec secede unilaterally?
3. In the event of a conflict between domestic and international law on the right of Québec to secede from Canada unilaterally, which would take precedence over the other?

[4]See Rosemary Speirs, Chrétien now has 2-track unity approach," *Toronto Star*, September 16, 1997.

The court's decision, in August 1998, was that Québec had no unilateral right to secede. But the judges went on to state that "the rights of other provinces and the federal government cannot deny the right of the government of Québec to pursue secession, should a clear majority of the people of Québec choose that goal." Indeed, they went further, and concluded that if the people of Québec were to win a referendum "by a clear majority on a clear question," then Canada has a "constitutional duty to negotiate."

These additional observations of the court were hardly what the federal side expected or desired. It is true that some analysts found the court ruling to be "even-handed," and felt that by giving something to

> Has the ruling given Québec, for the first time, a constitutional right to pursue secession?

both sides the judges had deprived the separatists of a rejection that they might have capitalized upon in a future referendum. Others, however, were dismayed that this ruling has given Québec a constitutional right to pursue secession—something not previously available to it under the provisions of Canada's constitution. It was also pointed out that since the court had not seen fit to define the terms 'clear majority' or 'clear question,' there were still some very important issues unresolved by the ruling. In early December 1999, Prime Minister Chrétien introduced legislation which will set rules governing how any separation vote must be conducted, prompting a very angry response from the Québec government, which will counter with legislation of its own. As debate heats up, Canadians may find themselves heading "once more into the Meech."

The Importance of the Charter

One of the reasons that the Meech and Charlottetown Accords were rejected is that something else very significant besides Québec's isolation happened when the constitution was patriated in 1982. Added to the constitution of Canada was a Charter of Rights and Freedoms. Canadians had always enjoyed a long list of rights and freedoms as part of common law. To a large extent, these rights might be considered part of the unwritten portion of our constitution—that portion referred to as custom or convention. Such things as freedom of speech, of the press, of assembly, of worship, freedom from discrimination and from censorship, and the right to the due process of law—all of these and more have always been considered part of one's heritage as a Canadian citizen.

However, one of Prime Minister Trudeau's main objectives in bringing home the constitution was to enshrine a charter of rights. This had the effect of codifying, in constitutional law, what had hitherto existed in less well defined fashion as part of the customs of the country. The specific rights provided in the Charter are summarized in *Appendix A* of this chapter. While the list is impressive, there are two qualifiers with great potential significance for the operations of the Charter.

Limitations on the Charter

The first qualifier is the statement that the rights in the Charter are subject to "such reasonable limits prescribed by law as can be demonstrably justified in a free and democratic society." This means that Charter rights can be ignored or overridden where such an infringement can be justified as a reasonable limitation. For example, anti-smoking legislation might be challenged as limiting freedom of assembly and movement—given all of the restrictions on where one is allowed to smoke. These restrictions, however, would presumably meet the test of a reasonable limitation for a free and democratic society, because of what is known about the health hazards of tobacco and about the dangers of second-hand smoke.

The second qualifier, the **notwithstanding clause**, is the "Achilles' heel" of the Charter. It authorizes the federal government or any province to declare that one of its statutes shall operate notwithstanding a provision in section 2 or sections 7 to 15 of the Charter. In other words, this clause allows a senior government to "opt out of" the Charter and carry on with legislation which is contrary to the Charter—by the simple expedient of passing legislation declaring that it is doing so. Any such action is limited to a five year period, after which the legislation must be re-enacted to continue the override.

How could such an escape clause be included in the Charter and in the constitution of Canada? Most provincial governments were strongly opposed to the Charter. Apparently the only way that Prime Minister Trudeau could achieve the inclusion of the Charter, which he so fervently wanted, was to accept inclusion of the notwithstanding clause. Presumably, the general feeling was that having this escape clause would be sufficient to placate provincial politicians, while at the same time public support for the Charter would be sufficiently strong to deter politicians from using—or at least from abusing—the clause.[5] Some supporters of this clause also argue that it makes the Charter more democratic by leaving final authority over these matters to elected representatives rather than judges. This rationale seems increasingly pertinent to those who are critical of what they see as excessive judicial discretion in the interpretation of the constitution and the Charter—an issue discussed later in this chapter.

Significance of the Charter

Even with these limitations, the addition of the Charter had significant implications for Canadian society.

1. It added a feature with which most Canadians were familiar as part of the American system of government. We had long been accustomed to hearing about the U.S. constitution's declaration of the right to life, liberty and the pursuit of happiness.

2. It altered the balance of power in our system of government. Before the Charter, Parliament was supreme—as it has always been in Britain. After the Charter, every action of Parliament became subject to the Charter. This meant that power shifted, from Parliament to the courts, whose role it is to interpret the Charter.

3. It emphasized that certain rights were enjoyed by all Canadians, regardless of their origins or their territorial location. On the positive side, this gave many Canadians a feeling of empowerment, a

---

[5]Ironically, it was Premier Bourassa's use of the notwithstanding clause, to support the continuation of the Québec Government's French-only sign legislation, which undermined the sympathy of many supporters in English Canada and contributed markedly to the defeat of the Meech Lake Accord.

feeling that they had equality under the constitution. On the negative side, this viewpoint was obviously contrary to the territorial claims being made by those French Canadians who wanted recognition of one geographic area—Québec—as a distinct society.[6]

> Groups which had little influence have gained by using Charter challenges.

With hindsight, it appears that there was a failure to recognize or understand the extent to which many Canadians had embraced the Charter and had come to value it as a protector of their rights. In the decade and a half since the Charter appeared, many groups which previously felt that they had little influence over a government system dominated by Parliament, and the political parties which controlled Parliament, have gained a great deal of influence through Charter challenges. We have seen the development of what some have termed a "court party," defined as "a loose alliance of judges, bureaucrats, lawyers, activists (who may also be bureaucrats and/or lawyers), academics and media personalities." They use the courts as "a new playing field for the pursuit of politics."[7]

LEAF, the feminist Legal Education and Action Fund, is a prime example of the new players and their strategies. By the early 1990s, it had become the most frequent non-government intervenor in Charter cases before the Supreme Court. It funded these challenges, in large part, through taxpayers' money provided through the Secretary of State and through the Court Challenges Program. Other members of the court party include the Canadian Disability Rights Council, the Charter Committee on Poverty Issues, the Canadian Prisoners' Rights Network, the Advocacy Group for the Environmentally Sensitive, and EGALE (Equality for Gays and Lesbians Everywhere).[8]

Whether or not you approve of this apparent shift of power in our society largely depends, presumably, on whether you were previously

---

[6]This discussion is largely based on Cairns, *op. cit.*, Chapter 10.

[7]Al Strachan, "The Hidden Opposition," *The Globe and Mail*, January 11, 1992, p. D3, reprinted in Gregory Mahler and Roman March (eds.), *Annual Editions, Canadian Politics*, Third Edition, Guilford, Dushkin Publishing Group, 1993, p. 46.

[8]*Ibid.*, p. 46.

one of the "ins" or the "outs." What is clear, however, is that the balance of power has shifted. One consequence is an enhanced role for the courts, and especially the Supreme Court of Canada, so it is time to take a closer look at this "third branch of government."

The Courts

Under the constitution of Canada, the provinces are responsible for the administration of justice. Each province has a superior or supreme court, usually divided into trial and appeal divisions. Some also have county or district courts with both civil and criminal jurisdiction. In addition, all provinces have courts presided over by judges appointed by the provinces to deal with lesser criminal and other matters. These include magistrates' courts and family and juvenile courts. In addition to the various provincial courts, there are two courts established by the Government of Canada—the Federal Court and the **Supreme Court of Canada**. The chart below depicts the general hierarchy of courts.

Structure of the Courts

	Supreme Court of Canada	
	Ontario Court of Appeal	
Divisional Court		
	Superior Ct of Justice	Unified Family Court
Provincial Court	Small Claims Court	
Family	Criminal	Provincial Offences

The preceding chart depicts the federal courts and those found in Ontario, but most provinces have a somewhat similar court structure. Since the appeal process and the sequence from court to court varies with the nature of the case, the chart is illustrative only.

Most of us equate the courts with the sort of dramatic criminal trials which hit the headlines or are popularized in television shows and movies. **Criminal law** deals with the relationship between the individual and the state. The national government is responsible for criminal law, which deals with such matters as murder, theft and assault. In contrast, **civil law** involves actions between or among individuals and corporations. It falls under provincial jurisdiction and includes such matters as wills, family law and torts (legal liability). For most Canadians, any encounter with the courts will revolve around such relatively minor matters as fighting a speeding ticket or suing a neighbour over a fence which supposedly encroaches on one's property.

The subject of law enforcement is an important one, which could easily merit a separate chapter of its own. Canadians often hold very strong views about the appropriateness of existing or pending legislation, or how rigorously it should be enforced—as is evident, for example, with respect to the federal "gun control" and "anti-smoking" legislation. Controversy also surrounds the cost and effectiveness of our criminal justice system. In 1992, Canadian taxpayers paid more than $9.5 billion to hunt down lawbreakers, prosecute and keep them locked up.[9] It cost about $46 000 to keep an inmate in a federal prison in 1993 and $40 000 more than that to keep a young offender in a secure custody facility in Ontario.[10] Yet many Canadians seem to feel that what is needed is to "get tough with" lawbreakers and to keep them incarcerated longer. Others question the logic of supporting what is essentially a policy of increased spending on policing and prisons while govern-

> Does it make sense to cut spending on child care and education and to increase it on policing and prisons?

---

[9] Rob Tripp, "Dollars and Pain: The Economics of the Justice System," *Kingston Whig Standard*, November 25, 1996.

[10] *Ibid.*

ments are cutting expenditures on programs such as child care, social assistance and education. They see it as one more example of our tendency to deal with problems after they occur rather than trying to prevent them. They point to research which estimates that $7 is saved in the costs of crime, welfare and education upgrading for every $1 spent on children when they are young.[11]

The administration of justice also illustrates well the intergovernmental nature of Canada. We have already noted the existence of both provincial and federal courts and judges. Policing is carried out by all three levels of government.[12] The Royal Canadian Mounted Police is responsible for enforcing all federal statutes and is also under contract to every province except Ontario and Québec and to over 100 municipalities to enforce criminal and provincial law. Ontario and Québec have their own provincial police forces, which may also contract to provide policing for municipalities. There are also many local police forces operated by municipalities, and there are local forces found in many native communities as well.

There is, however, an entirely different role which the courts play as key institutions within our machinery of government. They exist to enforce the principle of the **rule of law**. Simply put, this principle states that all government actions must be authorized by law; that there must be specific legal authority for the actions taken by government. This principle is an essential part of our democratic system. It helps to ensure that no one, even the most senior government personnel, is above the law. It helps to protect us from arbitrary or capricious actions taken by government.

The courts are particularly concerned to ensure that government decisions affecting individuals meet certain tests. ·

- Did the government have the legal authority to make the decision?
- In the process of arriving at the decision, did the government give any affected individuals the equivalent of their "day in court"? In other words, were the affected individuals given advance notice

---

[11] *Ibid.*

[12] This section is based on Robert Jackson and Doreen Jackson, *Canadian Government in Transition*, Scarborough, Prentice-Hall Canada Inc., 1996, pp. 207-208.

about the decision to be taken, the opportunity to attend, the right to hear and be heard, and reasons for the decision taken?
• Is the decision consistent with the provisions of the Charter?

If the courts determine that government decisions do not measure up to these tests, they will be quashed as *ultra vires* or contrary to the "proceedings of natural justice." The net result is protection for the individual from any abuse of power by government.

The courts or judiciary represent a "third branch of government," and one which is central to our democratic system. In countries which are not democratic, the courts usually exist as an arm of the ruling group and are used to enforce their actions. In contrast, the courts and judges in Canada are separate and independent. Judges of the two federal courts (the Supreme Court of Canada and the Federal Court of Canada) and of the higher level courts in the provinces enjoy a very secure tenure and can only be removed from office by a vote of both Houses of Parliament.

The issue of tenure for judges came to the fore in mid-1996 as a result of comments made by Québec Superior Court Justice Jean Bienvenue concerning women and Jews. A Canadian Judicial Council inquiry committee recommended his removal from the bench—the first time in this century that a federally appointed judge has been the subject of such action. In fact, only five cases of judicial misconduct have made it to Parliament since 1867 and the judges involved either died or resigned before a final vote was taken on their fate.[13]

♦ Something to Think About

The disparaging remarks made by Judge Bienvenue were deeply offensive and most Canadians who followed the incident probably welcomed the recommendation for his dismissal. But it is important to remember why judges have been given such secure tenure, and why they should be removed from the bench only in the most extreme circumstances.

---

[13]Lisa Fitterman, "Committee Wants Judge Removed from Bench," in *Kingston Whig Standard*, July 5, 1996. Bienvenue also chose to resign instead of awaiting a vote on the issue.

Judges must be free to carry out their duties without any political interference.[14] They must make decisions which often fly in the face of public opinion or anger powerful interest groups and lobbies. If we start holding judges responsible for remarks they make and opinions they have—however distasteful—we start down a very slippery slope. Would it not be even more dangerous and undesirable to have judges who think, but hide, unacceptable ideas? At least when judges reveal their true colours, a litigant can show an Appeal Court why unfair treatment occurred.

It is noteworthy that the day after the recommendation to remove Judge Bienvenue, the Québec Justice Minister announced that he would introduce measures to make judges "more accountable" in general. Any such action could undermine the independence of the judiciary and, ultimately, the protection of the rights of the public in a democracy. As a result, even those who found Bienvenue's words anything but "welcome," may want to reconsider defending his right to say them.

Supreme Court of Canada

As the highest court in the land, the Supreme Court's decisions are binding on all the lower courts. It deals mainly with cases that have been appealed at least once in the lower courts. It does not accept to hear all appeals. Rather, it is selective in its approach, allocating its limited time and resources to questions it regards as being of fundamental importance to Canadian society.[15]

Much of the work of the Supreme Court has centred around two very important types of case:

1. Those relating to the division of powers and the operations of Canadian federalism, and

2. Those dealing with Charter challenges.

---

[14]The discussion which follows is based on Julius Grey, "Bienvenue Case May Undermine Judicial Independence," in *Kingston Whig Standard*, July 12, 1996.

[15]This discussion is based on Robert J. Jackson and Doreen Jackson, *Politics in Canada*, 3rd Edition, Scarborough, Prentice-Hall Canada Inc., 1994, p. 180.

The Courts and the Division of Powers

Wherever there is a federal system of government, there will be uncertainty and debate over who is responsible for what. This uncertainty can arise because of a possible lack of clarity in the wording of the original division of powers. It may also arise because roles for government develop which were not even contemplated or covered in the original division of powers. Both of these factors apply in the Canadian case. In addition, the long delay in agreeing on an amending formula and in bringing home the constitution meant that Canada had to rely even more heavily on the Supreme Court and to hope that its interpretations could provide sufficient flexibility to allow an 1867 Act to meet the greatly changed conditions of the 20th century (and now the 21st).

Imagine that you are a Supreme Court justice. How would you respond to the following jurisdictional questions?

You Be the Judge

1. Under the constitution, provinces have ownership of mineral resources and the federal government controls navigable waters. Since technology now makes possible the "mining" of off-shore resources, which level of government has jurisdiction over resources under coastal waters?

2. The constitution does not directly deal with responsibility for management of the economy, since this was not a government function at the time of Confederation. Both the national and provincial levels have pursued a variety of economic policies over the past half century. The national government introduces wage and price controls and you are asked to rule if its action is constitutional and on what basis.

3. Canadians are concerned about a number of environmental issues, including the destruction of the ozone layer, clear-cutting of forests, and water pollution. Which level of government has jurisdiction to act?

___

And the answer is....

In the first instance, the Supreme Court ruled that the national government had jurisdiction over off-shore resources. In the second instance, there was a court challenge when the Liberal Government of Pierre Trudeau introduced wage and price controls after its reelection in 1974. The court held that the national government could take such action under its "Peace, Order and Good Government" clause, even though previous rulings had indicated that this blanket power was only to be exercised in a national emergency, which had been presumed to refer to matters such as war.

There is no one answer to the third instance posed above. Both the federal and provincial levels have passed environmental legislation, although most of the initiative in this area has been left to the provinces. Control over forests was specifically assigned to the provinces in section 92 of the BNA Act (and is also specified in the section 92a amendment added in 1982 when the Constitution Act was passed). Control over air pollution and over other activities harmful to the ozone layer can be exercised by both the federal and provincial governments. Both these levels, along with municipalities, can exercise responsibility with respect to water pollution—with municipalities often in the forefront.

This third example is all too typical. While the original division of powers was supposed to be based on "watertight compartments," the next chapter notes the growing overlap in the activities of the various levels of government. Today, there are very few areas of policy that are the exclusive responsibility of one level. One result is that much of the time of governments in Canada is spent in jurisdictional squabbles.

The Courts and the Charter

The Supreme Court now spends much of its time just dealing with Charter cases. It has made many important rulings dealing with such matters as Canada's abortion law, the federal immigration appeal process, and the issue of maternity leave provisions under the Unemployment Insurance Act. Three of its more widely publicized decisions over the past decade or so have been:

1. The "Askov" decision regarding the right to a speedy trial, which resulted in the dismissal (for undue delay) of more than 40 000 cases in Ontario alone;

2. The "drunkenness as a defence" decision, in which the Court accepted the defence argument that an accused was too drunk to know what he was doing and could not be held responsible for his actions; and

3. The Sue Rodriguez case in which the Court ruled against the doctor-assisted suicide being sought by Rodriguez.

There are strongly held and widely varying views about the role now played by the Supreme Court, especially as a result of the Charter. Some feel the judges have used moderation in their interpretation of the Charter, some complain that there is little consistency in the way the court deals with Charter challenges, while still others are very critical of the court for usurping the role of Parliament.

The latter view is well represented by Leishman, who points out that, prior to the Charter, judges attempted to uphold the law's essential purposes and principles in accordance with judicial precedents and *the legislative branch's original intentions* (emphasis added), and would never have considered amending the plain text of a statute duly passed. To illustrate the greatly changed situation since the Charter, he cites the following examples:[16]

- In the Federal Court of Appeal's 1990 *Schacter* decision, concerning the Unemployment Insurance Act's benefits for adoptive and natural parents, the court ruled that the law unfairly discriminated against natural parents and, to correct this deficiency, it unilaterally amended the Act. In reviewing this case, the Supreme Court asserted that the Charter had empowered the courts to read new provisions into a statute if, in the court's opinion, the change was necessary to bring the statute into conformity with the Charter.

- In the case of *Eldridge v. British Columbia (1997)*, the Supreme Court —contrary to the position taken by the British Columbia Supreme Court and Court of Appeal—gave the British Columbia government six months to change its Hospital Insurance Act regulations to provide free sign language interpretation for the deaf at all provincial hospitals.

---

[16]Rory Leishman, "Robed Dictators," *Next City*, Toronto, Fall 1998, pp. 37–38.

- In R. *v. Feeney (1997)*, the Supreme Court threw out the conviction of someone who had bludgeoned an 85 year old man to death and who had been found a few hours later still wearing a T-shirt splattered with the victim's blood. The court was troubled by the fact the police had entered Feeney's residence without a warrant, yet police have had this right for centuries, under common law, if an officer has reasonable grounds to believe that the suspect has committed an indictable offence.

- In *Vriend v. Alberta (1998)*, the Supreme Court's response to the fact that Alberta legislators repeatedly declined to amend the province's human rights code to include sexual orientation as a prohibited grounds for discrimination was to unilaterally amend the law.

A contrary view is that, while judges do exert great influence, what Canada suffers from is not so much judicial activism as legislative passivity.[17] In the matter of the Québec Secession reference, for example, the federal government—instead of developing and defending a position—referred the issue to the Supreme Court, exposing it to demonstrations and fierce criticism by separatists. Instead of adopting a policy with respect to gay and lesbian rights, the federal government was happy to let private groups force the Supreme Court to make decisions for the elected representatives. Instead of dealing with reforms to the Divorce Act and child custody and access awards, the politicians let judges decide children's lives on a case-by-case basis.

According to former Supreme Court Justice Bertha Wilson, all branches of government—legislative, executive and judicial—have an equal responsibility to carry out the Charter's mandate.[18] Legislatures should examine legislation before passing it to ensure it complies. If it is challenged after it passes, the courts must undertake the same review. If they find the legislation deficient, the courts must identify its defects as specifically as possible. The matter then goes back to the legislature

---

[17]See Felipe Morales, "It's time to change the judicial appointment process," *National*, Canadian Bar Association, August-September 1999, p. 6, on which this section is based.

[18]Hon. Bertha Wilson, "We Didn't Volunteer," *Policy Options*, Montreal, IRRP, April 1999, pp. 8-11. This issue features several articles on the power of judges, some of which are cited in subsequent footnotes.

for appropriate remedial action. So, in Wilson's view, "the courts' assessment of the legislation's constitutionality is not the last word; it is merely one step in the process."[19]

In a somewhat similar vein, Hogg and Thornton portray judicial review as a "dialogue" between judges and legislatures. As they see it, a judgment prompts public debate about Charter values and leaves the legislature, now better informed from that debate, in a position to decide on a course of action—which could involve re-enacting the old law, enacting a new one, or abandoning the initiative.[20] But Morton disputes this characterization, noting that if (as happens in most instances) a government responds by repealing offending legislation or amending it according to specifications laid down by the courts, this does not constitute dialogue. Rather, he argues, what unfolds is usually a monologue, "with the judges doing most of the talking and legislatures most of the listening."[21]

However one describes it, the result is a system in which, according to some, political accountability has disappeared.[22] Elected representatives don't want to make tough decisions, so they leave them to the judges, to whom they deflect the blame when there is criticism. The judges, in turn, claim that they had no choice but to decide in the absence of government leadership and legislation. Either the politicians must act or the judges must become more accountable. This leads to the issue of how judges are chosen.

The Appointment of Judges

Who are the members of the Supreme Court who allegedly wield such power? They are nine judges, appointed by the federal government— really by the Prime Minister of the day. They serve until age 75. Three of the judges are appointed from Québec in recognition of its different

---

[19]*Ibid.*, p. 10.

[20]Peter W. Hogg and Allison A. Thornton, "The Charter Dialogue Between Courts and Legislatures," *Policy Options*, April 1999, p. 20.

[21]F. L. Morton, "Dialogue or Monologue?" *Policy Options*, April 1999, p. 26.

[22]This point by Morales, *op. cit.*

system of civil law (based on the Napoleonic code, rather than on English common law). By tradition, three judges are from Ontario, two from the West and one from the Atlantic provinces. All are presumed to have distinguished legal careers, although not all have been on the bench in lower courts. For example, the late Bora Laskin, who became Chief Justice of the Supreme Court, was a law professor when appointed. John Sopinka, recently deceased, was a practising lawyer at the time of his appointment.

While their legal credentials are solid, what about their beliefs and values? These are obviously of equal importance, and may significantly affect the kinds of decisions which are made by the court. The short answer is that we don't know! Canadians do not have anything like the American system

The Unknown Nine

of "advise and consent" in which the U.S. President's nominees for the Supreme Court are examined by Congress in highly publicized hearings, before being approved (or not). Perhaps we would not wish such a system, especially after the spectacle of the Judge Thomas hearings and the Anita Hill accusations of sexual harassment against Thomas. Without some type of hearing process, however, Canadians have no way of knowing anything about the nine people who have acquired such substantial decision-making power.

It is reasonable to assume that a Prime Minister in power for a considerable period of time will have the opportunity to appoint several judges who share his philosophical or ideological bent. For example, there is some evidence[23] to support the notion that the appointments made by Brian Mulroney during his two terms in power were more conservative and less supportive of Charter challenges. Indeed, all but one of the judges serving in 1996 were Mulroney appointments, and half of those had some connection with the Conservative party.[24]

---

[23]Morton et al., "The Supreme Court's First Decade of Charter Decisions," in Paul Fox and Graham White (eds.), *Politics: Canada*, 8th Edition, Whitby, McGraw-Hill Ryerson Limited, 1995, p. 77.

[24]Jackson and Jackson, *op. cit.*, p. 198.

Since then, however, Prime Minister Chrétien has made a series of appointments. He created controversy in late 1997 by appointing to the court Michel Bastarache, a former law firm associate, avowed federalist and informal Liberal party adviser.[25] He then replaced John Sopinka, who died suddenly in November 1997, with Ian Binnie, and in the summer of 1999 replaced retiring member Peter Cory with Louise Arbour, who had gained much prominence during her assignment to the International War Crimes Tribunal. In late 1999, Chrétien appointed Beverley McLachlin to take over from Antonio Lamer as Chief Justice, and then appointed Louis LeBel to fill the vacancy left by Lamer's retirement. Views are divided on whether Chrétien is gradually installing a more activist court or is simply responding to vacancies with those available at the time.[26] One thing is clear, however. With one or two other justices expected to retire within a couple of years, the Supreme Court will be almost completely transformed during Chrétien's tenure.

It is clear that the role of the Supreme Court has become significantly more important since the advent of the Charter, however positively or negatively one views this development. At least some of its rulings have taken it into the realm of social policy and other matters traditionally decided by elected legislatures. Under the circumstances, perhaps a new method of appointing the court members is desirable— one which opens up the process somewhat without turning it into the "circus" atmosphere of the American method. One of a number of options suggested is that proposed by law professor Martin Friedland in a 1995 report for the Canadian Judicial Council.[27] It involves the creation of a committee to recommend two or three nominees. The committee would be composed of lawyers chosen by the Canadian Bar Association, representatives from the federal government, and members

---

[25]This characterization of Bastarache's background was found in a number of media reports, including David Vienneau, "Controversy likely to increase over high court appointments," *Toronto Star*, October 7, 1997.

[26]Janice Tibbetts, "The law according to Jean," *Ottawa Citizen*, September 13, 1999.

[27]As quoted in Jeffrey Simpson, "Needed: A better way to make Supreme Court appointments," *Globe and Mail*, August 29, 1997.

from the province or provinces from which a nominee hailed. If the Prime Minister chooses a name other than one of the nominees, some sort of confirmation hearing would have to be held. This arrangement would give the government the freedom to go outside the list and to have the final choice, but it was also put pressure on it not to do so.

Concluding Observations

After spending half a century before finally reaching agreement on the patriation of our constitution, Canada's governments have spent the last two decades wrestling with what amendments can be made to that constitution in an attempt to satisfy the one province (Québec) that did not agree to that patriation. While constitutional issues are important, especially as they relate to national unity, they have also claimed a great deal of the time and resources of Canada's governments. In the words of one who would know:

> We have developed our own peculiar cottage industry—highly paid and unproductive—in the field of constitutional reform. Imagine what might have been accomplished in, say, the field of medical research if the same amount of time and energy, talent and money, had been available as in the field of federal-provincial relations.

While this insight was offered by Brian Mulroney before he became Prime Minister,[28] it unfortunately has continued to ring true for most of the years since.

We are still coming to grips with the full implications of the Charter of Rights and Freedoms and the way it has altered the balance of power between governments and the courts. The courts have also altered the balance of power between the federal and provincial governments through their interpretation of the division of powers under the constitution. The changing nature of intergovernmental relations will be explored in the next chapter.

---

[28]Brian Mulroney, *Where I Stand*, Toronto, McClelland and Stewart, 1983, p. 57.

Appendix A
What Are your Charter Rights?

1. *Fundamental freedoms*

   of conscience and religion
   of thought, belief, opinion and expression
   (including freedom of the press and other media)
   of peaceful assembly (note the qualifier—"peaceful")
   of association

2. *Democratic rights*

   to vote and to be a candidate for office
   five year limit on the term of legislatures, (except in an extreme emergency)
   one sitting of a legislature at least once every 12 months

3. *Mobility rights*

   Every citizen has the right to enter, remain in, and leave Canada
   Every citizen and permanent resident has the right to move to any province and to pursue a livelihood in any province
   Programs favouring existing provincial residents are permitted if the rate of unemployment is below the national average

4. *Legal rights*

   To life, liberty and security of person
   To be secure against unreasonable search or seizure
   Not to be arbitrarily detained or imprisoned
   On arrest or detention, everyone has the right:
   - to be informed promptly of reasons
   - to be informed of the right to counsel, and to obtain counsel promptly
   - to have validity of detention confirmed
   ♦ If charged with an offence, everyone has due process rights
   Not to be subjected to cruel and unusual punishment
   ♦ To protection against self-incrimination
   To an interpreter

5. *Equality rights*

♦ Every person is equal before and under the law, free from discrimination based on: race, national or ethnic origin, colour, religion, sex, age, mental or physical disability
♦ Affirmative action programs permitted

6. *Language rights*

♦ English and French are the official languages of Canada and have equality of status as to their usage in all institutions of the government of Canada
♦ English and French are the official languages of New Brunswick, with the same equality provisions
♦ Either English or French may be used before any court established by the federal or New Brunswick governments
♦ The public can communicate with the federal government in English or French, where there is a significant demand for such language
♦ Minority language educational rights are guaranteed

The Last Word

Definition of Terms and Concepts

Calgary Accord:
Name given to set of seven principles agreed to by all Premiers except the Premier of Québec. It attempted to balance acknowledgement of Québec's unique character with a recognition that all provinces are diverse in their characteristics and equal in status.

Charlottetown Accord:
The name given to the comprehensive constitutional reform package on which Canadians voted (negatively) in October 1992.

Charter:
The Charter of Rights and Freedoms was added to the Canadian constitution when it was patriated in 1982. It provides a constitutional guarantee of certain rights for Canadians, to which Parliament and the provincial legislatures must adhere.

Civil Law:
This body of law deals with actions between or among individuals and corporations. It covers such matters as wills and family law.

Constitution:
The "rules of the game" concerning a governmental system and its operation, usually found in a central document or documents and in various customs and conventions.

Criminal Law:
The body of law which deals with the relationship between individuals and the state (government), including such matters as murder and assault.

Distinct Society:
A phrase open to many interpretations. At one extreme is the suggestion that this phrase merely recognizes the fact that Québec is different. At the other extreme is the contention that this phrase could be used to justify government actions otherwise contrary to the Charter

but directed toward protection and enhancement of Québec's distinct society. In short, there is no specific, commonly accepted definition.

Meech Lake Accord:
The name given to the constitutional amendment package which was agreed to by the Prime Minister and Premiers in 1987 but which failed to receive ratification by all provinces within the three year time frame required.

Notwithstanding Clause:
The override clause which allows the federal government or any province to opt out of the Charter (section 2 and sections 7 to 15) by the simple expedient of passing a law which declares that it (that law) is exempt. Any such legislation is limited to a five year term, but can be re-enacted.

Patriation:
Refers to the process of "bringing home" the constitution from Britain. This was accomplished in 1982 when the Constitution Act was passed by the Parliament of Canada, incorporating within it the British North America Act which hitherto could only be amended by the British Parliament which had originally passed it in 1867.

Rule of Law:
Fundamental principle that all government actions must be authorized by law. This principle is enforced by the courts which stand ready to declare *ultra vires* any government action which is without proper legal foundation.

Supreme Court of Canada:
The final court of the law for Canada. It consists of nine judges appointed by the federal government and devotes most of its time to Charter challenges and issues relating to the division of powers.

Points to Ponder

1. Given all that has happened since the Meech Lake Accord was introduced, do you think it should have been approved, and why or why not?

2. Before reading this chapter, what rights did you think you enjoyed as a Canadian, and how did they compare to the Charter rights as summarized in the Appendix to this chapter?

3. How do you feel about your constitutional rights being subject to a "notwithstanding" clause?

4. What do you think about the way the Charter has shifted the balance of power in Canadian society away from Parliament and those who control Parliament? Does the Charter empower more individuals and groups or does it mainly empower Supreme Court judges who are not elected by or accountable to anyone?

5. Does the important role which the courts play in protecting our rights and freedoms justify the kind of independence enjoyed by our judges? Should inappropriate comments and attitudes by judges be tolerated as the price to pay for judicial independence? Should the appointment of judges only be confirmed (as in the United States) after a public hearing which brings to light more about their backgrounds and values?

For Further Reading

Alan Cairns (edited by Douglas Williams), *Disruptions: Constitutional Struggles, from the Charter to Meech Lake*, Toronto, McClelland & Stewart Inc., 1991, provides an excellent analysis of the events during this period.

Paul Fox and Graham White, *Politics: Canada*, 8th Edition, Whitby, McGraw-Hill Ryerson Limited, 1995 has a number of articles in a section on the constitution and the Charter and also a section on the judiciary.

Robert Jackson and Doreen Jackson, *Politics in Canada*, 3rd Edition, Scarborough, Prentice-Hall Canada Inc., 1994, Chapter 5 provides a detailed examination of the evolution and patriation of the Canadian constitution. *Canadian Government in Transition*, 2nd Edition, 1999, by the same authors and publisher, includes both a chapter on the constitution and one on the courts.

Garth Stevenson (ed.), *Federalism in Canada*, Toronto, McClelland & Stewart Inc., 1989, contains articles on a wide-range of constitutional and federal-provincial issues.

Michael Whittington and Richard Van Loon, *Canadian Government and Politics*, Whitby, McGraw-Hill Ryerson Limited, 1996, has four chapters dealing with the constitution and the judicial process.

Information on the Supreme Court and various court decisions can be found at web site *www.scc.csc.gc.ca.*

Chapter 8

Who's On First?
Intergovernmental Relations in Canada

Objectives and Highlights

◆ To explain the shifts in dominance by the federal and provincial levels.

◆ To debate the merits of a strong federal government or strong provinces.

◆ To examine provincial-municipal relations and the impact of recent disentanglement initiatives.

Comics Abbott and Costello had a classic baseball routine entitled *"Who's on First?"* a conversation about names and positions which moved quickly into total confusion and hilarity. Much the same might be said of efforts to describe intergovernmental relations in Canada!

This chapter attempts to bring some clarity and order to this subject, in part by tracing shifts in the federal-provincial relationship over the years, from a dominant national level to increasingly assertive provinces. It examines the "fend-for-yourself" federalism that has been evolving, with each level attempting to deal with its debt problems by passing the buck to the next level down. Against this background, the chapter explores the main arguments typically advanced in favour of a strong national government and in favour of provinces. It also notes the increasing significance of international relationships, particularly those related to trade, and the impact of these on Canada's governments.

Provincial-local relations are also examined, along with the many parallels between this relationship and that found at the federal-provincial level. While efforts to disentangle and to reduce the overlap between the provincial and local level sound attractive, some cautionary comments are offered about this approach.

Introduction

As we saw in Chapter 2, Canadians have no shortage of governments supposedly attending to their needs. The result is a complex and confusing picture. It doesn't help that the governments often hide behind each other in trying to evade responsibility for unpopular or controversial situations. One such situation concerned the issue of toplessness which, in the summer of 1997, threatened to become a "tempest in a B-cup."[1] After an Ontario court ruled that a Guelph woman could stroll down the street without her top on, Premier Harris called for the federal government to amend the Criminal Code to deal with the matter. The federal Justice Minister replied that the issue might be better dealt with by local communities.

A story which has made the rounds for 20 years or more concerns the "International Conference on the Elephant"—an event to which learned scholars were invited to present a research paper on some aspect of the elephant. The highlights of the Conference featured four papers, from Britain, France, the United States and Canada. They were entitled as follows:

Britain: *The Elephant and the Empire*

France: *The Sex Life of the Elephant*

U.S.:   *How to Build Bigger and Better Elephants*

Canada: *Elephants: A Federal or Provincial Responsibility?*

That says it all. Whatever the issue, Canada usually manages to reduce it to a squabble over jurisdiction. It wasn't supposed to be this way. Sir John A. Macdonald, Canada's first Prime Minister and one of the chief architects of the governing arrangements for the new country, thought that he had allocated powers in such a way that the federal level would clearly dominate. Instead, we enter the 21st century with the

---

[1]Margaret Wente, "Tempest in a B-cup," *Globe and Mail*, June 28, 1997.

federal government reducing its role and provincial governments increasingly asserting their claims for expanded jurisdiction. What happened to Sir John's plan and what is happening to our federal system? What are the merits of a strong federal government and what are the merits of a stronger role for provinces? To answer these questions is a major purpose of this chapter.

Shifts in the Federal-Provincial Relationship

The story of the creation of the "Dominion of Canada" is familiar to most people, if only from their high school history classes. The challenge was how to establish a new country out of the separate colonies which then existed—Upper Canada or Canada West (Ontario), Lower Canada or Canada East (Québec), New Brunswick and Nova Scotia. All of the colonies were insistent on maintaining their separate identities and existence in whatever new governing structure might be formed. The solution agreed upon was the establishment of a federal state or federation. This simply means the bringing together of a number of different political communities with a common government for common purposes and separate "state" or "provincial" governments for the particular purposes of each community.[2]

Sir John A. Macdonald reluctantly accepted the idea of a federal system as the price necessary to create the new country. But he also made every effort to create a federation in which the national government was clearly the dominant level. The fact that the discussions leading up to the creation of Canada took place as civil war raged across the border in the United States certainly made an impact. The United States Constitution had attempted to provide for a strong level of state governments. The states had been given all "**residual powers**," that is, all powers not otherwise specifically assigned to the national or state level. The civil war was being fought over state rights, over which level of government in the United States would predominate. Not surprisingly, the Fathers of Confederation (led by Macdonald) took the view

---

[2]Eugene Forsey, *How Canadians Govern Themselves*, 3rd Edition, Ottawa, Ministry of Supply and Services, 1991, p. 7.

that Canada should avoid any such catastrophe by establishing a federal system in which the national level would clearly prevail.

The Division of Powers

The division of powers for the new federal system was set out in the British North America (BNA) Act of 1867,[3] particularly in sections 91 and 92 which outlined the main powers of the national and provincial levels, respectively.

Federal Government Powers
The federal government was given (among other matters):
a)   a blanket power to make laws for the "peace, order, and good government of Canada."
b)   29 examples (later increased to 31 through constitutional amendment) of this blanket power in the form of specific areas of responsibility. These included what were regarded as the most important responsibilities of government, including such areas as money and banking, defence, navigation and shipping, regulation of trade and commerce, and criminal law.
c)   unlimited taxing power.
d)   all residual power—that is, anything "left over" and not otherwise specifically assigned.
e)   the power (exercised through the office of Lieutenant Governor in each province) to reserve any provincial bill for consideration by the national government.
f)   the power to disallow any provincial Act for up to one year.
Provincial Government Powers
In contrast, the BNA Act limited the provinces to:
a)   16 specific responsibilities which were then regarded as being of a local or minor nature. These included such matters as municipal institutions, hospitals, and reform schools.
b)   direct taxation powers only.

---

[3]This Act was subsequently incorporated within the Constitution Act of 1982, as discussed in the preceding chapter.

Initial Federal Domination

Sir John A. Macdonald took full advantage of this one-sided division of powers, and the federal level dominated from 1867 until the closing years of the 19th century. In part, this domination stemmed from the leadership and sense of national vision provided by Sir John A. The railway was extended westward, to link Canada "from sea to sea," immigration policies populated the newly opened western territory, and tariff policies encouraged those in the west and east to buy the products produced by the manufacturing sector which was concentrated in Central Canada. Federal dominance was also reinforced by frequent use of the powers of **disallowance** and **reservation**.

Inevitably, of course, the provincial governments began to assert their rights and to demand that the federal government exercise more restraint, especially with respect to the use of the powers of reservation and disallowance. They received support from a series of decisions by the Judicial Committee of the British Privy Council (which was then the final court of law for Canada). These decisions had the effect of restricting the scope of the federal government while broadening the scope of the provinces.

It was during the "Roaring Twenties," however, that provincial governments enjoyed their first major expansion in power and importance. By this time, more than 50 years after Confederation, it was becoming apparent that a number of the powers given to the provinces were going to be among the most important responsibilities of government in the 20th century. While earlier economic growth had been stimulated by such national initiatives as railway construction and immigration, the 1920s saw the expansion of highways and the development of mineral wealth—both matters under provincial jurisdiction. In addition, this period saw increased provincial (and municipal) expenditures on education and public welfare.

The provincial momentum was short-lived, however, and various events conspired to promote a resurgence of national domination over the next 40 years. The main influences were:

> A number of factors led to federal dominance from the 1930s to the 1960s.

a) the Depression of the 1930s, which reduced several provinces to near bankruptcy and led the federal government to assume a substantial responsibility for relief payments (welfare).
b) the Second World War, in which the extreme centralization of activities brought Canada close to being a unitary state. By the end of the war in 1945, the federal government accounted for 82% of all government spending, with the provinces and local governments each spending roughly half of the rest.
c) the post-war management of the economy, which called for federal government actions with respect to the promotion of employment, economic growth and stable prices. By this time, most western nations had embraced "**Keynesian economics**,"[4] which was based on the use of government taxing and spending policies (and complementary monetary policies through the banking system) to offset fluctuations in the economy and ensure growth and prosperity.

There were also other factors at work in this post-war period. The federal government had built up a highly qualified group of civil servants during the war years and that gave it some extra credibility and "clout" for a time. Beginning during the war years, there had been considerable centralization of finances. The details need not concern us here, but essentially the provinces—in return for substantially enlarged grants from the federal level—stayed out of the three major tax fields of corporate tax, income tax and succession duties. This arrangement was intended to ensure better coordination of these tax fields (since both levels of government had been active in them) and to make easier the pursuit of Keynesian economics by the federal government.

Another major factor at this time was the expanded use of what became known as the "**federal spending power**." This is the power of the federal government to make payments to people or institutions or governments for purposes for which it does not necessarily have the power to legislate. During the period of economic growth and prosperity that followed World War II, it seemed appropriate that the federal government should use its powers to tax wealth wherever it might be concentrated in Canada and then to redistribute that wealth for the

---

[4]So-called because it was based on the writings of British economist John Maynard Keynes.

benefit of all by supporting various social programs. Since these programs helped to shore up incomes and maintain consumer spending, they were seen as making a positive contribution to economic growth. By the 1960s, approximately one-third of the expenditures of the federal government were largely based on this federal spending power—for such areas as family allowances, Canada Pension Plan, Old Age Security, Unemployment Insurance, Hospital Insurance, higher education, equalization payments, and regional economic development subsidies.

Many of these areas have been in the news in recent years. In most cases, they have become "an item" because the federal government has withdrawn or reduced its financial commitment to these programs, or is contemplating such action. This curtailment of the federal spending power reflects the greatly reduced role which the federal government has accepted (and has had forced upon it) in more recent times. What happened to the federal dominance which seemed so enduring from the 1930s through to the 1960s?

Pendulum Swings to Provinces

To some extent, it was a case of the pendulum having swung so far one way that it inevitably had to swing back. Among the factors contributing to this reversal were the following:

a) Post-war urbanization triggered a big increase in spending by provinces (and their municipalities), putting them in a "revenue squeeze." This led the provinces to demand more grant money from Ottawa or a greater proportion of the three tax fields which had been rented out to, or shared with, Ottawa since World War II.

b) As provinces developed highly qualified public services of their own, they were less inclined to defer to the expertise of the federal public service.

c) The long period of national dominance had featured Liberal governments in Ottawa; in fact, the Liberals were in power for 22 consecutive years from 1935 to 1957. John Diefenbaker's upset election victory in 1957 was partly based on an appeal to the "forgotten regions" outside of Central Canada and a promise to pay more attention to provincial rights. It would be 1968 before a Liberal government again enjoyed a majority in Ottawa, and by then a number of factors made it impossible to resume the old, centralist ways.

d) One of those factors was a marked shift in the position and demands of Québec after 1960. That year saw the election of a Liberal government under Jean Lesage which introduced a wide range of reforms to modernize Québec society. These reforms were very expensive and the provincial Liberals put increasing pressure on Ottawa for a greater share of the tax fields—demanding what became known as more **"tax room."**

e) Québec's demands fell on responsive ears when the Liberals returned to power in Ottawa with a minority government in 1963. Under Lester Pearson's leadership, the federal government presided over an era which became known as **cooperative federalism**. It has been praised for demonstrating the flexibility of federalism, thereby undermining (at the time) the separatist threat in Québec. It has also been condemned for making too many concessions to the provinces and undermining the role of the federal government.

f) While the issue of Québec separation has never been far below the surface in the intervening years, it should be noted that there have also been rumblings from other parts of the country as well. Western provinces expressed dissatisfaction with a number of policies of the federal government and decried Ottawa's failure to understand the needs of the west. Some organizations advocating western separation appeared and disappeared. At least some of the strong western support for the Reform Party is essentially a western protest vote. Maritime Union has also been discussed from time to time, but the Atlantic provinces have tended to be the most supportive of a strong role for the federal government because of their reliance on financial assistance from Ottawa.

g) By the 1980s, there was a general feeling of discontent with the size and prominence of the federal government and a fairly widespread viewpoint that further decentralization of power would be beneficial. This view was consistent with the right wing and somewhat anti-government sentiment which had become pronounced by this point in countries such as Britain (under Margaret Thatcher) and the United States (under Ronald Reagan). If "getting government off the backs of people" was the objective, the next best thing was to shift the responsibility for decision making by government as close to the people as possible. By this reasoning, a shift of powers from the national to the provincial level was a step in the right direction.

h) The rationale for a strong national government which had been provided by Keynesian economics was discredited by developments during the 1980s, as discussed in Chapter 10. While Keynesian policies were designed to address a problem of either inflation or unemployment, the 1980s saw a prolonged period of both problems—or what became known as stagflation. Attention shifted from fiscal policies pursued by a strong federal government to the elimination of inflation through monetary policies pursued by the Bank of Canada. Federal fiscal policies were also constrained by the fact that the provinces had become major players in spending and taxation, making it very difficult to pursue one, consistent policy for the nation. The fact that federal deficits and total public debt were climbing sharply through the 1980s also reduced the federal government's flexibility with respect to fiscal policies.

i) As the 1980s unfolded, even the federal government seemed willing to accept (or to promote) a reduction in its role. This was evident in the positions which had been taken by the governments of both Joe Clark and Brian Mulroney. In the case of the latter, Ottawa agreed to some decentralization of powers in unsuccessful attempts to amend the constitution of Canada through the Meech and then the Charlottetown Accords, both discussed in the previous chapter.

j) Even with the Liberals in office since 1993, the federal government has shown a continued willingness to accept a reduced national role. To some extent, the motivation is again one of hoping to placate the provinces (and especially Québec) by offering them greater jurisdiction in such areas as employment training, mines, forestry, tourism and recreation. In addition, however, the federal government was also strongly motivated by its desire to reduce its expenditures and bring its deficit and debt load under control. As noted earlier, much of the national expenditure has been on the exercise of the federal spending power, which has been criticized as allowing too much federal encroachment into areas of provincial jurisdiction. Ottawa's position almost seemed to be:

"Since our support for these programs isn't wanted, and we can't afford it anyway, we'll withdraw that support."

k) By the 1990s, the federal government felt itself to be increasingly constrained by global economic developments. As noted in Chapter 1, the increasing internationalization of economic activity put great pressure on national governments to accommodate business interests or run the risk of losing them to other jurisdictions. Much of this accommodation took the form of expenditure and program cuts and downloading of responsibilities and costs—all of which diminished the role and importance of the federal government. Thus power was flowing from the federal government in several directions—upward to the global and continental levels, outward to the market, and downward to the provinces. Indeed, Clarkson and Lewis goes so far as to suggest that the federal state in Canada "has become so tightly interconnected with governance above and below that it is now just one tier in an evolving and nested multi-level state structure."[5]

The Beginning of a new Social Union?

The pendulum swing to the provinces is also reflected in the various proposals which have been advanced for a new social union for Canada. Considerable impetus came from a paper by Courchene,[6] which served as the basis for Ontario's advancement of this concept at a conference of Premiers in 1996. This paper contended that the federal government now provided insufficient money to the provinces to give it the moral authority to enforce national standards. It also argued that Canada-wide identical standards were inappropriate anyway, given the diversity of provincial economies and the increasingly north-south economic pull of international trade. While it outlined an interim model that was less radical, the paper ultimately proposed that full responsibility for the design and delivery of health, welfare and education should be assigned to the provinces. It acknowledged the likelihood of spillovers (impacts extending beyond the boundaries of any one province), but explained that these would be handled through the development of an interprovincial accord and the establishment of a federal-provincial monitoring body. Response to the Courchene paper was divided, largely on the basis of whether one saw it as advocating more decentralization or providing a realistic adjustment to the decentralization already underway.

---

[5]Stephen Clarkson and Timothy Lewis, "The Contested State," in Leslie A. Pal (ed.), *How Ottawa Spends 1999-2000*, Toronto, Oxford University Press, 1999, p. 327.

[6]Thomas J. Courchene, *ACCESS: A Convention on the Canadian Economic and Social System*, a working paper prepared for the Ontario Ministry of Intergovernmental Affairs, August 1996.

At the annual Premiers' conference in August 1998, all 10 provinces agreed that:

- Ottawa should get the permission of the provinces before establishing any new social programs, *even* those that are entirely funded by the federal government.
- If an individual province did not concur, it could "opt out" and be fully compensated for the money that Ottawa would have spent in its jurisdiction.
- A framework agreement, to be called the social union, should be reached between Ottawa and the provinces, setting out mutually agreed upon rules for social programs.

On February 4, 1999, the federal government and nine of the provinces (not including Québec) signed a new social union agreement. Québec officials contend that the original social union deal restricting federal spending power, worked out the previous summer, had come unravelled when Ottawa threatened to withhold new money for health care. Under the new provisions:[7]

- the initiation of new social programs would require the agreement of the federal government and any six provinces.
- the provision for opting out of any new programs with full compensation is not part of the new agreement.
- there is a commitment to eliminate, in three years, policies that discriminate against newcomers from other provinces with respect to post-secondary education, training, health and other social services.
- funds transferred by Ottawa to the provinces must be used for the purpose for which they were intended. More than $5 billion in additional funds for health care will be transferred over a three year period.
- third party mediation will be sought, if both parties agree, whenever disputes arise over such things as what is permissible under the federal medicare legislation, which bans user fees and extra billing.
- regular reports will be made on the performance of social programs.
- Ottawa will give at least one year's notice before any future cuts to its financial support for social programs, and will consult with the

---

[7]The summary which follows is largely based on Edison Stewart, "Premiers cement 'new era' with PM," *Toronto Star*, February 5, 1999.

provinces before launching any new social programs that it finances exclusively.

How this new social union agreement will work in practice remains to be seen. Richard Gwyn finds little of significance in the agreement, which is mainly a vehicle through which Ottawa can give billions to the provinces for health care, and which the provinces (except Québec which didn't sign) have promised to spend on health care.[8] He is not surprised at Québec's relatively low key response to being left out of a joint agreement once again, noting that it still gets its full proportion of the new money being provided while not having to abide by the "mobility rights" clause in the new agreement which requires provinces not to discriminate against other Canadians. Gwyn contends that the new money for health care would have been forthcoming even without the social union agreement—simply because of the improved federal revenue position and the obvious public desire for health care spending. He concludes that "the entire social union debate thus has ended up as a device for Chrétien and the premiers to make themselves look good by spending other peoples' money (the taxpayer) the way those same people, as voters, most want it to be spent."[9]

Passing the Buck:
Changes in Federal-Provincial Financial Relations

From the time of Confederation, there has seldom been a very good balance between the expenditure commitments of a level of government and the revenues available to it. Because it was believed in 1867 that the federal government had been given all of the important powers, it also received unlimited taxing powers, whereas the provinces were limited to direct taxation.[10] As the provinces gradually expanded their

---

[8]Richard Gwyn, "Trying to swallow the fudge of the social union," *Toronto Star*, February 7, 1999.

[9]*Ibid.*

[10]The distinction is that a direct tax is levied upon the person expected to pay it, whereas an indirect tax is levied with the expectation that it will be passed on to a third party. A good example of an indirect tax is a wholesale tax which is absorbed and becomes part of the final price for a product paid by the consumer.

responsibilities, their expenditures inevitably increased beyond the level which had been anticipated. This change became particularly apparent during the 1920s, when provincial and municipal expenditures increased at more than five times the national rate annually.

By this time, the federal government was providing various subsidies to the provinces, including some conditional grants which had first been introduced in 1912. It was also providing special subsidies to the Maritime provinces in recognition of the economic disparities in this region. By this time as well, both the federal and provincial governments were levying corporate and income taxes, with the federal government having imposed the latter tax in 1917 *as a temporary measure* to finance the First World War.

The problems with this "double taxation" became particularly apparent when the Great Depression hit in the 1930s. One response, first introduced during World War II, was a series of five year agreements covering how the national and provincial government would share the fields of corporate tax, income tax and succession duties. However, as the provinces (and municipalities) increased their expenditures in response to the rapid urbanization following the war, there

Sharing the Taxes

was continued pressure on the federal government to increase the provincial share, to give the provinces more tax room.

By the late 1970s, **tax sharing** effectively ended. The federal government indicated that in setting its own rates it would "take account of" provincial rates. But the provinces became responsible for setting their own rates to meet their expenditure needs. In effect, the federal government told the provinces that they should accept responsibility for increasing their tax levels as needed, rather than expect the national level to forego its revenues by levying less tax to make more room for them.

Throughout this postwar period, a number of national government grants to the provinces had also developed. Briefly, these were:

Federal Grants in early post-war period
a) Federal payments to share in the costs of hospital care.
b) Federal payments to share in the cost of physicians' services.
c) Federal payments in support of post-secondary education.
d) The Canada Assistance Program (**CAP**) to support and bring more standardization to widely varied provincial social programs.
e) Equalization payments provided to the provinces with weaker tax bases so that they could provide services at an adequate level without imposing excessively high levels of taxation

In 1977 the federal government replaced the first three grant programs with something called **EPF** or Established Program Financing. This was a block grant which was essentially unconditional in nature—except that there were requirements relating to access in health care (which became a major issue) and to non-discrimination in education. The new arrangements were less satisfactory than the federal level had hoped. Its financial commitment continued to grow, but provinces took advantage of the relatively unconditional nature of the payments and used some of the money for priorities other than health and education. In response, the national government passed the Canada Health Act in 1984, with its financial penalty for provinces allowing extra-billing or user charges by hospitals—as discussed in the next chapter.

The following year (1985) saw the first in what became an ongoing series of cuts in federal transfers to the provinces as part of the national deficit reduction efforts. By 1990-1991 a two year freeze on payments under EPF was introduced, and then extended through to the end of 1994-95. The Ontario Government estimated that the total revenue loss to all provinces resulting from these changes to the EPF formula added up to $33.6 billion.[11] A similar pattern occurred with the Canada Assistance Plan. A 5% "cap" on the growth of payments to Ontario, British Columbia and Alberta was introduced in 1990-91 and then extended through 1994-95. With this cap in place, payments to those three provinces did not keep pace with the increase in welfare costs associated

---

[11]According to Paul Hobson, "Current Issues in Federal-Provincial Fiscal Relations," in Ronald Watts and Doug Brown (eds.), *Canada: The State of the Federation, 1993,* Queen's University, 1993, p. 181.

with the prolonged recession in the early 1990s. While the federal level had been paying 50% of the Canada Assistance Plan costs, the result of the cap is that this proportion fell to 47% for Alberta, 37% for British Columbia and 28% for Ontario.

Further major changes have been introduced by the federal Liberals since they assumed office in October 1993. Both EPF and the Canada Assistance Plan were replaced, effective

> Replacing EPF and CAP with the less conditional CHST was a major change.

the 1996-97 fiscal year, with a new Canada Health and Social Transfer (**CHST**). It is a block fund, like the EPF which it replaced. Soon after its introduction, the federal government announced that the CHST would be reduced by more than $6 billion over the period of 1996-98.

In his 1996 budget, Finance Minister Paul Martin pledged that the cash portion of the transfers under the CHST[12] would not be allowed to fall below $11 billion, and that this money could and would be used as a lever to ensure that provinces didn't cut corners and erode the social safety net. By the time of the federal election in 1997, the Liberals were promising to cancel any further cuts to the CHST.

As of the 1998-99 fiscal year, the following three programs represented 95% of all federal transfers to the provinces and territories.[13]

- CHST transfers in the amount of $26 billion—up from $25.1 billion in 1997-98 and projected to grow to $28.5 billion by 2002-03. The cash portion of these transfers was guaranteed to be $12.5 billion or more each year, up from the $11 billion pledged in 1996.

- Equalization payments of $8.5 billion to the "have-not" provinces.[14]

- Transfers to the territorial governments in the North of $1.1 billion.

---

[12]Even more money is transferred in the form of "tax room," which essentially converts what would have been federal tax revenues into provincial revenues.

[13]Ministry of Finance, *Federal Transfers to Provinces and Territories*, as downloaded on July 31, 1998 from its web site *www.fin.gc.ca/fed/prove*.

[14]These are the provinces which, according to a complex and controversial formula, are least prosperous—as distinct from the "have" provinces of Ontario, British Columbia and Alberta.

The provinces continued to call for restoration of the $6 billion which had been cut from the CHST in the mid-1990s, especially as the federal government moved from its chronic budget deficit situation to one in which a substantial surplus was anticipated. This issue became joined with provincial demands for a new social union (discussed above), in which the provinces would gain authority at the expense of Ottawa with respect to social programs. As noted above, a watered-down social union agreement was reached between the federal government and all provinces but Québec in February 1999, under which more than $5 billion of additional transfers for health care will come to the provinces over a three year period. The provinces are far from satisfied with these initial financial gains, however, and in late November 1999 they were demanding an emergency meeting with the Prime Minister to discuss their priorities for the growing federal cash surplus.[15]

Leaks in the Watertight Compartments

Underlying the shifts in the balance of power and financial arrangements between the federal and provincial levels, there has also been a growing overlap in activities, a growing encroachment by one level into the sphere of the other. This has happened in spite of the best intentions of the framers of the constitution who thought that they had so clearly divided the responsibilities of government that they were sealed in **watertight compartments**. Instead, a great deal of seepage has occurred over the years.

According to Stevenson, the only areas of exclusive federal jurisdiction appear to be military defence, veterans' affairs, Indian affairs and monetary policy; and provinces only have exclusive jurisdiction for municipal institutions, elementary and secondary education, and some areas of law related to property and to non-criminal matters.[16]

---

[15]Robert McKenzie, "Premiers demand cash crisis talks," *Toronto Star*, November 27, 1999.

[16]Garth Stevenson, "Federalism and Intergovernmental Relations," in Michael Whittington and Glen Williams (eds.), *Canadian Politics in the 1990s*, 4th Edition, Scarborough, Nelson Canada, 1995, p. 410.

The provinces claim that the overlapping of government activity has occurred because of federal encroachment into their fields, and in this regard we have already noted the use of the federal spending power with respect to social programs. But

> It's a two-way street:
>
> The provinces have also moved into various areas of federal jurisdiction.

it should also be recognized that provinces have intruded into a number of areas of federal jurisdiction.[17] Most larger provinces are active in the field of international trade and commerce, have departments dedicated to that field, and have trade missions in foreign capitals. The larger provinces also assert their right to deal directly with foreign governments on a variety of issues. Provinces such as Newfoundland and British Columbia have been active in fisheries, which is an area of federal jurisdiction. Western provinces and Québec have moved into the federal jurisdiction over "Indians and land reserved for Indians." Ontario and Québec are actively involved in television broadcasting, for which they claim jurisdiction because of the educational nature of the programs, even though broadcasting was placed under federal jurisdiction by court ruling in 1932.

We should also be careful not to assume that areas of overlap are automatically problem areas. Overlap, in which two governments are involved in the same field, is not necessarily the same as duplication, in which two governments are doing the same thing in the same field. Overlap also does not necessarily mean conflict. It can lead to beneficial collaboration and coordination. Indeed, it can be argued that overlap is preferable to watertight compartments (completely separate jurisdictions) as a way to govern because it provides some flexibility, encourages a variety of approaches through comparison and competition, and avoids a monopoly situation.

---

[17]The examples which follow are from Garth Stevenson, "The Division of Powers," in R. D. Olling and M. M. Westmacott (eds.), *Perspectives on Canadian Federalism*, Scarborough, Prentice-Hall Canada Inc., 1988, p. 44.

Draining the Watertight Compartments

Even those who might agree with the desirability of reducing overlap and clarifying the division of responsibilities between the federal and provincial governments worry about the end result of any such redefinition. The prevailing forces in the country appear to favour decentralization as the means of reducing overlap. Shifting powers from the federal level to the provinces would appear to meet the federal objective of reducing its financial obligations and the provincial objective (especially of provinces like Québec) of gaining increased jurisdiction.

♦ Something to Think About

But what are the implications for Canada of such a shift? What are the arguments for reasserting a strong role for the federal government versus strengthening the provincial level?

The Case for Strong Provinces

Defenders of the provinces start by noting that the reference to "levels" of government (as is found throughout this Guide) improperly implies some sort of superior-subordinate relationship. Instead, they argue that what we have is two "orders" of government, each with its own constitutional sphere of authority.[18] They contend that the national interest should not be defined and/or imposed by the federal government; rather, it should emerge from intergovernmental negotiations. They claim that provinces have shown themselves able to work together effectively. To those critical of provincial trade barriers, for example, they point to the June 1994 agreement to reform government procurement practices, to set rules to prevent provinces "poaching" investment from each other and to increase labour mobility between provinces.[19]

---

[18]The arguments in this section are partly based on R. A. Young, "What is Good About Provincial Governments?" in Mark Charlton and Paul Barker (eds.), *Crosscurrents: Contemporary Political Issues*, 2nd Edition, Scarborough, Nelson, 1994, pp. 124-136.

[19]Christopher Dunn, *Canadian Political Debates*, Toronto, McClelland & Stewart Inc., 1995, p. 136.

Provinces should play a prominent role, it is argued, because they have demonstrated a great deal of innovation and creativity, often stimulating the adoption of their approaches in other jurisdictions. Examples include the introduction of Medicare in Saskatchewan, the Québec Pension Plan, New Brunswick's introduction of the Ombudsman, the first condominium legislation from British Columbia, and the first law protecting historic sites in Québec.[20] Having a strong level of provincial governments, proponents claim, provides more outlets for experimentation and innovation, for comparisons and competitive pressures—all forces which contribute to better government. Moreover, if there are mistakes made, their impact is more limited in a provincial laboratory than had the flawed program been Canada-wide.

It is conceded that competition amongst the provinces can also become harmful and destructive, that it can lead to a "race to the bottom," in which—for example—provinces keep reducing environmental regulations or "rights of workers" legislation in an attempt to make their jurisdiction more attractive to business. But those favouring strong provinces point out that a dominant federal government which promotes centralized conformity to the lowest common denominator is also harmful. Such an arrangement results in the imposition of central standards which are unlikely to match the varying needs and preferences of different parts of the country.

Even those supporting strong provinces see a continued important role for the federal government. It must provide those public goods which provincial governments have little incentive to provide and those goods for which economies of scale are possible from delivery over the whole country. It must bring together and accommodate regional interests on truly national questions and it must act as a referee in cases of destructive interprovincial competition. It must "build the fundamental commonalities of Canadian citizenship."[21] But it should learn to play a more modest, limited role. It should gather and disseminate information as a way of promoting better public policy rather than trying to dictate policy on its terms. For example, comparative information on the stand-

---

[20]*Ibid.*, p. 128.

[21]*Ibid.*, p. 130.

ards and levels of service which exist in the various provinces would alert citizens to resist efforts by a province trying to downgrade services.

Young argues that the federal government would not lose, but gain, legitimacy, through decentralization of social programs—especially if it retains a monitoring function and becomes a source of information and expertise.[22] In his view, there is more to be gained from the federal government building a role as an umpire of interprovincial disputes than from it directly delivering programs which cause the provinces to criticize it as domineering.

The Case for a Strong National Government

One of the most forceful and best known proponents of a strong national government is former Prime Minister Pierre Trudeau. At a Montreal news conference in March 1990, he offered this challenge: "Canadians have to make up their minds. Do they want a loose confederation of provinces, that exists courtesy of the provincial governments—or do they want a real country with a real government?"

Advocates of a strong national government believe that it is the only institution capable of asserting and protecting the national interest.[23] They reject the notion that the sum total of the various separate provincial interests can somehow be added up and combined to form a national interest. They contend that Canada is a national community defined by the Charter, not a variety of distinct communities and cultures with their own collective rights which clash with the individual rights guaranteed to all Canadians by the Charter.

Proponents of a strong national government also see it as an essential vehicle for ensuring minimum standards of service in areas which help to define us as Canadians. They point to the marked disparities in economic health and income levels among the regions of Canada and argue that only a strong national government is in a position to tax the wealth wherever it may be concentrated in Canada, and then to redis-

---

[22]Robert Young, "Defending Decentralization," *Policy Options*, Montreal, Institute for Research on Public Policy, March 1997, p. 44.

[23]The arguments which follow are partly based on M. M. Westmacott, "Conflicting Constitutional Visions: Is There a Case for a Strong National Government?" in Charlton and Barker, *op. cit.*, pp. 117-123.

tribute it to where it is most needed. They reject the notion that desired national standards could somehow be achieved through interprovincial cooperation, pointing to the failure of the provinces (in spite of the June 1994 agreement cited above) even to eliminate the costly internal trade barriers which currently inhibit the free movement of goods and services in Canada.[24]

Those backing a strong national government concede that it must do a better job of articulating and accommodating provincial and regional interests. They acknowledge the need for reform of national institutions like the Senate, which was originally designed precisely for the purpose of representing and protecting regional interests within the new country of Canada. They even acknowledge that flexibility is needed to respond to the different needs of different provinces and concede that, to allow these arrangements, **asymmetrical federalism** may be necessary.[25] But they insist that the federal government should retain an over-riding constitutional authority to assert the national interest and that there should be no limits placed on the use of the federal spending power in support of such interests.

Both points of view have merit and deserve careful study. If we are facing a diminished role by government within our lives, it may still be important which level of government carries out that reduced role. In considering this issue, however, it should be borne in mind that Canada probably has the world's most decentralized federal system.[26] This assessment is based on the fact that:

---

[24]The Premiers did come close to an agreement on removing internal trade barriers during their annual conference in 1997, but the initiative apparently failed because of resistance from British Columbia's Premier Glen Clark.

[25]This cumbersome term is used to describe a federal system which would not have an identical relationship between the federal government and every province. Instead of that "symmetry," bilateral agreements would give some provinces different arrangements (such as greater decentralization of powers) than others — resulting in an asymmetrical federalism.

[26]This is certainly the view of Andrew Coyne, "The Case for Strengthening Federal Powers," *Policy Options*, Montreal, IRPP, April 1997, from which the following points are drawn.

- From a post-war peak of 70%, the federal government now retains only about one-third of all government revenues for its purposes.
- Canada is the only federation in the world without a working internal common market, nor any means of enforcing it.
- It is the only federation in the world in which any province may borrow money as it sees fit, without regard to the consequences for the rest.
- In no other federation, has the First Ministers Conference (or its equivalent) evolved into the sort of parallel government that it has become in Canada.

At a time when international developments and trading agreements are increasingly constraining the operations of the federal government (as discussed in Chapter 10), is it wise to weaken the federal government further through additional decentralization to the provinces?

Municipalities in the Canadian Federation

Intergovernmental relations in Canada involve more than the federal-provincial relationship. There have also been shifts and pendulum swings in the relationship between municipalities and the senior levels of government. There are, however, some fundamental differences in the nature of these relationships which should be noted at the outset.

Notwithstanding the best efforts of Sir John A. to establish a dominant national level, the relationship between the federal and provincial governments is essentially one between two equals. Each level of government has a guaranteed right to exist under the constitution of Canada, and each has a number of responsibilities specifically assigned to it. Neither level can abolish the other. In contrast, the relationship between municipal and provincial governments is completely different in law. The two levels are not equal; municipalities are in a distinctly subordinate position. Their existence is not guaranteed by the constitution. Nor are they given any specific powers under the constitution. They are only mentioned in the constitution as one of the powers given to the provinces. As a result, they only exist and have structures, functions, and finances to the extent that provincial governments see fit to provide for them. Legally, a provincial government could pass a law abolishing all of the municipalities within its jurisdiction—although there are solid practical and political reasons why it would not do so.

In spite of these very significant differences, the way in which the provincial-municipal relationship has evolved offers some striking similarities to federal-provincial relations.

> There are similarities in provincial-municipal and federal-provincial relations.

- Just as the provinces were expected to play a minor role in the new country of Canada, municipalities were expected to provide only a limited range of local services, mostly related to property.
- Just as the provinces were not expected to need significant revenue sources, it was assumed that the tax on real property would be adequate to meet municipal revenue needs.
- Just as the responsibilities given to the provinces became increasingly important in the 20th century, so too did the responsibilities given to municipalities—especially by the time of the rapid urbanization following World War II.
- Just as the national government responded to the provincial revenue shortfall with a number of conditional grants and shared cost programs (under the umbrella of the federal spending power discussed earlier), the provinces responded to municipal revenue needs by offering a variety of conditional grants. As a result, municipalities found themselves intertwined with provincial administrations, and correspondingly limited in their freedom to set local priorities. Provinces turned a deaf ear to these municipal concerns, even as they made exactly the same complaints to the national level about the way federal conditional grants were limiting provincial operating freedom.

The parallels have continued throughout the 1990s. As we have seen, financial restraint efforts of the federal government have led to cuts in the transfer payments made to the provinces. To "soften the blow," the payments are being made unconditional—as with the new Canada Health and Social Transfer—so that the provinces will at least have more freedom as to how they spend less money. In exactly the same fashion, provinces have responded to their financial problems by cutting grants to municipalities but offering them the reduced funds on an unconditional basis. The Klein Government in Alberta, for example, introduced in 1994 a new unconditional grant, rolled into it a number of the existing conditional grant programs (relating to areas such as parks, public transit, policing and family support services), and then reduced the amount of money transferred over subsequent years. In a strikingly similar move, the Harris government in Ontario announced in late 1995 that the existing roads grant would be lumped with other existing unconditional grants into a new block fund, the Ontario Municipal Support Grant (MSG), and that it would be reduced in amount by 47% over the next two years. (It has since been eliminated.) A number of other grants to municipalities and local boards were also cut or phased out.[27]

For a time in the 1980s, it appeared that the provinces would also follow the example of the national government and try to deal with some of their financial problems by downloading responsibilities and costs on municipalities. Examples of this trend cited by municipalities in Ontario included recycling and "blue box" programs, court-room security, and new initiatives on transit for the disabled.[28] In recent years, more attention has been paid to the concept of **disentanglement**, but as discussed below, this process can also bring downloading, as has been the case in Ontario.

Is Disentanglement the Answer?

Disentanglement is supposed to address the extensive overlap of provincial and municipal responsibilities and activities and to reduce that overlap. On the surface, it seems similar to federal-provincial efforts to drain the flooded watertight compartments found at those levels. But there are also some important differences.

The idea, in oversimplified terms, is that municipalities should retain responsibility for local functions and the province should have responsibility for matters of province-wide concern or matters which involve income redistribution such as social service programs. Since the func-

---

[27]See Association of Municipal Clerks and Treasurers, *Municipal Administration Program*, Mississauga, AMCTO, Unit Three, Revised 1998, Lesson 1.

[28]These and other examples were given by the Association of Municipalities of Ontario and reported in *Municipal World*, St. Thomas, July 1990, p.3.

tions retained by municipalities will be local in nature, there will be less need for provincial intervention on the grounds of protecting some provincial interest. Proponents of disentanglement contend that it will result in a simpler and more streamlined system, leading to cost-savings and a more understandable and accountable arrangement for the public. In practice, however, the approaches taken by different provinces, the underlying objectives, and the results achieved have varied widely, as will be seen from the three examples which follow.[29]

The New Brunswick Experience

The earliest disentanglement initiative, and one of the most substantial, was introduced in a 1967 Program for Equal Opportunity, which addressed problems with varying service standards at the local level and financially strapped municipalities. The New Brunswick government took over responsibility for the administration of justice, welfare, and public health, and also financial responsibility for the provision of education. Property assessment and property tax collection also became provincial responsibilities. The extent of the provincial take-over, and the fact that the province replaced municipalities in providing services in rural New Brunswick, caused many to worry that the improvement in service allocation and delivery had been achieved at the price of municipal government.

The Nova Scotia Experience

The disentanglement process in Nova Scotia arose out of a provincial initiative which was originally focused on reducing the number of municipalities in the province. When the *Task Force on Local Government* reported in April 1992, it cited the position of the Union of Nova Scotia Municipalities that:[30]

> Property services should be supported by property taxes and delivered by municipal government. People services are the responsibility of the provincial government and should be financed by general provincial

---

[29]These examples are from C. Richard Tindal and Susan Nobes Tindal, *Local Government in Canada*, 5th Edition, Scarborough, Nelson, 2000, pp. 213-220.

[30]Report to the Government of Nova Scotia, *Task Force on Local Government*, April 1992, p. 11.

revenues. Both orders of government should continue efforts to reallocate the delivery and financing of services recognizing this basic principle.

The report also called for any reallocation of services to be revenue-neutral, again reflecting the position of the municipal association. More specifically, the Task Force proposed that rural municipalities would have to start providing their own policing and roads (as urban municipalities had been doing) and that the province would take over the municipal share of the administration and financing of general welfare assistance.[31]

The Liberal government elected in 1993 adopted the principle of service exchange proposed in the 1992 Task Force report. The province would provide a five year period of transition payments and, during this time, municipalities would "be relieved of responsibility for social welfare services and contributions to the cost of correctional services."[32] To offset this shift and to maintain the **fiscal neutrality** of the swap, rural municipalities would take over the costs of policing and residential streets (services already being paid for by urban municipalities). But as these changes were being implemented, the province became increasingly preoccupied with deficit reduction. As a result, it capped the amount available for equalization payments to financially weak municipalities, causing particular hardship to a number of coastal towns formerly dependent on the ground fishery.[33]

In April 1998, the province and the Union of Nova Scotia Municipalities signed a memorandum of understanding under which the municipal contribution to social service costs is to be phased out between 1998-1999 and 2002-2003. A comprehensive review of roles and responsibilities was initiated, the first phase of which involved the identification of issues affecting the provincial-local relationship. One of the concerns expressed by municipalities was that they should have more

---

[31] Allan O'Brien, *Municipal Consolidation in Canada and Its Alternatives*, Toronto, ICURR Press, May 1993, p. 18.

[32] Kell Antoft and Jack Novack, *Grassroots Democracy: Local Government in the Maritimes*, Halifax, Dalhousie University, 1998, p. 11.

[33] *Ibid.*, p. 12.

say with respect to services for which they have a financial responsibility. For example, it was argued that if municipalities are required to contribute to the cost of roads, they should have some say about the roads standards, presently determined by the province.[34] It remains to be seen whether there will be any further service exchange in Nova Scotia as a result of this ongoing review.[35]

Ontario's Disentanglement Experience

Social services figured prominently in the reallocation of responsibilities in New Brunswick and Nova Scotia, and it was also social services which launched the disentanglement process in Ontario. The *Report of the Provincial-Municipal Social Services Review* (PMSSR) recommended in 1990 that Ontario follow the lead of most other provinces and take complete responsibility for the cost of social assistance. The province agreed in principle but was not prepared to absorb the approximately $800 million in extra costs that this would entail. It also agreed in principle, but demurred in practice, when faced with the shift in services recommended by the Hopcroft report in 1991.[36] However, further discussions between the province and the Association of Municipalities of Ontario (AMO) led to a tentative agreement in January 1993, under which the province would take over municipal share of the cost of general welfare assistance. To keep the service exchange fiscally neutral, municipalities would assume responsibility for certain provincial highways and for the cost of property assessment services, and would receive reduced grant payments from the province. But within a few months AMO had rejected this agreement because of municipal anger over other initiatives taken by the province.

---

[34]These examples are from Richard Ramsay, *Report to the Union of Nova Scotia Municipalities and the Department of Housing and Municipal Affairs*, October 23, 1998, p. 8.

[35]Further information about the review process can be obtained from its web site, which is *www.munisource.org/unsm/review*.

[36]Officially titled the *Report of the Advisory Committee to the Minister of Municipal Affairs on the Provincial-Municipal Financial Relationship*, it soon became known as the Hopcroft Report after its chair.

Disentanglement returned, albeit with some important changes in approach and emphasis, following the election of the Harris government in June 1995. A *Who Does What* panel, chaired by former Toronto mayor David Crombie, was appointed on May 30, 1996, to begin a complete overhaul of who does what in the delivery and funding of many government services. The stated goal of the panel was "to ensure the very best service delivery by reducing waste, duplication and the overall cost of government at the provincial and local government levels."[37] The panel's recommendations culminated in a summary report in December 1996, which largely followed a services to property versus services to people distinction. It called for increased municipal responsibility with respect to roads, transit, ferries, airports, water and sewer systems, and policing, and increased provincial responsibility for social services (notably social assistance and child care) and education.

The Ontario government's response was a flurry of announcements in one week in mid-January of 1997, in what became known as "megaweek." Its proposed realignment of responsibilities ignored the recommendations of *Who Does What* in several key respects. In particular, the province proposed to download to municipalities increased responsibility for a number of social programs, including public housing, public health, homes for special care, long-term care, and general welfare assistance. In return, the province would assume all of the education costs previously borne by residential property tax payers.

In the face of mounting criticism and evidence that the proposed service swap was financially unfair to municipalities, the province—after consultations with the Association of Municipalities—announced a new division of responsibilities on May 1, 1997. Central to the new agreement is the fact that residential property tax payers continue to pay half of the education costs they had been financing (about $2.5 billion). However, the province now sets the education tax rate, which is to remain frozen for several years. With the money saved from not taking over all of the education financing from residential property tax payers, the province found itself able to retain a number of responsibilities

---

[37]According to Ministry of Municipal Affairs and Housing *News Release*, August 14, 1996.

relating to social programs that were to be shifted to the local level. It has kept full responsibility for long-term care and for homes for special care, rather than shifting half or all of these costs to municipalities as had been announced. The province also abandoned its plan to split welfare costs 50/50, and has continued with the existing 80/20 formula. However, this cost-sharing formula has been extended to Family Benefits Assistance, which had been 100% provincially funded, so the net result was still to shift some social assistance costs to the local level. In a further concession to municipal concerns, the province indicated that before shifting responsibility for social housing to the local level it would spend some $200 million on capital upgrades.

Since these changes were introduced, the province has dropped use of the "who does what" terminology and now refers to the exercise as a local services realignment, or LSR. There have been continuing adjustments, especially in relation to the various transition funds which were created to ensure the fiscal neutrality of the exercise. In March 1999, the province announced that effective January 1, 1999, it would share half of the municipal costs for public health and land ambulances, in part to ensure provincial standards in the delivery of these services.[38] Since provincial grant support is being adjusted to reflect this change, there is no net financial gain for municipalities. But the initiative may indicate some provincial sensitivity to the complaint that municipalities should not have to pay for services whose standards are set by the province. This is essentially the same complaint about violation of "pay for say" noted above with respect to Nova Scotia municipalities.

More Download Than Disentangle?

Consider the markedly different approaches taken in New Brunswick and Ontario. Under the Program for Equal Opportunity, the New Brunswick government took over responsibility for the administration of justice, welfare, and public health, and also financial responsibility for the provision of education. In so doing, it diminished the role of municipal governments, even to the point of abolishing rural counties and taking over direct provision of some services to rural areas. In contrast,

---

[38]Ministry of Finance Backgrounder, *Local Services Realignment—1999 Enhancements*, March 23, 1999.

the municipal level in Ontario appears to have been strengthened, not diminished, by assuming a number of additional responsibilities. At this point, however, it is unclear whether Ontario municipalities have really gained responsibilities or just additional costs. So far, the province apparently intends to continue dictating service levels and standards, contrary to the "pay for say" principle.

Municipal opinions differ on the desirability of the additional responsibilities being shifted downward, especially as between urban and rural municipalities—just as they did in response to the previous disentanglement exercise at the beginning of the 1990s. Small and rural municipalities, which are heavily represented in the Association of Municipalities of Ontario, generally supported the services to property versus services to people distinction, and were opposed to the downloading of social programs. However, the regional governments and a number of the large cities recognized the importance of social programs as a way of "connecting to diverse communities and promoting quality of life" and they also recognized that the quality of life in urban areas is "the key instrument of economic development in a global economy."[39] They were interested in the possibility of greater responsibility for social programs, *if* commensurate financial resources were also provided.

> Disentanglement became a numbers game to adhere to fiscal neutrality.

The objective of fiscal neutrality for any service swap has been a primary issue, one which has seriously compromised the whole exercise. A true disentanglement exercise would determine what services were best handled by what level of government and would then shift them accordingly, *regardless of* the financial impact. There would be "winners" and "losers" as between levels of government, but since there is only one set of taxpayers in Canada (as politicians are fond of repeating), then the overall impact would balance out. If provincial costs went up as a result of a service swap, municipal costs would go down by a corresponding amount and the total provincial and municipal taxes paid should remain about the same.

---

[39]Katherine A. Graham and Susan D. Phillips, "Who Does What in Ontario: The Process of Provincial-Municipal Disentanglement." *Canadian Public Administration*, Summer 1998, pp. 194 and 205.

Whatever superficial logic this theoretical argument has, it totally ig-nores political reality. It matters greatly to governments which level is perceived as spending more or less—especially in the current climate. As a result, the disentanglement exercises of the 1990s have had as an over-riding objective the achievement of fiscal neutrality, a pledge that neither level of government will be better or worse off financially as a result of any service swap. The requirement of this objective is under-standable on one level, but it effectively destroys the disentanglement exercise. One cannot shift functions to the level where they most logically belong; one must manipulate the final service swap in such a way as to balance the books.

The extent to which this financial requirement can distort disen-tanglement is painfully apparent in Ontario. Logic, and the recommen-dations of a series of previous studies including those of the *Who Does What* panel, suggested that the province should retain, or assume even greater responsibility for, various social programs. If it wished to take over responsibility for education as well, so be it. The result would be an increase in provincial costs and a corresponding decrease in munici-pal costs. Instead, the combined forces of the fiscal neutrality pledge and the provincial government's own financial and tax-cutting priorities reduced the disentanglement exercise to "basic arithmetic." Since the province wanted education, it needed to download enough other ser-vices to offset that cost. This largely explains why social housing, which wasn't even part of the *Who Does What* panel's deliberations, got tossed into the mix.[40]

The Ontario experience is also instructive in another regard. If inappropriate responsibilities are downloaded, the end result is to in-crease entanglement, not to decrease it. The services which most logi-cally belong under municipal jurisdiction are those which can vary in their provision and their standards from place to place. The great attrac-tion of a separate level of municipal government is that it allows citizens in different jurisdictions to choose different servicing priorities through their elected councils. But such variations are not an advantage if they occur with respect to services which need to be provided at a minimum

---

[40]*Ibid.*, p. 187.

standard across Ontario. If those services fall under municipal jurisdiction, then concerns arise about a lack of common standards, and
about problems caused by spillovers and externalities. This is the situation we now face in Ontario. The province has downloaded responsibilities with respect to water and sewage treatment facilities, social
housing, public health programs, highways, public transit, and a variety
of other matters. Will service standards be maintained, especially by
municipal governments facing a serious financial squeeze?

Lessons on the Road to Amberley

This is essentially the same question which has
long been posed in the federal-provincial domain, when provinces demand greater freedom
to make their own service arrangements. It is
epitomized by the public concern over medicare and whether a strong federal presence is
the best way of resisting the development of a
two tier (private and public) health care system. The questions have been nicely joined in
an article by Thomas Walkom,[41] in which he
invited those who support the provincial call
for a social union in which they would have
more say over social programs to hold their
meetings (in the winter of 1999) in Amberley, Ontario. They would find
that they could not get there, which is the point he wants to make.

Amberley is a small community near the Lake Huron shoreline,
which used to be accessed from no fewer than four provincial highways.
All of these highways have been downloaded to the municipal level. As
a result, road standards, snowplowing, even speed limits, abruptly
change as one moves from one county jurisdiction to another. According to Walkom, in the winter of 1999 the radio routinely reported that
county authorities had pulled their plows off the roads. The police
responded by closing the roads, and local residents were advised to
"hunker down and wait out the weather." In his view, the lesson from

---

[41]Thomas Walkom, "Drive slowly: Offloading dangers ahead," *Toronto Star*,
January 12, 1999.

all this is that function follows form. "If you want to destroy a provincial highway network, hand off responsibility for roads to local government. If you want to disable a national medicare system, give more authority over enforcement to the provinces."[42]

One need not go as far as Walkom to have reservations about the impact of downloading responsibilities. The Ontario government appears to recognize the potential dangers by providing that municipal performance must adhere to provincial standards which will be developed or enhanced. These standards may well be desirable or necessary to ensure at least minimum conditions with respect to such services as water supply, sewage disposal, or public health programs. But the result is a provincial-municipal relationship which is arguably more entangled, not less.

Ultimately, it may be that efforts at disentanglement are not only flawed in ways described above, but pointless or inappropriate. The needs of citizens may best be addressed by more than one level of government. For example, "acknowledging the legitimate local interest in human-service delivery, while retaining responsibility for income redistribution at the provincial level, would contribute to recognition of the diversity of circumstances and need across communities and affirm a vital role for local governments in the social domain."[43]

Concluding Observations

Canada enters the 21st century with the distribution of powers and financial resources in its federal system fundamentally changed. The long period of national domination is clearly over, and has been for some time. The federal government has allowed itself to be weakened and constrained by a variety of forces, both internal and external.

Its prominent role in managing the economy has been largely reduced to one of holding inflation down, mostly through the efforts of the Bank of Canada. Keynesian economic policies have lost favour and,

---

[42] *Ibid.*

[43] Graham and Phillips, *op. cit.*, p. 205.

in any event, the federal government's ability to pursue fiscal policies has been limited by the fact that the provincial level is now a major player in terms of government expenditures and taxation. The widely held view that government must continue decreasing expenditures to offset past spending excesses also rules out the use of expansionist fiscal policies to stimulate growth and employment. Transferring powers to the provinces is one way of trying to reduce federal expenditures, and it serves the added purpose of responding to the incessant demands (from many, but not all, provinces) for expanded jurisdiction. Another way of reducing federal expenditures is by cutting transfer payments to the provinces. These cuts are made more palatable by reducing the conditions attached to the use of the money, which also reduces the influence of the federal government and its ability to maintain and enforce national standards. A further constraint is the global economy, in which any kind of government management of, or intervention in, the operation of the economy is not welcome.

With the use of the federal spending power sharply curtailed, it is unlikely that the federal government will launch major new national programs underwritten by substantial funding. As noted earlier in this chapter, the provinces didn't limit federal spending initiatives as much as they had originally hoped, but under the social union agreement reached in February 1999, the concurrence of the federal government and any six provinces is required for the initiation of any new national social programs and the federal government is even obliged to consult with the provinces before launching any new social programs which it finances exclusively.

While acknowledging the federal government's decreased ability to enforce national standards, Gibbins argues that the universality of social programs will be maintained through court action. He points out that "the Supreme Court as a national institution has far greater potential than Parliament to impose a degree of policy homogeneity from sea to sea, for its jurisdiction is not limited to the federal sphere."[44]

---

[44]Roger Gibbins, "Taking Stock: Canadian Federalism and Its Constitutional Framework," in Pal, *op. cit.*, p. 207.

While the provinces might be expected to step into the vacuum at the centre created by the declining role of the federal government, that development is by no means automatic. The provinces have great difficulty in presenting a united front on most subjects, not only because of Québec's isolation but also because a number of the have-not provinces prefer to see a continued strong role for the federal government, from which they have benefited. In addition, most provincial governments are preoccupied with the same cutback and downsizing mentality that has gripped the federal government, which limits their ability to take on a larger role.

If the senior levels of government continue to "pass the buck" downward—both literally and figuratively—what does this mean for the local level? Will the level of government which has usually been regarded as the least important (if regarded at all) emerge as the most important level of government for the 21st century? The pendulum is unlikely to swing that far, but the reallocation of responsibilities currently underway in Ontario, for example, certainly suggests that municipalities will become more prominent—if they can survive the functional and financial load being thrust upon them. Ironically, the amalgamations being forced on municipalities in several provinces are producing some very large cities and regions which may become increasingly important players in the global economy, players who will become reluctant to stay under the thumb of the provinces that created them. Under the circumstances, it would seem wise for the 6 voters in 10 who typically do not vote in municipal elections to start paying more attention to those chosen to govern at this level

The Last Word

Definition of Terms and Concepts

Asymmetrical Federalism:
A term to describe the fact that Canada's federal system does not involve identical relationships (perfect symmetry) between the federal government and all provinces.

CAP:
Canada Assistance Program, under which the federal government paid 50% of certain provincial social assistance programs.

CHST:
Canada Health and Social Transfer, a new block grant from the federal government, replacing CAP and EPF.

Cooperative Federalism:
A term given to describe the era of enhanced consultation and cooperation in federal-provincial relations which was particularly associated with the period when Lester Pearson was Prime Minister in the 1960s.

Disallowance:
Power of the federal government (now fallen into disuse) to disallow or quash any provincial act up to one year after its passage.

Disentanglement:
A process designed to redistribute responsibilities between levels of government, so that there is less overlap. The objective is to simplify the allocation of functions so that citizens can more easily see which level of government is responsible for what, and enforce accountability.

EPF:
Established Program Funding (or Financing), a block grant introduced in 1977 to replace three conditional grants for hospitals, physicians' services and post-secondary education.

Federal Spending Power:
> The power of the federal government to spend money in areas in which it does not necessarily have the power to legislate. Used to underwrite and promote national standards in a variety of programs, especially social programs.

Fiscal Neutrality:
> A pledge that neither level of government would be better or worse off financially as a result of any service swap between them.

Keynesian Economics:
> Derived from the writings of British economist John Maynard Keynes, and based on the notion that government could — and should — accept responsibility for the performance of the economy by pursuing various monetary and fiscal policies.

Reservation:
> The power of the Lieutenant-Governor to reserve any provincial bill for review by the federal government, presumably at federal request. Like disallowance, this power has fallen into disuse.

Residual Powers:
> All powers left over and not otherwise specifically assigned to a level of government.

Tax Room:
> When there were tax rental and tax sharing agreements to avoid double taxation within the fields of income and corporate tax, the amount of tax room referred to the portion of the tax field available to one level of government without intruding on the portion reserved to the other. (Also known as tax points or tax credits.)

Tax Sharing:
> Process through which the federal and provincial governments, through a series of five year agreements, coordinated their joint occupancy of key tax fields, especially income and corporate tax.

Watertight Compartments:
> Term to describe the complete separation of federal and provincial responsibilities, in such a way as to avoid any overlap.

Points to Ponder

1. It appears likely that use of the "federal spending power" will be curtailed sharply in the future. What is your view of this prospect? Are there any new initiatives that you can think of that could benefit from the use of the federal spending power?

2. Discussions to disentangle provincial-municipal responsibilities usually give special attention to the handling of education and social services. Which level of government do you think should look after these areas, and why?

3. This chapter has raised a number of concerns about the vacuum being created at the centre. Has this discussion caused you to rethink your views about whether Canada should continue to decentralize its government operations?

For Further Reading

Mark Charlton and Paul Barker (eds.), *Crosscurrents: Contemporary Political Issues*, 2nd Edition, Scarborough, Nelson Canada, 1994, explores the merits of strong national/ provincial governments.

Paul Fox and Graham White, *Politics: Canada*, 8th Edition, Whitby, McGraw-Hill Ryerson Limited, 1995, has several pertinent sections.

Robert Jackson and Doreen Jackson, *Politics in Canada*, 3rd Edition, 1994, Scarborough, Prentice-Hall Canada Inc., Chapter 6, discusses federalism including the financial relationships. See also *Canadian Government in Transition*, 2nd Edition, 1999, from the same authors and publisher.

Leslie A. Pal (ed.), *How Ottawa Spends 1999-2000*, Toronto, Oxford University Press, 1999, especially Chapters 6 and 9.

C. Richard Tindal and Susan Nobes Tindal, *Local Government in Canada*, 5th Edition, Scarborough, Nelson, Chapter 8, explores provincial-municipal relations, including the issue of disentanglement.

Chapter 9

The Unravelling Social Safety Net

Objectives and Highlights

◆ To outline the main components of Canada's social safety net.

◆ To examine the changes eroding our social programs.

◆ To explore the choices and challenges we face today.

As discussed in the preceding chapter, the shift over the past decade or so to a kind of fend-for-yourself federalism has raised concerns about the future of Canada's social programs and the enduring nature of our much-touted social safety net. It is not only the lack of adequate financial support which threatens these programs, however. It is the fact that there has been growing criticism of their effectiveness and even of their justification. In part, this change in the tenor of public debate reflects the neoconservatism which has loomed so large of late. At a time when the virtues of the market place are emphasized and the merits of government programs questioned, it is not surprising that social programs would come under critical scrutiny. The current philosophy that individuals should take more responsibility for their own circumstances also invites such scrutiny.

Even those who support social programs concede that they have not been very effective in keeping Canadians above the **poverty line** and in narrowing the gap between the "have-nots" and the "haves" in Canadian society. But they are insistent that any savings achieved by undermining the social safety net will be more than offset by the increased costs which will result later. We can, they argue, address child poverty now, or spend far more money later on things such as health care, policing, courts, and prisons.

Obviously we are dealing with a complex subject and one about which emotions run high. This chapter will attempt to "unravel" the issues involved and give you a basis on which to judge the appropriateness of government actions in this area. Before looking at what has been happening to the **welfare state** in Canada, it is useful to recall when and why it was established.

The Evolution of the Welfare State

The decline in individual self-sufficiency and the rise of dependence on government coincided with fundamental changes in the nature of the Canadian economy and society inherent in the shift from an agricultural and rural society to an urban and industrial one. It was the Great Depression of the 1930s, however, and the almost total collapse of the Canadian economy, which dramatized the need for government intervention and support for those in need. Consider these images:[1]

> Atlantic Canada was devastated. Fish exports plummeted and unemployment soared. Unemployment in Ontario rose from 2% in 1929 to 36% in 1936. The collapse in the Prairies was aggravated by drought and shrinking world markets for wheat. By 1936, one-third of Saskatchewan farmers were on relief; two-thirds by the following year. In some districts every single family was on relief. At the height of the Depression, half of the wage earners in Canada were on some form of relief. That "relief" was administered by provinces and municipalities, who were generally punitive in their approach. There was a terrible stigma attached to the "dole." To be eligible for relief, a family had to demonstrate that it was nearly destitute. Inspectors would come to the home, and if they found any signs of food, new clothes, liquor or, in some cases, even a radio, relief was denied. Most municipalities had a one year residency requirement even for emergency health care, and immigrants were not only turned down for help but deported for requesting it. Medical aid was scarce and far too expensive for many Canadians and, of course, there wasn't any universal health care.

---

[1] The description which follows is based on Maude Barlow and Bruce Campbell, *Straight Through the Heart*, Toronto, HarperCollins Publishers Limited, 1995, pp. 14-16.

As the Depression deepened and dragged on, the federal government gradually assumed some responsibility for unemployment relief, in part to bail out provincial governments which were virtually bankrupt from trying to make these payments. Many municipalities had gone bankrupt—defaulting on debt obligations incurred for expansion of roads, water and sewer systems, and other infrastructure during the boom period of the "Roaring Twenties." The Depression eventually ended because of the upsurge in economic activity associated with World War II, and by the end of the war most Western nations were embracing the economic ideas of John Maynard Keynes. Central to Keynesian economics was the view that governments could pursue deliberate policies which would help to minimize unemployment and maintain rising incomes, stable prices and other desirable economic objectives. As a result, government payments to the unemployed and other forms of income support gained favour, not as a form of welfare, but as a stimulus to the purchasing power of Canadian citizens and thus to economic growth. Consider these developments:

> Income support programs were seen as promoting economic growth, not as a form of welfare.

1941	Introduction of a federal unemployment insurance program
1945	Family allowance payments ("baby bonus") introduced
1952	Old age pension of $40 per month to Canadians 70 and older
1965	Canada Pension Plan, payments at age 65 to contributors
1966	Comprehensive public assistance plan, Canada Assistance Plan or CAP, to coordinate provincial plans
1966	National health care program ("Medicare") introduced

Thus over a period of 25 years many of the key components of Canada's modern welfare state were put into place. They were established during a period in which the Canadian economy enjoyed almost continuous growth and in which revenue sources for government seemed inexhaustible. During these heady times, it was widely accepted that the provision of a social safety net was a defining characteristic of the civilized way of life available in Canada.

The Withering of the Welfare State

The stagflation of the 1970s and several economic downturns in the 1980s and 1990s have had a sobering impact. As fiscal concerns took centre stage, governments reduced their commitment to social programs and the safety net began to unravel.

From Universal to Targeted Programs

The family allowance program was abolished in the early 1990s, and replaced with a child tax credit. Instead of a universal program, available to all, we moved to a targeted program, provided on the basis of income. It is true that family allowance payments (and old age security, for that matter) had long been treated as income for tax purposes, making them targeted in practice. But this feature became much more evident with the abolition of family allowances. Many may find merit in targeting scarce government funds to those most in need, but experience shows that targeted programs are difficult to maintain because political support for them comes only from that segment of the population that receives them. In contrast, **universal programs** that benefit all have a much stronger support base. Bakker charges that this change was one of a number of steps taken during the Mulroney years which transformed social policy "by stealth" and undermined the egalitarian goals of the welfare state.[2]

Changes to UI

The Liberal government elected in 1993 introduced a number of changes to the Unemployment Insurance program, including a new

---

[2]Isabella Bakker, "The Politics of Scarcity: Deficits and the Debt," in Michael Whittington and Glen Williams (eds.), *Canadian Politics in the 1990s*, Scarborough, Nelson Canada, 1995, p. 66.

name—Employment Insurance program.[3] One of its objectives was to reduce the cost of the **UI** program by some $2 billion. The other main objective was to redirect some of these savings into measures to help people get back into the workforce. In proportional terms, the cuts fell most heavily on claimants with family incomes above $50 000 a year, moving UI away from a universal program toward one that is means-tested. The Minister responsible for these changes, Lloyd Axworthy, freely admitted that he wanted to make work more rewarding and the collection of UI less so. The reforms also targeted seasonal workers who still qualify for UI, but take home less money and for a shorter time. The success(?) of these reforms is evident from the results of a fall 1998 study from the federal department of Human Resources which showed that only 42% of the jobless qualified for benefits as compared to 83% a decade earlier.[4]

Changes to Pensions

There are three federal programs providing assistance to senior citizens. One of these is the Canada Pension Plan (**CPP**)[5], which is funded by contributions made by employers and employees, on the basis of past earnings. These contributions have not been keeping up with demands on the plan, especially with Canada's aging population. A 1995 report from the Federal Superintendent of Financial Institutions stated that the CPP would be wiped out in 20 years, just as baby boomers started to hit age 65, unless contributions were more than doubled or benefits somehow cut.[6] By the year 2030, the number of pensioners is expected to more than double, and there will only be three Canadians of working age to support each of these pensioners, compared to five now.[7]

---

[3]Edward Greenspon, "Axworthy undoes Mackasey's work," *Globe and Mail*, December 2, 1995.

[4]Editorial, "EI system fails Canada's jobless," *Toronto Star*, October 22, 1998.

[5]The CPP covers workers in all provinces but Québec, which has a very similar Québec Pension Plan (QPP) covering its workers.

[6]Quoted in the *Kingston Whig Standard*, February 25, 1995.

[7]Editorial, "Seniors Benefit plan worth repairing," *Toronto Star*, July 5, 1998.

The government's response was to introduce legislation in 1997 under which contribution rates are climbing by more than 70% over six years to build up a far larger fund. A new CPP Investment Board will invest the money in securities markets to try to boost the rate of return, following the approach which has been taken with Québec's Pension Plan. While most agree that contributions had to jump significantly if the CPP was to remain solvent, critics have labelled the move a massive tax increase for Canadians and there have been some calls for a private pension plan in which individuals make their own mandatory contributions into a registered retirement plan. The new, aggressive investment strategy has been criticized as gambling with the savings of Canadians.

The other two federal programs for seniors are the Old Age Security (**OAS**) and the Guaranteed Income Supplement (**GIS**). The OAS is a universal program financed out of general revenue, whereas the GIS is means-tested. Only about half of Canadians have low enough incomes to receive GIS benefits. The 1995 federal budget brought major changes to these two programs. They were then costing over $20 billion, and were expected to grow by 60% over the next 15 years as the "baby boomers" turned into senior citizens. It was announced that, effective 2001, the OAS and GIS programs would be replaced by a Seniors Benefit program. It would be tax-free and fully indexed to inflation, but the size of the benefit would be reduced and then eliminated, based on income. However, the Minister of Finance announced in mid-1998[8] that the improved fiscal situation no longer made these changes necessary, and that the existing OAS and GIS system would be fully maintained. While the proposed changes had been quite controversial, most feel that some reform of the programs is still needed, since the increased costs associated with the aging population remains a challenge.

Cuts in Federal Social Transfers

As discussed in the preceding chapter, the decade of the 1990s saw a significant reduction in federal financial support for social programs, in the name of deficit and debt reduction. Highlights included:

---

[8]Department of Finance *News Release*, "Finance Minister's Statement on the Seniors Benefit," July 28, 1998.

- a freeze on payments under EPF (Established Program Funding), introduced in 1990-91 and extended through1994-95.
- a cap on CAP (the Canada Assistance Plan), beginning in 1990-91, which placed a ceiling of 5% on the growth of CAP payments to the three "have" provinces of Ontario, Alberta, and British Columbia, regardless of their actual social assistance costs, and which remained in effect through 1994-95.
- the replacement of both EPF and CAP, effective 1996-97, with a Canada Health and Social Transfer (CHST), to be reduced by more than $6 billion over the period from 1996 to 1998.

By the time of the 1997 federal election, the Liberals promised to cancel any further cuts to the CHST, and they have since pledged that the cash portion of this transfer payment will not fall below $12.5 billion a year—an amount supposedly large enough to ensure that the federal level retains bargaining leverage with respect to the enforcement of national standards. Under the social union agreement reached by the federal government and all provinces except Québec in February 1999, several billion dollars of additional transfers for health care is supposed to come to the provinces over a three year period. But the damage had been done well before this action, and various provincial governments had responded in kind, further undermining the social safety net.

Provincial Cuts As Well

Faced with cuts in transfer payments from the federal level, provincial governments could presumably have increased their expenditures to make up the shortfall. But, most provinces had become equally concerned with deficit and debt questions. As a result, their reaction was to make cuts of their own, including cuts in transfers to municipalities and other local governing bodies. Ralph Klein led the way in Alberta with a series of sharp cuts in funding for municipalities, school boards, hospitals and other social agencies.

Since his election in June 1995, Mike Harris has done his best to match the Alberta example in Ontario. One of his first acts was to introduce a 21% cut in welfare payments. Further cuts were announced in a Fiscal and Economic Statement from the Minister of Finance in November 1995. As discussed in the previous chapter, municipal grants

: combined (into a General Support Grant), made less conditional, a.._1 then eliminated. In addition, the Province announced substantial cuts in grants for such programs and services as libraries, public transit, education and child care spaces. In 1997, the province introduced a new local service alignment under which the responsibility and/or cost of a number of social programs were shifted to the municipal level, as also discussed in the preceding chapter. This was supposed to be a revenue-neutral exchange, but has served to shift costs downward, while leaving maintenance of social standards to municipalities of widely varying financial strength— an arrangement contrary to developments in most other provinces and contrary to the recommendations of a number of past Ontario studies.

From Welfare to Workfare

When the federal government replaced its EPF and CAP programs with the CHST block grant, one of the concerns was that the open-ended nature of the new financial arrangement would leave it (the federal level) with even less means of enforcing national standards in health, education and social assistance. While CAP was in existence, the federal funding was conditional. A well publicized example was when a $46 million payment was temporarily withheld from British Columbia until it removed a three month residency requirement which it had imposed in violation of CAP provisions.

With CAP and its limited conditions gone, provinces have been experimenting with their social assistance programs. Of particular interest has been the concept of **workfare**, the requirement that able-bodied welfare recipients work for their cheques. Ideally, according to proponents of workfare, it will ease welfare recipients into the work force, restoring their self-confidence and upgrading skills made rusty by inactivity. Another motivation, not always as openly admitted, was the perception held by some that people preferred to stay on welfare, or at least found it more attractive and financially rewarding than the minimum wage jobs that might be available. Yet many studies have shown that the overwhelming majority of those on welfare are very anxious to find work. In addition, citing examples where social assistance pays more than minimum wage ignores the more fundamental issue that *neither* option provides enough income for decent living conditions. It ignores the fact that while the minimum wage in every province but Ontario in 1976 provided an income that was above the poverty line, 20 years later the proceeds of the minimum wage were well below the poverty line in every province.[9] It ignores the fact that many who want to get off social assistance are trapped because the financial return from work does not recognize the cost of raising children, personal supports, or work-related expenses.[10]

Alberta decreed that welfare recipients would be cut off if they refused jobs in programs such as Community Employment, which gave up to 26 weeks of work performing such tasks as tree-planting.[11] It had some success in moving people off welfare rolls, but mainly because of a jump in oil prices which created additional jobs. Québec offered higher benefits to those who accept work or training, and New Brunswick had a workfare program, but neither of these has been very successful because jobs could not be found for welfare recipients.[12]

The Ontario government launched a workfare program in 1996, promising that by the end of September that year, 54 000 people would be working for their benefits in 20 pilot municipalities. When the end of September came, *not one job* had been found. Three years later, barely 5% of Ontario welfare recipients are in some form of workfare. The province's response is to blame municipalities and to introduce financial incentives and penalties in an attempt to increase participation.[13] But part of the difficulty in Ontario is that its initiative appears to have been motivated by a desire to cut costs rather than necessarily to provide the best experience for the individuals affected by the process. The state of

---

[9]Walter Stewart, *Dismantling the State*, Toronto, Stoddart, 1998, p. 273.

[10]Christopher Clark, "Work and Welfare: Looking at both sides of the equation," *Perception*, Volume 19, No. 1, 1995, Ottawa, Canadian Council on Social Development.

[11]Mary Janigan, "Wading into the Welfare Mess," *Maclean's*, November 27, 1995, p. 34.

[12]Clarke, *op. cit.*

[13]Editorial, "Aim workfare at realistic targets," *Ottawa Citizen*, November 24, 1999.

> To be effective, workfare programs require more money than the cost of welfare payments.

Wisconsin is widely held to have one of the most successful workfare programs, and one of the lessons learned there is that welfare reform is very expensive. Wisconsin's per family payments have soared because instead of just sending out welfare cheques, it is now paying for child care, training, counselling, wage subsidies and health care.[14] In contrast, a massive shortage of child care spaces in Ontario is cited as a major obstacle preventing people from breaking free of welfare, according to a very critical study by the consulting firm KPMG.[15]

A Sick Health Care System?

Nowhere have government cutbacks been more dramatic and worrisome to Canadians than in the area of health care. That term is something of a misnomer. What Canada really has is a national sickness care system, since the overwhelming emphasis of government policies and commitment of resources is on the treatment of sickness not the maintenance of health. But this was not always the case and the original public health movement focused on preventing contagious disease and epidemics—that is, with preventing sickness by keeping people healthy. Local governments were in the forefront of this activity, dealing with sanitation, sewage and the treatment of drinking water. As the 20th century unfolded, however, powerful diagnostic and therapeutic tools such as x-rays, antibiotics and effective anaesthesia appeared in medicine. Clinical supremacy (what was often termed the medical model) took over from the public health movement and better health became equated—in the minds of the public and their politicians—with doctors and hospitals. In response, the senior levels of government became increasingly involved in supporting the newer tools of health care. As a result, expenditures and emphasis on prevention programs declined.

---

[14]Richard Gwyn, "Wisconsin workfare a Clinton triumph," *Toronto Star*, August 29, 1997.

[15]Richard Mackie, "Study finds workfare not working," *Globe and Mail*, September 25, 1999.

In contrast, expenditures on hospital construction, the acquisition of new technology, drugs, and payments to physicians expanded dramatically throughout the 20th century. The new technology and increasingly sophisticated treatment techniques did not hold down medical costs, however. To the contrary, these advances have extended the life span of the ill, without contributing to the health of society. The aging of the population is another major cost contributor, inevitably leading to an increased demand for medical care, for beds in hospitals and chronic care facilities, and for home care services. According to demographer Robert Evans, people over 65 use over half of the hospital days in Canada, undergo about half the surgical procedures, account for roughly one-quarter of the physician billings, and use about 40% of all prescription drugs—even though they represent only one-eighth of the population of Canada.[16] As the baby boomers age and make senior citizens an increasing proportion of the total population of Canada, the upward pressure on health costs will increase further.

As these upward pressures on health costs have intensified, governments have become less and less willing to find the necessary funding, given their preoccupation with debt and deficit reduction. Since the money being transferred by the federal government (even back in the days of EPF) was relatively unconditional, there were concerns that individual provinces might take, or allow, actions which would undermine public health care in Canada. In response, the federal government passed the Canada Health Act in 1984, with its financial penalty for provinces allowing **extra-billing** by doctors or user charges by hospitals. The Act provided for a reduction in transfer payments to a province by an amount equal to the total value of these "outlawed" activities. These reductions were applied against Ontario in the mid-1980s, forcing the Ontario government to confront extra-billing, precipitating a strike by doctors in 1986, but ultimately resulting in compliance with the federal

Health care cuts painful

---

[16]Quoted in *Alberta Report*, September 25, 1995, p. 12.

requirements. Ten years later this scene was repeated, with Alberta agreeing not to allow private health care facilities to extra-bill patients seeking essential medical care, but only after a lengthy stand-off that cost the province almost $4 million in penalties.[17] The relatively modest size of the financial penalty reflects the erosion in federal transfers for health which had been occurring.

Faced with reduced federal transfers, provincial governments have responded by cutting their expenditures on health care, partly through reducing the number of hospital beds and through closing some hospitals. Alberta was again in the forefront of this activity in the early 1990s. The NDP government in Saskatchewan, the birthplace of government-funded health care, closed 52 hospitals, mostly in rural areas, in the mid-1990s. 1996 saw the reduction of hospital beds in Manitoba and several hospital closings in Montreal. The Parti Québécois cut more than $1.4 billion from the health care system during its first mandate. The Ontario government announced that funding for hospitals would be reduced by $1.3 billion over the three years from 1996-97 to 1998-99, and Bill 26 (the Savings and Restructuring Act) gave the Minister of Health new powers to close hospitals. The Province set up a Health Services Restructuring Commission whose recommendations (still not complete) have led to the closing or merger of more than 40 hospitals across Ontario in the second half of the 1990s.

According to Statistics Canada, there were 6.9 hospital beds per 1000 population in 1987-88, but by 1995-96 that ratio had fallen to 4.8—and it is lower still today. Fewer beds were sufficient, it was argued, if people were looked after in various lower cost community facilities or through home care. But the shift in resources to make this happen has been slow to materialize. For example, when Ontario lost 15.4% of its acute care beds between 1986 and 1996, its residential beds didn't increase proportionally, but actually declined by 3.9%.[18] The health care restructuring exercise launched by the Harris government in

---

[17]Brian Laghi, "Alberta gives in to Ottawa on billing," *Globe and Mail*, May 31, 1996.

[18]The statistics in this section are from Jennifer Sass, "Curing Health Care," *CBC News Online*, as downloaded on August 10, 1999 from web site *cbcnews.cbc. ca/news/indepth/healthcare*.

the second half of the 1990s has also shown a lack of proper planning and sequencing. The first thing needed is an adequate supply of low cost beds and of home care. These allow pa-tients to be shifted from costly beds

> Hospitals have been closed before adequate home care and community facilities are in place.

in hospitals, which can then be closed. Ontario has moved quickly to close hospital beds and entire hospitals, but critics claim that it has done so *before* providing the alternative services.

The additional $2.5 billion in federal funding for health care announced in 1999 is welcome news, but it is far from sufficient to address the heavy and increasing demands being made on the system. The underfunding of health care is reflected in an ongoing series of "horror stories" about patients lying neglected on cots in the hallways of overcrowded hospitals, about ambulances turned away or surgeries postponed, about cancer patients sent to the United States for treat-ment, even about deaths occurring as a result of lack of response from a system overstretched. The only solution, according to some, is to allow the development—or more accurately, the expansion—of a two tier system of **medicare**, in which private medical facilities, available at a price, exist side-by-side with the publicly funded system. Those who opt to pay for private health care, it is argued, will reduce the load and shorten the queues with respect to public health care.

Alberta, once again, has been in the forefront, with the Klein government arguing for increased privatization of the system. It allowed private clinics for cataract surgery to operate and charge patients $1000 over the provincial reimbursement fee. Premier Klein has stated that he might sell some of Alberta's surplus hospitals to private companies which could offer "for-profit health care" for Americans.[19] Canada's first for-profit hospital opened in September 1997 on the site of the former Grace Hospital which had been closed as part of a series of budget cuts which saw the health budget for Alberta reduced by 20%. Strong public objections caused the government to withdraw a 1998 bill

---

[19]Joan Price Boase, "Trends in Social Policy" in Christopher Dunn (ed.), *Canadian Provincial Politics*, Peterborough, Broadview Press, 1996, p. 467.

which would have given the Minister of Health the final say in approving or rejecting private health facilities.[20] However, in November 1999, Premier Klein announced plans to introduce legislation in the spring of 2000 which will allow health authorities to contract with privately operated facilities for surgical services, "if it will improve access, improve efficiency, or reduce waiting lists in the public system."[21] He insisted that the new arrangements would adhere to the provisions of medicare, and that those using private facilities will be covered by their health insurance cards. The federal government and a number of health care groups have expressed concerns, and the debate on this initiative will doubtless continue for some time. On the surface, the Klein proposal does not appear to contemplate the kind of two tier health care system discussed below, in which fee for service and publicly funded health care co-exist. But it is still unclear why the provincial government felt it necessary to cut the health care budget and close public hospitals and then to offer additional funding for *private* health care facilities.

Ontario introduced new user charges related to health care soon after the election of the Conservatives in 1995. Seniors earning more than $16 000 a year as singles and $24 000 a year as families were for the first time forced to pay a $100 per year user fee, plus up to $6.11 per prescription. Welfare recipients and low income seniors had to pay a $2 prescription fee. Through such means the government presumably hoped to recoup some of the $1.3 billion it was spending annually on drugs for seniors and welfare recipients.[22] At this time, Ontario also had close to 100 non-hospital clinics, funded by OHIP, and providing services that included diagnostic tests such as ultra-sound and tuberculosis and pneumonia tests, plus treatment facilities for laser dermatology, plastic surgery, and gynaecological surgery.[23]

---

[20]Mike Sadava, "Government retreats on private hospital bill," *Edmonton Journal*, November 25, 1998.

[21]Ashley Geddes, "Klein sees role for private hospitals," *Edmonton Journal*, November 17, 1999.

[22]These figures are all from William Walker, "U.S.-Style Health Care Heads North," *Toronto Star*, December 9, 1995, B4.

[23]*Ibid.*

Monique Begin, former federal Minister of Health and the main architect of the 1984 Canada Health Act, claims that growing privatization, government underfunding, the de-listing of services, the imposition of extra charges and user fees, and the failure to enforce the Canada Health Act are combining to erode medicare in Canada. She cites as examples a patient in hospital with a broken ankle who is given the choice between a regular, heavy cast, which is free of charge, or an ultra-light cast, which costs $85, and the case of a patient needing an MRI scan who is encouraged to avoid a long waiting period by going to a private clinic where the procedure is available at once, but for $750.[24]

Two Tier Already Here?

A few statistics illustrate dramatically how far Canada has already moved toward a two tier health care system. Private care represented 23.6% of Canada's health bill as far back as 1975, and it has increased to 27.2% in 1993 and to over 30% today. The federal government's cash share of medicare's bill dropped from 27% in 1978 to 11% in 1998.[25] With some $24.3 billion of Canada's $80 billion health care tab now being paid by Canadians out of their own pockets or by their private insurers, the $2.5 billion in extra funding pledged by the federal government in early 1999 is only a drop in the bucket. While Canada is fourth among 28 OECD countries in combined public and private spending on health, it ranks 17th in *public* spending on health care.

> Among OECD countries, Canada is 17th in public spending on health care.

About 250 large corporations, most of them based in the United States, are involved in the Canadian health sector. In the new era of free trade agreements, they threaten to dominate the provision of services, with the support of some provincial governments (such as Alberta and Ontario), most large employers, and large sections of organized

---

[24]Monique Begin, *The Future of Medicare: Recovering the Canada Health Act*, Canadian Centre for Policy Alternatives, September 1999. The discussion in this section is based on a release on this publication, obtained in October 1999 from the Centre's web site at *www.policyalternatives.ca/whatsnew/healthpr.html*.

[25]Mark Kennedy, "Critical Condition," *Montreal Gazette*, February 13, 1999.

medicine.[26] Multinational drug companies have been key contributors to the increase in the health care bill. Since the deregulation of Canada's drug industry, the cost of prescriptions in Canada rose by 93% between 1987 and 1996, compared to an increase in all consumer prices of 23%. With hospital expenditures decreasing over this period by about the same amount as drug costs went up, it could be said that we exchanged less hospital care for increased revenues for the drug companies.[27]

Medicare High on Drugs

Walter Stewart[28] is even more critical of a drug pricing process which appears to him to be aimed at protecting large pharmaceutical companies, nearly all foreign owned. Patent legislation passed by the Conservative government in 1992 prevents Canadian generic drug manufacturers from producing cheaper versions of drugs for up to 20 years—supposedly to keep jobs in Canada and to promote research in this country. Instead, he finds that no new jobs have been created but that 2300 jobs were lost in Montreal and Toronto as a result of foreign firms closing or merging operations. Stewart also reports that the drug companies spent $1 billion annually on product promotion and $89 million (after tax write-offs) on basic research, while generating a rate of return on equity about twice that of banks. To those who might wonder why we hand such large profits to drug companies while laying off thousands of nurses to ease health care costs, he contends that "drug firms have an active and effective lobby in the old-boy network in Ottawa, while nurses do not."

♦ Something to Think About

If passive or "creeping" privatization is occurring anyway, should we face reality and plan for a two tier system of health care, public and private? What are the pros and cons of such a step?

---

[26]Colleen Fuller, "Canada's Health Care Crisis," *The CPPA Monitor*, Canadian Centre for Policy Alternatives, March 1998.

[27]Robert Chernomas, "Why Medicare Is In Trouble," *The CPPA Monitor*, Canadian Centre for Policy Alternatives, July/August 1999.

[28]Stewart, *op. cit.*, pp. 58-59.

Under a two-tier system, patients would continue to have access to publicly funded, "free" core medical services, but could obtain treatment from private clinics if they wanted to pay for it, either from their own pockets or from private insurance. The private clinics, proponents argue, would divert some patients away from the overloaded public health care system. Since governments aren't going to provide sufficient money for public health care, the only answer is to move to a two tier system. Those with money will "jump the queue" and obtain faster service from private clinics. But their departure will reduce the current overload on the publicly funded system.

However, any scheme which introduces fees or charges for medicare touches a nerve for many Canadians. Critics claim that "the direct charge concept is an idea whose time has gone." According to most literature on the subject:

> extra billing, user fees, and the like impede equality of access to medical care, deter utilization by the poor, redistribute the burden of paying for health care from taxpayers to the sick, violate the principles on which the Canadian health care system was established, do not make a contribution to overall expenditure control, and serve the interests of not the public, but providers, private insurance companies, and provincial governments."[29]

Critics of a two tier system also argue that it inevitably leads to a deterioration of the first or public system.[30] Doctors would steer their patients toward the second or private system because it would pay them more. Patients, in turn, would take out private insurance to cover their costs for this second tier. Gradually, they would resent having to pay taxes for those left behind in the first tier, and would be inclined to support candidates and parties promising to cut funding for that tier. As a result, the first tier would deteriorate and waiting lists would get longer, not shorter.

---

[29]Mike Burke and Michael Stevenson, "The Politics and Political Science of Health Care in Canada," in Paul Fox and Graham White (eds.), *Politics: Canada*, 8th Edition, Whitby, McGraw-Hill Ryerson Limited, 1995, p. 570.

[30]This section is based on editorial, "Two tier system not the answer," *Toronto Star*, January 3, 1997.

This is the danger with the new private facilities being promoted by Premier Klein for Alberta.[31] He has pledged that no one will have to pay for services covered by medicare, insisting that he will adhere to the requirements of the Canada Health Act. But in addition to providing services covered by medicare, these private facilities will offer a variety of additional services deemed not "medically necessary," but attractive to the patient—such as a better quality of artificial lens available during cataract surgery. The private facilities will promote these extras, since that is where they will derive their profits. The more people pay extra for such niceties, they more they will want private insurance to cover such costs. It is private insurance that has the capacity to destroy medicare, by underwriting the expansion of private, fee-for-service facilities alongside an eroded public system mainly used by the poor.

Supporters of medicare also reject the argument that a two tier system is preferable because it will introduce "market solutions" to health care problems, with competition reducing costs and stimulating innovation. They point out that the most competitive health care system in the world, that of the United States, is also the most expensive by far.

But Canadians may be basing their identity on a health care system that exists more in theory than in the reality of hospital closings and waiting lists for medical services. It is also true that public and private systems co-exist in a number of other jurisdictions. For example, Great Britain has a network of private hospitals, Sweden still imposes user fees, France allows private hospitals and over-billing, and 10% of the German population uses private health services.[32]

Poverty Amidst Plenty

Even those who despair at the recent cuts to Canada's social programs, tend to concede that the social safety net has not been especially effec-

---

[31]The discussion in this section is based on Thomas Walkom, "Back from the Grave," *Toronto Star*, December 4, 1999.

[32]According to Alain Dubuc, as quoted in Lysiane Gagnon, "Courchene plan crumbled before the unity train arrived in Jasper," *Globe and Mail*, August 24, 1996.

tive in improving the distribution of income in Canada or reducing the incidence of poverty. In 1951 the top 20% of income earners in Canada accounted for 42.8% of total money income and the bottom 20% accounted for 4.4%. In 1990, the top 20% accounted for 40.2% and the bottom 20% had 6.9%. The gap was much wider in 1990 if social security benefits are excluded from the picture, leaving the bottom fifth of income earners with 1.1% of income before government transfers, while the top fifth had 47.7%.[33] The combined wealth of the 50 richest Canadians exceeds that of the five million lowest income Canadians.[34]

> Canada's 50 richest people have more wealth than its 5 million least well off.

The National Council on Welfare reported in 1995[35] that the number of people living in poverty in Canada had grown to 4.8 million in 1993, up from 4.3 million in 1992. Poor single mothers were the most impoverished, averaging $8500 below the poverty line (defined below). In fact, 90% of families headed by a single mother were below the poverty line. The Council also reported that more than 1.4 million children, representing 20.8% of all Canadians under 18, were below the poverty line—the highest level yet recorded.

Conditions have not improved over the second half of the 1990s. While Canada has enjoyed considerable economic growth, the gap between rich and poor has intensified and concerns over child poverty and homelessness have deepened. A new report from the Centre for Social Justice includes the following findings:[36]

---

[33] All figures are from Stephen Brooks, *Public Policy in Canada*, 2nd Edition, Toronto, McClelland & Stewart Inc., 1993, p. 190.

[34] Ed Finn, "Child Poverty Keeps Rising, and —Surprise!—So Does the Number of Millionaires," *Canadian Forum*, March 1997, as quoted in Stewart, *op. cit.*, p. 273.

[35] *Globe and Mail*, April 6, 1995.

[36] Armine Yalnizyan, *The Growing Gap Report*, Centre for Social Justice, October 1998. The points listed above are from the summary downloaded in October 1999 from its web site *www.socialjustice.org/gap-summary.html*.

- While the richest 10% of Canadian families made 21 times more than the poorest 10% of Canadian families in 1973, they made 314 times as much in 1996.
- Real (inflation-adjusted) average family market incomes are lower today than they were in 1981. Sixty percent of families with children were earning less than in 1981.
- While about two-thirds of the employed labour force worked in a full time 35-40 hour a week job a generation ago, now only half of workers have such jobs. About one in five jobs are part-time and the fastest growing segment of the labour market is "casualized" jobs—temporary, contract, irregular—which account for about 15% of the total.
- Welfare rates, welfare eligibility, and/or shelter allowances have been reduced in almost every province since 1995.
- Government decisions in recent years to cut back transfer payments and scale back the provision of public goods have hit hardest the poorest families, and the youth of Canada.

This last point was driven home by a hard-hitting report from the United Nations which charged that Ottawa and the provinces had deliberately "adopted policies...which exacerbated poverty and homelessness among vulnerable groups during a time of strong economic growth and increasing affluence."[37] The report criticized the 1.5 million children living below the poverty line. It noted that Canadian politicians had taken credit for Canada's top ranking for five years on the UN list for standard of living, while ignoring the fact that Canada ranked 10th on the human poverty index for industrialized countries.

What Is Poverty?

If beauty is in the eye of the beholder, poverty is also a very subjective concept. A university or college student might live on an income considered barely above subsistence and yet not feel impoverished because of optimism about future prospects. While any precise definition of poverty in terms of income must be arbitrary, Statistics Canada publishes a set of low income cut-offs that are usually referred to as poverty

---

[37]Report by the U.N. Committee on Economic, Social and Cultural Rights, December 1998, as reported in *Toronto Star*, December 5, 1998.

lines. These cut-offs are established in relation to what the average Canadian family spends on food, shelter and clothing. Any family that spends more than 20% more than the average family spends to buy these three essentials is considered to have low income (or to be below the poverty line). For example, in 1992, the average family spent 34.7% of its gross income on these items, so the low income cut-off was established at 54.7%. Statistics Canada then calculates a whole series of these cut-offs, reflecting different family sizes, urban versus rural, and population, and these are adjusted each year for inflation.[38]

This method of measuring poverty is often criticized by those on the right, who claim that it is a relative measurement which rises with improvements in living standards. According to this view, the low income cut-offs are not really a measure of poverty at all, in the diction-ary sense of "absolute deprivation," but instead are more accurately a measure of inequality, or of relative poverty.[39] As a result, the low income threshold today is equivalent in real terms to what would have been considered a middle class income 20 or 30 years ago.

This point of view, not surprisingly, is expressed in a study pub-lished by the Fraser Institute. It complained that almost one in five households below the poverty line in 1990 owned their own homes, 97% had colour television sets, and 53% owned a car—all "extras" not associated with poverty. A more accurate measure, according to this study, would be to cost "basic needs" which, it turns out, total far less than the low income cut-off point.[40] However, the needs list as en-dorsed by the Fraser Institute is far too basic in the view of many. For example:[41]

---

[38]This description of low income cut-offs is based on C. Michael Fellows, Greg Flanagan, and Standford Shedd, *Economic Issues: A Canadian Perspective*, Whitby, McGraw-Hill Ryerson Limited, 1997, pp. 196-197.

[39]Andrew Coyne, "StatsCan's poverty measure of relative worth," *Ottawa Citizen*, July 17, 1997.

[40]Chris Sarlo, *Poverty in Canada*, 2nd Edition, Vancouver, Fraser Institute, 1996. The discussion of this study is based on a June 11, 1996 news release "Canadian Poverty Rate Exaggerated Fivefold."

[41]These examples are from Richard Shillington, "How poor are the really poor?" *Toronto Star*, December 30, 1997.

- it costs the minimum caloric requirement of an elderly women at $22 per week for food, including 14 servings of fruit for $2.11.
- it allows less than $400 a year for transportation, regardless of family size, employment status, or urban/rural setting.
- it provides no funds for school supplies, which are "assumed to be offset by part-time or summer earnings."
- it excludes such items as radios, televisions, VCRs, magazines and newspapers, "which cannot in any way be described as physical necessities." Nor are such items as children's toys, books and writing materials included, for the same reason.

There may well be imperfections in the low income cut-off definition of poverty, and because it is a relative measure it will always show a substantial number of poor, even as (in fact, because) economic conditions improve in the country. But it is surely preferable to the mean-spirited approach outlined in the Fraser Institute study. The exclusion of radios from the list of basic needs is striking when one recalls the lengthy quote at the beginning of this chapter, citing the harsh application of the "dole" in the 1930s, and the fact that relief could be denied if inspectors found as much as a radio in the home. More fundamentally, the Fraser Institute approach is cruel because it argues for a universal definition of poverty which can apply anywhere in the world. According to its study, a poor family in Canada is no less poor than a family in the same situation in India or Haiti.[42] But does such a comparison make any sense? People are poor in those other countries because of a lack of resources, not a problem that exists in Canada. Using an absolute poverty measure of the sort advocated by the Fraser Institute serves to deny the poor in Canada of any claim on the growing wealth in this country. It seeks to perpetuate and even to increase the gap between the haves and the have-nots.

A Benefit or a Right?

One of the responses of those concerned with the deterioration of the social safety net has been to advocate a **social charter** which would

---

[42]Quoted in *ibid.*

somehow provide constitutional protection of social rights just as the Charter of Rights and Freedoms protects other rights. This was a major objective of former Ontario Premier Bob Rae, who succeeded in getting a social charter included in the ill-fated Charlottetown Accord. Rae's position was that a national system of health care, an array of income support programs, free public and secondary education, and affordable post-secondary education had become common values shared by Canadians and expected from their governments.[43]

Proponents of the social charter argued that entrenchment would prevent erosion of these rights by governments obsessed with deficit and debt reduction.[44] They claimed that equality of treatment across provinces would be ensured, instead of the danger of harmful competition in which provincial governments would reduce social programs as a part of a strategy to reduce taxes and thereby attract more economic growth—a possibility usually referred to as "the race to the bottom." They further argued that entrenchment would provide protection in the face of economic harmonization efforts, especially those related to free trade. Canadian businesses demanding "a level playing field" constantly pressured for tax reductions which, in turn, threatened established social programs.

Critics of an entrenched social charter argued that we could not and should not bind future governments financially, and that guaranteeing certain social programs in the constitution would prevent future governments from responding to the preferences of their electorates. Such a step would further elevate the role of the courts and dilute the role and responsibility of elected legislatures. Entrenchment opponents also pointed out that the judicial process is slow, relatively inflexible, and not accountable. The social charter died with the Charlottetown Accord and little has been heard of it since.

Those on the right contend that social benefits have been incorrectly labelled as democratic rights. They argue that our democratic

---

[43]See Ontario Ministry of Intergovernmental Affairs, *A Canadian Social Charter: Making Our Shared Values Stronger*, September 1991.

[44]For an examination of this topic, see Issue 23 in Mark Charlton and Paul Barker (eds.), *Crosscurrents: Contemporary Political Issues*, 2nd Edition, Scarborough, Nelson, 1994, pp. 493-511.

rights deal with such matters as free speech, free association, freedom from arbitrary arrest, and the right to due process of law, and have evolved over many centuries. In contrast, they object to the notion of economic and social "rights" and the implication that these are something we have as a birthright.[45] From the perspective of those on the right, all citizens are born with the right to free speech, but they are not all born with medical insurance. If the latter is seen as a right, and if some individuals can't afford such insurance, then other people must pay through taxation. If they decide to do so, they are conferring a benefit, not acknowledging a right. By the same token, a government can remove such benefits if there is no longer a willingness to support them financially.

Maintaining National Standards

Whether social programs are provided as a right or as a benefit, there are growing concerns about how to maintain national standards with respect to these programs. It has traditionally been assumed that any such standards would be maintained by the federal government, and could only be maintained by that body. Only the federal government is in a position to tax the wealth of Canada wherever it may be located and then to redistribute that wealth in ways that help to equalize (and therefore to standardize). Because of the extent of federal money transferred in support of provincial social programs, it was also felt that the federal government had the leverage necessary to enforce national standards.

As discussed in the previous chapter, this conventional way of looking at the issue was challenged by a paper from Thomas Courchene which formed the basis for discussions at the 1996 conference of Premiers.[46] Essentially, this paper argued the federal government now transferred insufficient money to give it the moral authority to enforce

---

[45]This viewpoint is well expressed in a *National Post* editorial, "Calling a benefit a right is wrong," November 28, 1998, on which this discussion is based.

[46]Thomas J. Courchene, *ACCESS: A Convention on the Canadian Economic and Social System*, a working paper prepared for the Ontario Ministry of Intergovernmental Affairs, August 1996.

national standards, and that identical, Canada-wide standards were inappropriate anyway. It envisaged a much greater provincial role in the development of standards and proposed a federal-provincial monitoring body to enforce them.

For now, the federal government continues to be the body which is expected to enforce national standards, and yet as the previous chapter indicated, the federal role in this regard has been greatly reduced. The key change in this regard was the replacement of two conditional grant programs (EPF and CAP) with the block grant known as the Canada Health and Social Transfer (CHST). Under CAP, the federal and provincial governments had agreed on four national standards that each provincial regime would meet in order to qualify for federal money.[47] All that remains under the CHST is a ban on residency requirements, and a number of provinces have moved to introduce work-for-welfare schemes that were previously not permitted. While health care standards were to be enforced through continued adherence to the five conditions of the Canada Health Care Act, there has been little federal reaction when a number of provinces have introduced or tolerated health care policies or practices which appear inconsistent with the Act. To the contrary, there is speculation that Ottawa is tacitly encouraging the expansion of a two tier health care system as a way of reducing future financial demands upon it.

Concluding Observations

If government is all about "who gets what, when, and how,"[48] Canada's experience with social programs offers some fascinating insights. For most of the post-war period, we operated on a kind of understanding or unwritten agreement that might be summarized as follows:

---

[47]See Ronald Manzer, "'And Dog Will Have His Day': National Standards in Canadian Social Policy," in Mark Charlton and Paul Barker (eds.), *Crosscurrents: Contemporary Political Issues*, 3rd Edition, Scarborough, Nelson, 1998, p. 151. This article is one side of Issue Seven, which deals with national standards.

[48]As in the title of the classic work by Harold Laswell, *Politics: Who gets what, when and how*, New York, Meridian Books, 1958.

> Citizens made a commitment to work and to pay taxes in return for state-funded insurance against temporary unemployment, old age, poor health and certain family responsibilities. The state committed to introduce policies that would ensure high levels of employment.[49]

The prolonged period of economic growth in the second half of the 20th century facilitated implementation of this social contract. Increasing tax revenues financed a welfare state and both employees and employers appeared to benefit and prosper, thereby contributing to expanding tax revenues.

This mutually reinforcing set of arrangements has largely fallen apart, for a variety of reasons. A perception developed that government had grown too large, levied excessive levels of taxation, and allowed programs of temporary relief from life's uncertainties to become on-going social benefits that were viewed as permanent entitlements, thus encouraging dependency. More difficult economic conditions in the 1980s and 1990s slowed the flow of tax revenues. Governments increasingly preoccupied with deficit and debt reduction changed their view of social programs. Once seen as contributing to economic growth by maintaining purchasing power, they were increasingly viewed as an expense that is no longer manageable. They were also portrayed as an impediment to Canada's competitiveness in the global market place.

The Canadian society which enters the 21st century has been significantly altered as a result of these changes. Our economic and fiscal health seems improved, to the extent that the federal government and most provinces have moved from annual deficits to balanced budgets or even budget surpluses and levels of unemployment have fallen steadily to about 7% at the end of 1999. But our social health and our social cohesion (the sense of mutual commitment among citizens) have not fared nearly as well. A growing number of Canadians feel insecure about their future and believe that

> Our fiscal health has improved, but at the expense of our social health and sense of social cohesion.

---

[49]Judith Maxwell, "Rethinking Government," in *Perspectives on Public Management*, Ottawa, Canadian Centre for Management Development, 1994, p. 49.

we are becoming a more divided and polarized society.[50] These feelings stem from developments such as these:

- the average income of Canadians declined in the 1990s.
- the real annual earnings (before tax/transfers) among young people declined by 30%.
- income polarization is increasing between a core group of older and more highly skilled workers and a group of younger workers with low skills and precarious jobs.
- the 1990s saw the "casualization" of the labour market, because of the growing use of contracting out by large companies and governments and the increased contract, temporary and seasonal work.
- the incidence of poverty has risen in the 1990s and those who are poor are getting poorer.

These developments paint a disturbing picture. They challenge the contention of those who put their faith in the market economy as the solution to society's needs. It seems increasingly clear that "a rising (economic) tide does not lift all boats." The economic growth of the recent past has not been shared at all equally. Canada's top 10 chief executive officers took home more than $10 million in 1998, and on average the top 100 CEOs enjoyed a hike of 56% in compensation.[51] In contrast, rank and file employees (in government as well as in the private sector) have endured wage freezes throughout much of the past decade, and those in need of government assistance are constantly told that such largesse can no longer be afforded.

The image of the "new Canada" includes over 2000 food banks[52] and a rate of homelessness which has been labelled a national disgrace. Many of the adults living on the streets are a product of past provincial initiatives to "deinstitutionalize" the mentally ill—without providing

---

[50]According to polls conducted throughout the 1990s by Ekos Research and quoted in The Senate Standing Committee on Social Affairs, Science and Technology, *Final Report*, June 1999. The discussion in this section is based on this report.

[51]Sue Bailey, "Gap growing between rich and poor," *Kingston Whig Standard*, February 25, 1999.

[52]Michael J. Prince, "From Health and Welfare to Stealth and Farewell: Federal Social Policy, 1980-2000," in Pal, *op. cit.*, p. 189.

other community facilities and supports for them. According to a study by the Clarke Institute of Psychiatry, 86% of the homeless have suffered from mental illness or substance abuse at some point in their lives.[53] Our governments have tightened employment insurance regulations so that fewer than half of those unemployed can now qualify, they have slashed welfare payments, and they have downloaded responsibility for public housing. When one of the consequences of these various government actions is increasingly pesky "squeegee kids," looming up at every traffic light, aggressively seeking to wash your car windows in return for some cash, the response of the newly reelected Conservative government in Ontario in mid-1999 was to promise a police crackdown and tougher measures to rid society of this nuisance.

> The government cutbacks of the past decade will end up costing *more* money in the long run.

One of the greatest ironies, even tragedies, of the fiscally-inspired government cutbacks of the past decade or so is that they will almost certainly end up costing *more* money in the long run. Especially distressing and short-sighted is our treatment of young children, far too many of whom live below the poverty line. The promise of a new national day care program has remained just that for a decade, even while governments have cut support for day care spaces and for junior kindergarten programs. Leading experts, like Dr. Fraser Mustard of the Canadian Institute for Advanced Research, emphasize that quality child care, specifically pre-school care, is one of the three or four major social instruments for correcting the effects of bad parenting, severely dysfunctional family life, social trauma, and violent behaviour.[54] For some reason, we have great difficulty getting through to politicians that what is invested in child care now carries a huge return down the road, saving great sums that would otherwise be spent on police, prosecutors, judges and jails. Yet long-term studies in the United States have concluded that

---

[53] As quoted in Carol Goar, "Punishing needy is not the answer," *Toronto Star*, June 27, 1999.

[54] Quoted in Michael Valpy, "Child Care: Why Politicians Still Matter," *Globe and Mail*, January 25, 1996.

$1 spent on quality pre-school care saves $7 that would have been spent later on welfare, policing, social services, and prisons.[55]

The response by governments to the problem of child poverty has been disgraceful. In the words of Linda Goyette of the *Edmonton Journal*:

> Back in 1989, after a unanimous resolution in Parliament, Canada promised the United Nations that it would work tirelessly to eradicate child poverty by the year 2000. In their curious wisdom, Ottawa and the provinces decided to reach this goal by cutting billions of dollars out of health, education and social programs; reducing the employment insurance and welfare payments to families; replacing the Canada Assistance Plan with a watery substitute; and abandoning the promise of a national day-care program.[56]

We know that children from poor families are undernourished and that this condition can lead to weight loss, stunted growth, weakened resistance to infection, and impaired cognitive development.[57] They are also more likely to use drugs, have problems with alcohol, or come into conflict with the law. The death rate due to fires, drowning, accident, suicides, and homicides is up to 10 times higher for poor children than for the general population.[58] So in our efforts to save money, we are creating a population that will help to fill our jails, courts and mental institutions. More perverse still, we seem more willing to spend money on jails, alarm systems, and private police than on the social programs which might prevent these problems from arising.

Equally short-sighted has been the government's approach to health care. As noted earlier in this chapter, what has really evolved is a sickness care system, in which only 5% of the health budget is actually devoted to prevention. Hospitals and doctors provide valuable, even

---

[55]Michael Valpy, "Taking it out on Child Care," *Globe and Mail*, January 24, 1996.

[56]Quoted in Stewart, *op. cit.*, p. 272. The fall 1999 Throne Speech from the Liberals has promised an action plan for children; time will tell.

[57]J. Larry Brown and Ernest Pollitt, "Malnutrition, Poverty and Intellectual Development," *Scientific American*, February 1996, p. 36, as quoted in Stewart, pp. 269-270.

[58]*Ibid.*, p. 274.

life-saving, treatment of sickness or illness, but they are not involved in health care—except to the extent that they may provide some education or counselling about maintaining a healthy lifestyle. According to the 1986 Ottawa Charter on Health Promotion, the prerequisites for health include peace, shelter, education, food, income, a stable ecosystem, social justice and equity. The Premier's Council on Health, Well-Being and Social Justice in Ontario came to similar conclusions. According to the Chair of the Determinants of Health Committee of the Premier's Council, "Canadians should be more concerned about job creation than hospital bed closures, if we are to improve the health of our population."[59] The findings of this Committee are that human health and longevity are linked to national wealth, household income, employment status, social support networks, level of education, early childhood development, and the quality of our natural and built environment. To put it in simplest terms, the number one determinant of health is wealth!

Dr. Fraser Mustard, a member of the Ontario Premier's Council on Health, emphasizes that health gains can best be achieved by integrating social and economic policies. He points out that life expectancy in Scandinavian countries, where governments have consciously used social policy to provide equal opportunities, is higher than in countries with higher average incomes, like the United States. He adds that research has shown that when income gaps are narrower, such as in Japan and Sweden, the population as a whole is healthier.[60]

In light of the above evidence, government policies have been doubly harmful with respect to health care. In a narrow sense, the policies have been misguided because they have focused on closing hospitals and cutting back on hospital beds before alternative community facilities are sufficiently in place and without adequate resources devoted to the maintenance of good health. In the broader sense, the policies have been very harmful because, in cutting back on social programs, downsizing their staff, and leaving job creation to the uncertainties of the market place, governments have undermined the very features which are widely held to be the key determinants of health. As

---

[59]Dr. Andrew Pipe, in a press release dated January 20, 1993.

[60]Quoted in *ibid.*

David Foot reminds us, "a mountain of evidence exists to prove that unemployment and poverty are the prime causes of poor health, yet this fact is rarely discussed in the context of our health care system."[61]

Instead of pursuing social justice and promoting social cohesion, too many of Canada's decisions with respect to social programs have been designed to serve economic objectives—whether domestic goals of fiscal restraint or global economic imperatives. A closer look at the economic context of government decision making is long overdue.

[61]David Foot (with Daniel Stoffman). *Boom, Bust & Echo*, Toronto, Macfarlane Walter & Ross, 1996, p. 180.

The Last Word

Definition of Terms and Concepts

CPP:
  Canada Pension Plan, which provides payments at 65 to those who have made payments into it.

Extra-billing:
  Charges by doctors which exceed the fee approved by the provincial health insurance program.

GIS:
  Guaranteed Income Supplement, providing a supplementary pension to the elderly who have no means of support other than old age security.

Medicare:
  Canada's national health care program, under which Canadians receive "free" hospital care and physicians' services on the basis of financing provided by the provinces, supported by federal funding and legislated standards under the Canada Health Act.

OAS:
  Old age security payments made by the federal government to all Canadians over 65 who meet basic residency requirements. (Not to be confused with the CPP which is only paid to those who have made contributions to it.)

Poverty Line:
  The point at which a family spends more than 20% more than the average family spends on food, shelter and clothing.

Social Charter:
  A constitutional declaration of certain social rights guaranteed to Canadians, similar to the Charter of Rights and Freedoms.

UI:
  Unemployment insurance (now called employment insurance), which provides insurance—through contributions made by both the employer

and the employee—against an interruption of income due to unemployment, illness or pregnancy.

Universal Programs:

Social programs provided to all Canadians regardless of need or circumstance—in contrast to targetted or means-tested programs, which are provided only to those who qualify.

Welfare State:

A network of government programs providing comprehensive social services for the population.

Workfare:

Government programs designed to require able-bodied welfare recipients to accept some form of employment (usually through community projects) in return for their cheques.

Points to Ponder

1. Are our social programs a primary cause of the deficit and debt problems of government, or have they been unfairly singled out?

2. What do you think of the concept of targeting social programs more specifically, so that the money gets to those most in need? What do you see as the pros and cons of universal versus targeted programs?

3. Do we need a strong federal commitment, including funding, to ensure national standards, or could such standards be set and maintained by the provinces?

4. Does the way we define poverty lines inflate the number who are classified as poor? How do you think poverty should be defined?

5. If Canada has already moved toward "passive privatization" and some elements of a two tier system of health care, should we formalize this development and encourage private, fee-for-service clinics as a way of freeing up our over-extended public health care system?

| For Further Reading |

Maude Barlow and Bruce Campbell, *Straight Through the Heart,* Toronto, HarperCollins Publishers Limited, 1995, present their case that Canada's social programs are under siege.

Stephen Brooks, *Public Policy in Canada,* 2nd Edition, Toronto, Mc-Clelland and Stewart, 1993, examines health policy in the context of a general chapter dealing with social policy in Canada.

Mike Burke and Michael Stevenson, "The Politics and Political Science of Health Care in Canada," in Paul Fox and Graham White (eds.), *Politics: Canada,* 8th Edition, Whitby, McGraw-Hill Ryerson Limited, 1995, pp. 564-576, examines the current state of health policy and funding in Canada.

The pros and cons of entrenching social rights in the constitution are explored by Brian Howe and Janet Ajzenstat in Mark Charlton and Paul Barker (eds.), *Crosscurrents: Contemporary Political Issues,* 2nd Edition, Scarborough, Nelson Canada, 1994.

For a good overview and analysis of developments in the last 20 years, see Michael J. Prince, "From Health and Welfare to Stealth and Farewell: Federal Social Policy, 1980-2000," in Leslie A. Pal (ed.), *How Ottawa Spends 1999-2000,* Toronto, Oxford University Press, 1999.

William G. Watson, "The View from the Right," in William Watson, John Richards and David Brown, *The Case for Change: Re-inventing the Welfare State,* Toronto, C.D. Howe Institute, 1994, provides the right wing perspective on Canada's social state, complete with numerous examples to illustrate the abuses of the system.

A great deal of information is available on the Internet on "both sides" of the story. See previously cited organizations such as the Fraser Institute (*www.fraserinstitute.ca*) and the Canadian Centre for Policy Alternatives (*www.policyalternatives.ca*), and also the Canadian Council on Social Development (*www.ccsd.ca*). On health matters see the Canadian Health Coalition (*www.healthcoalition.ca*) dedicated since 1979 to the preservation of medicare.

Chapter 10

It's the Economy, Stupid

Objectives and Highlights

◆ To examine the effectiveness of Canada's economic policies.

◆ To illustrate the economic limits on government actions.

◆ To describe the international economic framework within which Canada's governments operate.

The title of this chapter was used by Bill Clinton when, as Governor of Arkansas, he sought the United States presidency in 1992. He had these words on signs posted prominently on his campaign bus and in his campaign offices, as a reminder to keep his successful campaign focused on the single item that was identified as being most important to voters. Jean Chrétien, leader of the Liberal Party of Canada, similarly focused his successful federal election campaign of 1993 on the economy. The Liberal "Red Book" highlighted economic issues of importance to Canadians, particularly *"Jobs, Jobs, Jobs."* The Progressive Conservative Party of Ontario was the third party in the Ontario Legislature and in pre-election polls when the 1995 provincial election was called. But the party swept to power on the basis of its political manifesto labelled the "Common Sense Revolution," which stressed the party's desire to reduce the **deficit** and to get Ontario's economy back on track. The upswing in the economy which followed was presumably a major factor in its reelection in 1999. Politicians at the municipal level are similarly elected on the basis of their promises to keep property taxes down and to attract new businesses to their communities. The debt and deficit, inflation, jobs, and taxes are all economic themes of concern to the citizen, and are critical to the success of politicians at all three levels.

Government influences the economy, but economic forces have even more influence on government.

The actions which government can take to deal with economic concerns will be examined in this chapter, and illustrated by examples from the Canadian experience. But it has become increasingly clear that whatever influence governments may have on the economy, economic forces have even greater, and growing, influence over government. This influence is evident in the way in which governments have responded to their deficit and debt programs. It is also reflected in the frequent government assertions that their hands are tied because of the dictates or demands of the global economy. So the blunt title of this chapter is not only suggesting that jobs are important, but is also drawing attention to the real determinant of many government actions. Its intention is to provide enough background to allow you to form your own opinion about the extent to which Canada's governments are free to pursue Canadian policies and objectives.

Post-War Economic Management

The 1945 White Paper on Employment and Income committed the federal government to the pursuit of four main economic goals: (1) full employment, (2) price stability, (3) economic growth, and (4) balance of payments stability. These goals were to be achieved by applying the theories of British economist John Maynard Keynes. In simplest terms, Keynesian economics started with the position that government policies could be adopted to smooth out fluctuations in the economic cycles which countries experience Because of the cyclical nature of economic activity, with growth followed gradually by decline, and then by renewed growth, governments were expected to face at one time only one of the following key economic problems:

- an increase in **unemployment** as growth declined *or*

- an increase in prices or **inflation** as the economy took off again.

Keynesian policies addressed each of these as a separate problem. Faced with high unemployment, governments should pursue **fiscal policies** which "prime the pump" by increasing government spending and/or by introducing tax cuts to stimulate spending by consumers and businesses. In either case, the result would be a deficit budget, but the spending stimulus would lead to economic growth and the resulting tax revenues would allow the government to balance its budget again. **Monetary policies** to create "easy money," notably through a lowering of interest rates, would also help to stimulate growth.

Faced with high inflation, governments could dampen down economic activity and reduce the upward pressure on prices by decreasing government spending and/or increasing taxes to discourage consumer and business spending. The result would be a surplus budget, which would have the effect of taking money out of circulation and helping to "cool off" the economy. The accompanying monetary policy in this case would be "tight money" reflected in higher interest rates, which would tend to discourage business investment and consumer spending.

In addition to these deliberate adjustments to fiscal and monetary policy to manage the economy, governments also developed a number of what were known as "**automatic stabilizers.**" Most of these took the form of income maintenance programs that helped to ensure incomes and therefore purchasing power in the hands of Canadian consumers, which—in turn—would help to ensure consumer spending and economic growth.

Example of Automatic Stabilizer

A good example of an automatic stabilizer has been employment insurance. When the economy is booming, employment is high, more and more people are paying employment insurance premiums, and the surplus in the Fund is increasing. The premium payments, by taking money out of the economy, can be seen as helping to slow down the pace of economic growth and to reduce the upward pressure on prices (inflation). When the economy declines, unemployed workers draw upon the Fund, thereby increasing their purchasing power and helping to maintain spending and economic growth. Thus the Fund expands and contracts automatically in ways which help to offset whatever economic forces are underway.

Keynesian economics supported a strong role for government. It also justified the various social programs which were being introduced Whatever their merits as a humanitarian initiative, most of these programs were supported because they helped to shore up incomes and spending; they were an integral part of the economic policies of the time. The success of these policies, and the almost continuous expansion of the economy from 1945 until the early 1970s, generated the growing revenues needed to finance the social programs. Economic and social policies appeared to be mutually reinforcing.

As the 1970s unfolded, however, governments found themselves facing a combination of economic problems that were not supposed to occur together, according to Keynesian economics. Levels of unemployment and inflation both climbed and persisted together, creating what became known as "**stagflation**." Much of the inflation was triggered by the creation of OPEC in 1973. OPEC stands for oil producing and exporting countries, and it is essentially a cartel which was established to limit the supply of oil made available for sale, thereby forcing up its price. The resultant quadrupling of oil prices helped to push inflation to 10.8% and also contributed to job loss. The same results occurred when OPEC again restricted petroleum exports to Western countries in 1979. Inflation rose to a new high of 12% in 1981, and remained stubbornly high throughout that decade.

As these combined economic problems persisted, Keynesian economics fell out of favour. Economists began to believe that unemployment levels were not just the result of normal business cycles but were more related to rigidities in wage rates and prices. Inflation came to be seen as the most pressing economic problem. Whereas Keynesian theories had presumed that judicious use of fiscal and monetary policies could moderate business cycles and keep both unemployment and inflation low, the new view was that unemployment could not be reduced below a "natural" rate without triggering rapid inflation. The non-accelerating inflation rate of unemployment (NAIRU) was estimated to be about 9% in Canada.[1]

---

[1]Peter Leslie, "The Economic Framework: Fiscal and Monetary Policy," in Andrew F. Johnson and Andrew Stritch (eds.), *Canadian Public Policy: Globalization and Political Parties*, Toronto, Copp Clark Ltd., 1997, p. 32.

It was felt that governments would find it politically difficult, if not impossible, to pursue the tough fiscal policies needed to hold down inflation, given the accompanying

> Monetarist views focused on inflation replaced Keynesian economics.

high levels of unemployment that must result. Therefore, monetary policies began to receive increasing attention, sparked by the writings of such economists as Milton Friedman. The views of the monetarists, as they became known, gradually gained widespread acceptance and included the following policy implications:[2]

Policy Implications of Monetarism

- Inflation must be fought with monetary policy, preferably pursued by an independent central bank, insulated from government and public pressure. Fiscal policy should not counteract or undermine the thrust of the monetary policy.
- Fiscal policy should not be used to force unemployment below the NAIRU because that will inevitably trigger higher inflation. The only effective way to reduce unemployment is through "economic adjustment" policies which eliminate rigidities in prices and especially in wages. [Translation: Policies which weaken unions, deregulate the workplace, and remove employment security, so that wages can be reduced whenever employers risk becoming uncompetitive and so that superfluous staff can be shed as needed.]
- Policies for income security must not impede the operation of the labour market. Minimum wage laws, employment insurance, and welfare were considered economically inefficient because of their focus on equity.

The Bank of Canada embraced monetarism in the mid-1970s and ever since has been in the forefront of the battles against inflation. It originally proposed to reduce the rate of growth in the supply of money very gradually over a period of years, but developments in the United States forced a change. At the end of the 1970s, the American Federal Reserve System (its central bank) responded to the inflation induced by OPEC (and the heavy military spending on the war in Vietnam) by

---

[2]*Ibid.*, pp. 33-34.

introducing tight money policies featuring high interest rates. Canadian interest rates rose in tandem, because of a fear that American funds invested in Canada would otherwise move back south of the border— since money goes where it can gain the highest rate of return.

From the mid-1980s, the Bank of Canada became even more obsessed with inflation; its objective was not just to reduce it but to achieve "zero inflation." There were even suggestions that the legislation governing the Bank's operations be amended to remove any reference to its responsibilities with respect to growth and employment and to make its only goal that of controlling inflation. In pursuit of its economic objective, the Bank limited growth in the money supply and kept interest rates high (to discourage excessive spending which might drive up prices). The anti-inflation extremism exhibited by Canada at this time was dubbed by one critic as sado-monetarism.[3]

There were two very significant side effects of such monetary policies: (1) they increased the cost of borrowing for the government and, therefore, the cost of financing its debt and (2) they contributed to higher unemployment in Canada. On the latter point, Economist Pierre Fortin[4] argues that Canada's much weaker economic performance in comparison to the United States can be explained by an overly tight monetary policy compounded by fiscal restraint brought on by sharp cuts in government expenditures. He points out that the U.S. Federal Reserve has been content to achieve an inflation target of 3% which has not stood in the way of growth and relatively full employment in that country. In contrast, the Bank of Canada's actions in pursuit of its goal of 1% inflation have been the major cause of unemployment rates remaining almost double those found in the United States.

As the economy slid into a major recession at the end of the 1980s, inflation all but disappeared, with the **Consumer Price Index** (CPI) rising less than 2% a year. But unemployment soared to close to 12% (or more than 1.6 million Canadians looking for work) and interest pay-

[3]Unnamed critic is quoted in Linda McQuaig, *The Cult of Impotence: Selling the Myth of Powerlessness in the Global Economy*, Toronto, Penguin Books Canada Ltd, 1998, p. 124.

[4]Pierre Fortin, "Raise the Inflation Targets and Let Canada Recover," *Globe and Mail*, September 26, 1996.

ments on the debt of the federal government became greater than its spending on pensions, health care and education combined!

The Deficit and the Debt

The amount of **public debt** replaced inflation as the central preoccupation of government as the 1990s unfolded. This debt represents the total of all net budget deficits (not offset by budget surpluses) accrued by government over time. Since Confederation the federal public debt has increased almost every year in absolute terms.[5] Much of this debt arose because of the series of annual budget deficits which inevitably resulted from fighting two world wars and from dealing with the prolonged depression of the 1930s. A good deal of the debt took the form of investments in the basic infrastructure of Canada, the provision of railways, dams, power plants, airports, and other facilities which laid the foundation for expansion of the economy. This debt is similar to that incurred by a private company when it expands its plant or equipment to increase its productive capacity. It is seen as worthwhile debt, which will more than pay for itself in the long term. An increase in public debt is also viewed with less concern if the economy, and the ability to sustain that debt, is increasing even more rapidly— just as individuals increase their debt to purchase a new home without undue concern if they are experiencing increasing annual incomes.

But certain features of Canada's debt were worrisome by the 1990s. One was the rapid growth of the debt, fuelled by more than 25 consecutive annual budget deficits—deficits which grew larger each year until they reached more than $40 billion at their peak. Of particular concern was the fact that by the 1990s the total public debt had become so large that much of each year's annual deficit was made up of the cost of servicing that debt. By the 1990s, the federal government was taking in more revenues than it required for program spending, but the cost of repaying the public debt pushed it into a deficit position each year. As a result, Canada found itself in the grip of a vicious downward spiral.

[5]C. Michael Fellows, Greg Flanagan and Stanford Shedd, *Economic Issues: A Canadian Perspective*, Toronto, Irwin, 1997, p. 499.

Each year it had to borrow more money, mostly to cover interest charges on previously borrowed money, and each new borrowing only increased the interest charges that it would have to finance from borrowing the next year.

An added concern was that the nature of the debt was changing significantly. At one time, the debt was almost totally owned by Canadians, and there was comfort in the thought that "we owe it to ourselves." But foreign holdings of government securities increased substantially in the 1980s and 1990s, reaching 35% by 1995.[6] Thus Canada was not only generally vulnerable to shifts in investor confidence because of its high level of debt, but this vulnerability was intensified by the high proportion of debt owned by foreigners.

As this problem deepened, it was widely held that the cause of Canada's deficit and debt problems was excessive spending on social programs. This view was vigorously advanced by the business community, which also claimed that the cost of these programs added a financial burden which made it more difficult for Canadian companies to compete in the global market. Ironically, the social programs which had once been viewed as an essential component of economic policy in Canada, were now dismissed as a barrier to economic growth. The erosion of the social programs which resulted has been summarized in the preceding chapter.

The Real Causes of the Debt

The allegation that social programs caused Canada's debt problems does not hold up to close examination. Wolfe's 1985 observation that no new social programs have been instituted in Canada since 1975 is still valid.[7] The cost of the programs already in place increased mainly because of recessions in 1981-83 and 1989-1992—recessions which some would argue were prolonged and made worse by government higher interest rate policies overly preoccupied with curbing inflation to the neglect of

---

[6] *Ibid.*, p. 504.

[7] David Wolfe, "The Politics of the Deficit," in Bruce Doern, *The Politics of Economic Policy*, Volume 40 of the research studies for the Macdonald Commission, Toronto, University of Toronto Press, 1985, p. 141.

unemployment. Moreover, according to Wolfe the key factor in explaining the growing debt has been the unwillingness of the federal government to increase the level of taxation, especially of business and the wealthy, to keep pace with expenditure growth.

Statistics Canada studies support this contention by showing that government spending, and specifically social spending, held steady from 1975 to 1991. The increase in deficits after 1975 was caused, not by any surge in spending, but by a drop in federal revenues relative to the growth of the economy and by rising debt charges. Revenues dropped partly because of a variety of tax concessions introduced by the federal government, particularly concessions to business. These are usually termed "**tax expenditures**" to reflect the cost they impose on the federal treasury and they have added up to many billions a year over the past couple of decades. They are a form of welfare or social spending for business which somehow gets overlooked when the business community is criticizing social programs.

> Deficits increased because of a drop in revenues caused by tax concessions, especially to business.

McQuaig cites a 1991 study by an official in Statistics Canada that calculates how much each social program contributed to the growth of the federal debt.[8] It found unemployment insurance responsible for only 1% of the debt problem, welfare 4.5%, and old age pensions 6%. It found that family allowance benefits had been cut so severely after 1975 that they helped to *reduce* the debt growth by 11%. Overall, the study found that Canada was spending roughly the same portion of its **Gross Domestic Product** on social programs in 1991 as it had been in the mid-1970s, when the debt was considered small and manageable.

The Statistics Canada study also found that by far the biggest cause of the debt was rising interest costs, which accounted for 44% of the growth of the national debt between 1974-75 and 1988-89. In the fiscal year 1988-89 alone, interest charges accounted for 72% of the deficit. These interest charges were largely the result of deliberate government

---

[8]Linda McQuaig, *Shooting the Hippo*, Toronto, Penguin Books, 1995, pp. 56-58 and p. 117, on which this section is based.

policies directed toward eliminating inflation, an objective strongly urged by the business community.

The evidence seems clear. Canada's deficit and debt crisis was *not* caused by excessive spending on social programs. It is true that since these programs accounted for some two-thirds of government spending, it was difficult for them to escape the "axe" when deficit reduction efforts focused on cutting expenditures rather than increasing revenues. But the fact that they became part of the solution does not mean that they were the cause of the problem, a key point not to be forgotten.

By the end of the 1990s the federal government had succeeded in eliminating the string of annual deficits and had a budget surplus of some $10 billion. While some of this turnaround was achieved through expenditure cuts, including cuts in transfers to the provinces, much of it can be attributed to a combination of lower interest rates which reduced the carrying cost of the debt and increased government revenues from a growing economy. Both of these positive influences were largely the result of a prolonged expansion of the United States economy throughout the 1990s, accompanied by sufficiently low inflationary pressures that American interest rates have remained low (thus allowing Canadian rates to remain low as well).[9]

With a budget surplus now, and with surpluses projected for the next several years, presumably spending will be directed to shoring up Canada's eroded social programs. Not necessarily. The business community remains adamant that any surplus must be used to finance tax cuts, so that they can be more competitive in international markets. Others insist that the surplus be used to begin paying down Canada's huge public debt, lest the international financial community lose confidence in Canada's fiscal prudence. The International Monetary Fund advocated this approach in late November 1999, in its annual review of Canada (an exercise it carries out for all of its member countries). It is critical of Canada's ratio of debt to Gross Domestic Product and calls for tax cuts as well as debt repayment to be the two priorities for Canada's budget surpluses, along with "moderate" spending initiatives

---

[9]It is noteworthy that the American experience of very low unemployment rates not triggering inflation should cast doubt on the NAIRU concept and its implicit argument for keeping unemployment high.

in education and health care.[10] The debate over what will be done with the surplus draws attention to the extent that outside forces influence Canadian economic decision making.

The Truth About Taxes

In recent years, there have been growing demands for tax cuts, especially as the federal government has moved from chronic annual deficits to the prospect of ongoing annual budget surpluses. Largely through the efforts of the business community and business-backed "think tanks" such as the Fraser and C.D. Howe Institutes, there has been widespread acceptance of the notion that Canadians are severely over-taxed compared to most other Western countries, and that this excessive tax burden is contributing to a growing brain drain south of our "best and brightest." A closer examination, however, raises a number of questions about these tax allegations.

As indicated in the table below, Canada places very close to the middle of the **OECD** countries, both overall and for most individual taxes being compared.

Tax Revenue as a share of GDP, 1996[11]

	Personal Income	Corporate	Social Security	Goods & Services	Other Taxes	Total Tax Revenues
Canada	13.9	3.3	5.9	9.1	4.6	36.8
United States	10.7	2.7	6.7	4.9	3.5	28.5
European Union	11.0	3.2	11.2	13.3	3.7	42.4
OECD average	10.1	3.1	8.4	12.3	3.8	37.7

[10]Tim Harper, "IMF tells Canada: Cut debt and taxes," *Toronto Star*, November 20, 1999.

[11]From OECD statistics quoted in Murray Dobbin, *Ten Tax Myths*, Canadian Centre for Policy Alternatives, October 1999, p. 9.

Personal income taxes are higher in Canada, and there is no denying that they have increased substantially over the past few decades. According to the Fraser Institute, the average Canadian family's tax bill rose from 33.5% to 46.4% of family income between 1961 and 1998, and the tax bill now accounts for more of the budget than shelter, food and clothing combined.[12] This latter comparison is quite misleading according to Dobbin, because the use of averages produces skewed results that ascribe tax rates to the average person that are actually paid only by taxpayers at considerably higher income levels. Using 1997 data from Statistics Canada, he shows that for 40% of Canadian households, income taxes represented the *smallest* share of expenditures and that only for the top two income groups were taxes the major household expenditure.[13]

A good portion of the tax bite is caused by **"bracket creep"** as a result of changes introduced by the Mulroney government in 1986. Between 1973 and 1985 the personal income tax system was fully indexed, which simply meant that personal exemptions and tax brackets were adjusted each year to take account of inflation and thus to protect taxpayers from having to pay higher taxes because of incomes increased by inflation. This protection cost the government a good deal in tax revenues and a partial de-indexing was brought in, under which tax brackets and the amounts used to calculate personal tax credits were only adjusted by the amount of inflation over 3%.

How does this growing level of personal income tax compare with other countries? Critics of tax levels always draw comparisons with the United States, so let's use that as our frame of reference.[14] The table which follows compares federal tax brackets only, but the impact of state and provincial taxes is also discussed below.

---

[12] As quoted in Luiza Chwialkowska, "Taxes exceed total for food, shelter and clothing," *National Post*, March 12, 1999.

[13] Dobbin, *op. cit.*, p. 5.

[14] The discussion which follows is based on Marc Lee, *The Lowdown on High Taxes*, Canadian Centre for Policy Alternatives, September 10, 1999.

Federal Tax Brackets, Canada and the US, 1999	
1 United States Canada	15% on the first $23 500 of income 17% on the first $29 590 of income
2 United States Canada	28% on income between $25 351 and $61 400 26% on income between $29 591 and $59 180
3 United States Canada	31% on income between $611,401 and $128 100 29% on income over $59 181 (But a 5% surcharge effectively raises the top federal marginal tax rate to 31.3%)
4 United States	36% on income between $128 101 and $278 450
5 United States	39.6% on income over $278 450

What do these figures indicate?

- 1999 federal income tax rates by tax bracket in Canada and the United States for a single individual taxpayer are very similar, except that the United States has two additional brackets that apply to high income earners.
- the big difference in the overall tax levels between the two countries comes from income taxes at the provincial or state level. Canadian provinces have income tax based on a percentage of the value of federal income taxes owing, ranging from 44% in Alberta to 69% in Newfoundland.[15] Income taxes at the state level vary widely, but they are lower than those of Canada's provinces, resulting in a combined tax burden which is lower in the United States than that found in Canada.
- much of the difference in tax levels reflects public policy choices about social programs, which account for at least two-thirds of provincial budgets (and which explain their higher tax burden). According to a study by DRI

> The higher tax levels in Canada compared to the United States reflect enriched social programs.

[15]Although Alberta, and more recently Ontario, have announced plans to de-link their provincial taxes, so that their revenue yield won't be affected by changes in federal rates.

Canada (a subsidiary of Standard and Poor's), when private medical and education costs in the United States are factored in, the difference in the tax burden disappears.[16]

What about business taxes? According to the business community and its advocates, these taxes are also far too high in Canada as compared to other countries, and are reaching an intolerable level. But the fact is that the tax burden has been shifting from business to individual taxpayers for the past 50 years. In the early 1950s, revenues from personal and corporate taxation were roughly in balance. Since then, the balance has swung heavily against personal taxpayers. This pattern intensified during the Mulroney years in the 1980s. One study of this period notes that after the Conservatives came to power in 1984, corporate taxes increased by only 8%, income taxes by 45%, and the sales tax (not counting the GST) by 67%.[17]

A number of studies by KPMG indicate that the taxes affecting corporations in Canada are extremely competitive with those in other developed countries. One such study, comparing the cost of doing business in Canada, the United States, the United Kingdom, France, Germany, Italy, and Sweden, showed that Canada had the *lowest* effective corporate income tax rate—that is, the tax rate actually paid after all the tax breaks and credits were deducted. Canada's rate (including federal and provincial taxes) was 27.4%, while the United States rate was 40%, placing it in fifth place among the countries studied.[18]

However, corporate taxes have been reduced in a number of countries in recent years, placing continuing pressure on Canada to lower its rates. Britain, Denmark, France, Italy, Switzerland, and Turkey are among the countries that have cut corporate taxes since 1996. A 1998 report to Finance Minister Paul Martin by a committee of experts

---

[16]Lee, *op. cit.*

[17]Isabella Bakker, "The Size and Scope of Government: Robin Hood Sent Packing?" in Michael Whittington and Glen Williams (eds.), *Canadian Politics in the 1990s*, 3rd Edition, Scarborough, Nelson, 1990, p. 444.

[18]*The Competitive Alternative: A comparison of business costs in Canada, Europe and the United States*, KPMG, Prospectus Inc., October 1997, as quoted in Dobbin, *op. cit.*, p. 12.

concluded that Canada had a comparatively heavier business tax burden than many other major economies and called for tax cuts.[19]

Given the tax realities described above, how do we explain the persistence of the argument that taxes must be reduced dramatically, even at the expense of further erosion of Canada's social programs? The short answer is that this has become the prevailing ideology. But this situation also reflects the fact that even those who believe in maintaining social programs through whatever level of taxation that requires, find themselves increasingly constrained by forces beyond their control. More and more, global interests are taking precedence over domestic interests, and a closer look at that international context is long overdue.

The International Economic Context

While it is only in recent years that the term "global economy" has come to the fore, Canada has always been a trading nation, dependent on external markets for its products. Long before Confederation, Canada developed primarily as a supplier of certain staple commodities such as fur, cod, and timber. After Confederation, the "National Policy" of Macdonald (emphasizing state-subsidized railway construction and immigration policies geared to settlement of the wheat-growing Prairies) reinforced Canada's role as a resource-producing hinterland in the international division of labour.[20] We did gradually develop our secondary manufacturing, but mainly on the basis of foreign—mostly United States—investment, which brought outside influence and control over the operations of our domestic economy. Over 70% of Canada's import and export trade were accounted for by the American market, even before the Canada-U.S. free trade agreement of 1988 (discussed later in this chapter) ensured the further integration of our two economies.

---

[19]Neville Nankivell, "Reducing corporate rates cannot be delayed too long," *National Post*, March 12, 1999.

[20]This discussion is based on Stephen Brooks, *Public Policy in Canada*, Toronto, McClelland & Stewart Inc., 1993, Chapter 3.

The main reason that countries trade is that the earth's resources are not equally distributed across its surface and therefore each nation must trade with others to acquire what it lacks. International trade allows each party that enters into a trading agreement to benefit from the exchange.[21] This happens because products are redistributed in such a way that both parties end up having a combination of goods that best meets their preferences than the goods they held before the trade. In effect, a trading nation specializes in producing those goods it can produce best, exports what is surplus to its needs, and uses the money earned from the exports to import the goods that it cannot produce as well.

This process is analogous to the specialization which individuals pursue in the modern age. At one time, we operated in a much more self-sufficient manner, clearing the land and building a home, growing our own food, even making our own clothes. Today, we find it much more efficient to specialize in a particular activity and then to use the money earned from this activity to purchase the goods and services we need from others who have also specialized. But with our modern efficiency, we also find ourselves much less self-sufficient. Depending on others to provide for us can leave us vulnerable to the caprices of the unreliable tradesperson or "handyman." In much the same way, countries that specialize gain efficiencies and lose self-sufficiency. They must depend for certain goods and services on other countries, and their source of supply can be disrupted by events totally beyond their control.

Nations which trade face the challenge of maintaining a balance in their international payments. Since Canada purchases extensive imports from the United States, for example, it requires a sufficient supply of American dollars to pay for these imports. It can earn these dollars by selling enough exports to the United States, but a perfect balance in these exchanges is most unlikely. United States and Canadian dollars also flow back and forth across the borders of the two countries as a result of such things as travel, tourism and investment (both direct and indirect). The balance between these flows affects the exchange rate of the currencies of Canada and the United States—that is, the value that

---

[21] The inevitability of this beneficial result arises from the principles of absolute and comparative advantage, as described in any introductory economics text.

each has in relation to the other. The exchange rate for the Canadian dollar (in relation to the American dollar) has been around 66 cents throughout most of 1999, meaning that our dollar is worth only two-thirds of an American dollar.

This low value for the Canadian dollar reflects the fact that, for much of the post-war period, Canada has had a shortage of American dollars to balance its international payments. This has not been caused by an export-import imbalance, but by the fact that so much American direct investment flowed into Canada in the early post-war period that it has given rise to a continuous outflow of American dollars in the form of interest and dividend payments to American lenders and share-holders. If American dollars are in short supply in Canada, their value goes up, which, in turn, pushes down the value of the Canadian dollar. As the Canadian dollar devalues, it costs Canadians more to purchase American imports, increasing the cost of living for us. To avoid or to minimize this situation, it has been Canadian policy over the years to maintain interest rates at least slightly higher than those prevailing in the United States so as to attract American dollars and thus keep the ex-change rate stable. The problem with this policy is that high interest rates, however appropriate for maintaining our exchange rate, are at times entirely inappropriate for the conditions of our domestic economy which may be experiencing a depression and should be stimulated by a policy of low interest rates. As this admittedly oversimplified example illustrates, economic policies often face a clash between international and domestic consideration.

> International and domestic needs may not call for the same economic policy.

Free Trade Agreements

Canada has been involved in a number of free trade agreements over the years, beginning with Commonwealth preference treaties with Britain. Since 1948 it has been a member of the General Agreement on Tariffs and Trade (GATT)—now known as the **World Trade Organization**—a body which has negotiated gradually lower trade barriers among its member nations. In 1965 Canada entered into an Auto Pact agreement with the United States which provided for free trade in cars, trucks, buses, and auto parts. 1988 saw the signing of a very controversial free trade agreement with the United States. This was followed by an agreement with the United States and Mexico which ushered in the North American Free Trade Association (NAFTA), the largest trading area in the world, accounting for nearly 30% of the global economy.[22] Why has Canada taken these steps, and what are the implications?

Pros and Cons of FTA and NAFTA

Proponents of free trade argued that the 1988 deal was critical to ensure Canada's continued access to its largest market, in the face of growing **protectionist** sentiment in the United States. With the world increasingly moving toward a series of large trading blocs, there was a concern that Canada might be left "outside" and a feeling that it should lock in a permanent relationship with its main trading partner. More generally, it was argued that free trade agreements would give Canadian companies unrestricted access to much larger markets in which they would grow and prosper. Under the stimulus of expanded free trade, the produc-tivity of Canadian companies would increase as well.

Opponents of free trade worried about the massive adjustments which would occur in the economy of Canada as resources were shifted to respond to the new trading arrangements, and the higher unemployment which would result—at least in the short term. They argued that sufficient progress toward freer trade was being made under the auspices of GATT (now the World Trade Organization) and that it was both unnecessary and unwise to tie our economic future so closely to the American economy. Without a tariff wall in place, they predicted that United States branch plants in Canada would shut down and move back home since they could ship their products back into Canada without any trade barriers. Most of all, critics of the FTA worried about the potential loss of Canadian independence as we became increasingly intertwined with the United States economy.[23] Among their key concerns

---

[22]This discussion is partly based on James John Guy, *How We Are Governed*, Toronto, Harcourt Brace & Company, 1995, p. 417.

[23]This was certainly not a new fear, given that the Liberals had lost the election of 1911 when they ran on a platform of free trade with the United States.

were the potential threat to Canadian culture and the possible loss of control over our supply of fresh water.

A little over 10 years later, what has been the effect of the new trading arrangements? According to Jeffrey Simpson, they "neither produced all the wondrous gains supporters predicted nor caused the calamities critics so menacingly foretold."[24] Among the effects are:

- There is general agreement that the FTA is at least partly responsible for a very dramatic increase in Canada-U.S. trade. During the first decade of the agreement, Canadian exports to the United States rose by 169% and imports from the United States rose by 149%.[25]
- Given this development, it is surprising that the expected productivity gains have not materialized, although measurements in this area are complex and subject to varying interpretations.
- The overall impact on jobs and economic growth is also difficult to determine. Under free trade, Canada's unemployment rate rose from 7.5% to more than 11%, before gradually falling back to the 7% range in late 1999. This pattern could suggest that the restructuring of the economy prompted by the FTA produced higher unemployment but only of a short term nature. But it can also be argued that ineffective domestic economic policies in Canada prolonged the country's recovery from the severe recession at the beginning of the 1990s. A study by Trefler[26] found that job losses in manufacturing between 1988 and 1996 were significantly compounded by the FTA and that restructuring prompted by tariff cuts may have accounted for as many as one in three of the lost manufacturing jobs.
- By a number of measures the Canadian economy has done worse than the American economy since the signing of the FTA. For example, the Canadian unemployment rate is almost double that of the United States and our living standards (as measured by inflation-adjusted personal disposal income per person) have declined by 5%

---

[24]Jeffrey Simpson, "Free-trade deal the right choice," *Globe and Mail*, June 4, 1999.

[25]John McCallum, "Two Cheers for the FTA," *Policy Options*, Montreal, IRRP, June 1999, p. 6. There are several articles on free trade in this issue.

[26]Daniel Trefler of the University of Toronto, as quoted in Andrew Jackson, "From Leaps of Faith to Lapses of Logic," *Policy Options*, June 1999, p. 16.

as compared to a 12% increase in the United States.[27] But here again, the differences may be the result of domestic economic policies in the two countries as much or more than because of the FTA.

- The dispute settlement processes established under both the FTA and NAFTA have been used extensively (more than 50 times) and their busy history shows that they are preferable to other previously available options.[28] On the other hand, the binational panels set up under these processes are required to apply the law "as it may be amended from time to time," and the Americans have shown themselves willing to use this avenue to protect their domestic interests.

- Concerns over cultural sovereignty appear to be valid. NAFTA does contain a "cultural industries" exception which Canada had used to protect its domestic magazine industry, but the United States filed a complaint with the World Trade Organization which ruled against Canada's tax on American magazines. Canada then tried another avenue with Bill C-55, which was designed to keep U.S. "split-run" magazines out of Canada by imposing a ban on Canadian advertising in them. The Americans threatened various forms of retaliation and our government was forced to back down.

- More than cultural sovereignty appears to be lost as a result of NAFTA giving foreign firms new rights to challenge almost any regulatory action that might "expropriate" their future earnings. Consider the example of the federal government's effort to legislate a ban on the gasoline additive MMT, a product which allegedly poses a significant health hazard. The manufacturer of this product, Ethyl Corporation of the United States, launched a $251 million lawsuit against the Canadian government, claiming it had expropriated its future profits by the ban. The federal government retreated and withdrew the ban, an action which shows "how dramatically power has been lost to the foreign marketplace."[29]

---

[27]McCallum, *op. cit.*, pp. 6-7.

[28]Peter Watson, "Dispute Settlement Under FTA-NAFTA," *Policy Options*, June 1999.

[29]Stephen Clarkson and Timothy Lewis, "The Contested State: Canada in the Post-Cold War, Post-Keynesian, Post-Fordist, Post-National Era," in Leslie Pal (ed.), *How Ottawa Spends 1999-2000*, Toronto, Oxford University Press, 1999, p. 316.

- Concerns over Canadian fresh water continue to surface as well.[30] British Columbia banned bulk exports of water in 1995 before any of the firms planning to ship it to California could get their operations up and running. In 1998 Ontario gave a permit to a group planning to ship Lake Superior water to Asia, but then withdrew it in the face of strong public opposition. Free trade critics like Maude Barlow of the Council of Canadians argue that if any bulk water export is allowed, all water will have to be treated as a trade good, subject to strict NAFTA rules. The federal government concedes that this is a contentious area of trade law and announced plans, in February 1999, to outlaw all bulk water exports—if the provinces agree (something which hadn't happened as of the end of 1999).

Taking into account all of the above, it is hard to conclude that the free trade agreements have been a success for Canada. The productivity gains that were supposed to be the most important benefit have not materialized. Nor has the economic restructuring under free trade led to an upsurge in large Canadian companies carving out new markets in North America and beyond. While some such companies have flourished, Canada's overall economic dependence on the U.S. market has grown, not declined, and at an accelerating rate. Americans paid more than $25 billion for 127 Canadian companies in the first 11 months of 1999, compared with $16 billion for 121 companies in all of 1998.[31] Nor has gaining secure access to the U.S. market removed trade disputes, as the extensive activities under the dispute settlement processes indicate. "Whatever the Americans could not secure during the negotiations —agriculture, cultural policies, lumber-stumpage rates—they have continued to seek through a variety of means."[32]

If the main result of the free trade agreements has been to expand Canada's already extensive trade with the United States, it is not clear why

> **Is even closer integration with the U.S. economy advantageous for Canada?**

---

[30]The discussion which follows is based on John Geddes, "Hot Water," *Maclean's*, May 17, 1999, pp. 26-28.

[31]Peter C. Newman, "The Year of Living Dangerously," *Maclean's*, December 20, 1999.

[32]*Ibid.*

this is advantageous. Integrating our economy even more closely with that of the United States will make it that much more difficult to pursue independent economic policies. It will also increase the pressure for a "harmonization" with the American way of doing business, which is a euphemism for such changes as reducing taxes, environmental standards, collective bargaining rights, and any other factors considered as impediments to the free market and the pursuit of profit.

What makes the pressure so difficult to resist is that it is presented as an inevitable by-product of the global economy, as simply recognizing "competitive realities." But the global economy is being used as an excuse or a scapegoat. The reality is that these problems arise because big business and international capital are no longer subject to some of the controls and "checks and balances" that used to apply to them. To explain this statement requires a little historical background.

The Post-War Framework and its Demise[33]

When World War II was drawing to a close, political leaders like Roosevelt and Churchill were determined not to have a repeat of the problems which had occurred before World War I. Trade volumes between North American and Europe had increased continuously from the late 19th century, but the inequalities in the distribution of wealth generated by this trade went largely unaddressed because of the laissez faire[34] governing philosophy of the time. It was widely believed that these inequalities contributed over time to political turbulence, revolution, depression, and the two world wars.

As a result, the new economic order after World War II entailed new multilateral organizations set up to ensure cooperation among trading partners. Stability and predictability in international economic transactions was provided through the establishment of fixed exchange

---

[33]The discussion which follows is largely based on Ethan B. Kapstein, "A Global Third Way: Social Justice and the World Economy," *World Policy Journal*, Winter 1998/99, Vol. 15, pp. 23-35.

[34]This expression literally means to leave alone and depicts a view that government play a very limited role and not interfere with the operations of the private sector.

rates, equated to the Unites States dollar, with this currency essentially replacing gold as "the standard." An International Monetary Fund (IMF) was established to handle any exchange rate adjustments that might be needed, so as to prevent countries

> Stability in international economic transactions was based on fixed exchange rates and new bodies such as the IMF.

from devaluing their currencies unilaterally[35] to gain a trade advantage on others. The Fund was also authorized to make emergency loans when countries suffered a balance-of-payments crisis, so that they would not be tempted to adopt protectionist trade measures of the sort which aggravated the depression of the 1930s. A World Bank was also created, to provide funds for postwar reconstruction and aid and technical assistance to developing countries. The overall concept was to support and encourage all member states to move along the path to a liberalized global economy.

For more than 25 years, these postwar arrangements worked very well. In fact, between 1950 and 1973, the world enjoyed the greatest growth spurt in its history.[36] To a considerable extent, the resulting wealth was shared, because of the social programs being put into place in most Western nations during this period, Canada included. The dream of economic growth *and* social justice seemed achievable.

Then, as noted earlier in this chapter, the Western world was rocked by the Organization of Petroleum Exporting Countries (OPEC) oil embargo. When the OPEC countries restricted production of oil, so essential to most production processes, its price rose dramatically, leading to both higher unemployment and an increase in inflation. The same "double whammy" occurred when OPEC again restricted petroleum exports to western countries in 1979. Unemployment and inflation both climbed to over 10%, creating a condition which became known as stagflation. As it persisted, governments began to turn away from the

---

[35]By devaluating its currency, a country makes it worth less in relation to the currencies of its trading partners. As a result, it is cheaper for those countries to import goods for the country which has devalued.

[36]Kapstein, *op. cit.*

Keynesian economic policies they had followed since the end of WWII and they embraced monetary policies almost exclusively concerned with eliminating inflation.

As dramatic and high profile as the OPEC crisis was, with motorists lined up for blocks to "top up" their gas tanks, it is clear that the collapse of the postwar economic order actually began two years earlier, with the abandonment of fixed exchange rates. This move was precipitated by the United States, whose currency faced strong downward pressure because it had been over-committed in helping to finance much of the postwar economic expansion. But once exchange rates were allowed to float, currencies themselves became the object of speculation, creating entirely new financial markets. "Banks invested heavily in computer technologies that enabled them to exploit arbitrage opportunities—that is, any mismatch between the price and underlying value of currencies—buying and selling foreign exchange in response to a state's actual and projected economic conditions."[37] Economic agents sought to diversify their currency holdings and to exploit the opportunities offered by floating rates.

As Linda McQuaig points out, daily trading in foreign exchange markets around the world grew from almost nothing to $150 billion by the mid-1980s, to $880 billion by 1992, and to $1.2 billion by 1995. Most of this trading is not a reflection of the healthy flow of capital involved in nations trading and investing in each other; it is short-term, speculative buying and selling of currencies to generate profits. Two-thirds of the currency exchanges in 1995, for example, were for fewer than seven days and only 1% lasted as long as a year.[38] According to Michalos, only about 2% of all global foreign currency exchange activity is connected to the export and import of real goods.[39]

Under these new circumstances, it became much harder for countries to maintain capital controls, since financial institutions were anxious to diversify their currency holdings and to exploit the opportunities

---

[37]*Ibid.*

[38]McQuaig, *The Cult of Impotence, op. cit.* pp. 153-158.

[39]Alex C. Michalos, "The Tobin Tax: A Good Idea Whose Time Has *Not* Passed," *Policy Options*, Montreal, IRRP, October 1999, p. 64.

provided by floating exchange rates. Mobile capital was now free to roam the planet, giving it tremendous power over economic policy making, and forcing countries to get their monetary and fiscal houses in order if they wished to be on the receiving end of international investment.[40] The ability of national governments to pursue domestic policies was severely constrained as a result. "With a click of the mouse, after entering a few numbers into the computer, bond markets and transnational corporations can change the course of any nation's development."[41] When Moody's Investor Services put Canada's AAA credit rating under review a few weeks prior to the 1995 federal budget, the message received by the government was that it had no choice but to cut spending, two-thirds of which was made up of social programs.[42] As one observer sees the situation:[43]

> ...we live again in a two superpower world. There is the U.S. and there is Moody's. The U.S. can destroy a country with bombs. Moody's can destroy a country by downgrading its bonds.

Besides undermining the independence of nation states, the unrestricted flow of capital has become a source of great instability in the world today. This instability was reflected in the Asian meltdown in 1997-98, just as it had been in the collapse of the Mexican peso and the upheaval in Latin American countries, notably Argentina, in 1994-95. There is no reason to expect this instability to lessen, especially since our response has been to bail out the financial institutions who get in trouble from their speculation by imposing harsh sanctions on the countries in difficulty. This strategy has been pursued by the International Monetary Fund which has taken on the role of "economic consulting agency" to countries in trouble. But it should be clear that the $50 billion aid package put together by the IMF and others for

---

[40]Kapstein, *op. cit.*

[41]Howard Pawley, "Is Globalization Good For Canada?" *Toronto Star*, February 2, 1998.

[42]Andrew Johnson, "Strengthening Society III: Social Security," in Johnson and Stritch, *op. cit.*, p. 180.

[43]Thomas L. Friedman, quoted in *ibid.*, p. 181.

Mexico was not really for the Mexicans, but for the foreign banks and other financial institutions who had made loans to Mexico that were now in jeopardy.[44] Milton Friedman argues that this bailout helped to fuel the East Asian crisis that followed two years later, by encouraging lenders to invest without sufficient regard for the consequences on the assumption that the IMF would bail them out too, if necessary.

> Government intervention in the "free" market is bad unless the interests of capital are threatened.

We have thus evolved into a paradoxical situation in which economic activities harmful to the domestic interests of countries and to the living standards of their citizens go unchecked on the grounds that this is the inevitable working of the free market system and yet in which governments intervene to prevent the market from operating freely when the interests of capital are threatened. We have been persuaded that the events taking place must be accepted because they are an integral part of the new global economy in which we now find ourselves. Yet as *The Economist* has pointed out,[45] capital was just as mobile in earlier periods. What has changed—besides modern computer technology obviously—is that the capital controls and regulations put into place after World War II (as described above) no longer exist. *The Economist* notes that these controls served to insulate domestic markets and gave governments more control over their domestic economies.

The WTO and its Significance

Instead of controls over capital and the operations of transnational corporations, we are getting increasing international controls over the operations of national governments as a result of the establishment of the World Trade Organization (WTO). It came into existence on January 1, 1995 following an eight year process of trade negotiations under GATT (General Agreement on Tariffs and Trade) known as the

---

[44]The discussion in this section is based on Milton Friedman, "It's time to kill the IMF," *National Post*, November 2, 1998.

[45]An article titled "Back to the Future," quoted in McQuaig, *The Cult of Impotence, op. cit.*, pp. 24-25.

Uruguay Round. It was Canada that proposed introducing the more authoritarian institutional structure that transformed GATT, which had been so ineffective that it was often referred to as the "General Agreement to Talk and Talk." Apparently Canada believed that as a mid-sized state it was better off in a rules-based system with a dispute settlement mechanism strong enough to enforce these rules.[46]

The WTO has over 130 member countries which account for 90% of world trade. Decisions are made by the entire membership, typically by consensus, and the resultant agreements are then ratified in the parliaments of members.[47] While the WTO evolved from GATT, it also differs from it in two profound ways. The first difference is one of scope. Whereas trade rules used to focus on the movement of raw materials and goods across borders, trade agreements under the WTO now include investment measures, intellectual property rights, every type of domestic regulation, and services. As a result, "it would be difficult to identify an issue of social, economic, or environmental significance that does not come under the scrutiny of trade regulation."[48] The second difference is the more powerful enforcement tools that exist under the WTO to ensure compliance with its rules. In the first trade complaint to be resolved under the WTO, for example, the United States Clean Air Act regulations were held to violate trade rules and the U.S. was given the choice of removing the regulations or facing trade sanctions of $150 million a year.

Having an organization to monitor international trade agreements is advantageous in some respects. Unless there is compliance with such agreements, countries can raise various barriers to trade which negate the agreements, and can pursue the sort of "beggar thy neighbour" policies which aggravated the depression of the 1930s. But the main concern of the WTO seems to be the compilation of detailed rules which prohibit a vast array of government regulations that might interfere with the actions of large corporations. Some of these prohibitions

---

[46]Clarkson and Lewis, *op. cit.*, pp. 315 and 299.

[47]According to information at the WTO's web site, *www.wto.org*.

[48]The discussion in this section is based on West Coast Environmental Law, *The WTO and the Global Economy*, available at web site *www.wcel.org*.

relate to regulations or programs that might only indirectly influence trade, such as recycling regulations, energy efficiency standards, or toxic substance bans.

Examples of the impact of the WTO on Canada include:

- Reference has previously been made to the ruling against Canada's efforts to protect its domestic magazine industry. Although the Canada-U.S. FTA had grandfathered such Canadian cultural policies as prohibiting split-run editions of American magazines appearing in Canada with Canadian advertising, a case was launched at the WTO against the blocking of a Canadian edition of *Sports Illustrated*. In ruling against Canada, the WTO dispute panel declared cultural policies that were democratically legislated decades ago to be invalid according to Geneva's 1995 trade rules.[49]
- Trade-related intellectual property rights (TRIPS) were included in NAFTA and became part of the WTO regulations as well. When Ottawa was pressured by Washington into complying with these regulations, the result was to give "foreign-owned pharmaceutical subsidiaries generous protection for their branded drugs and to eliminate the legal base for the Canadian public health system's much cheaper generic drug suppliers."[50]
- In late 1999, the WTO ruled against some provisions of Canada's historic Auto Pact with the United States, which has been successful in keeping substantial automotive production within this country, arguing that these provisions discriminated in favour of the "Big Three" automakers.

Even efforts by national governments to ensure the quality of food consumed by their citizens are likely to be thwarted by the WTO, which has already levied fines against the European Union for refusing to admit British beef in the wake of the "mad cow disease" crisis. While there is growing concern in many countries, including Canada, about genetically altered foods, the multi-billion dollar business interests involved in their production are certain to turn to the WTO to block any restrictions which national governments may impose. A study of the 167 contested trade issues brought to the WTO as of March 1999 found

---

[49]Clarkson and Lewis, *op. cit.*, p. 300.

[50]*Ibid.*

that in every case in which an environmental, health, or food safety law was challenged at the WTO, these laws were declared illegal barriers to trade.[51]

Sleepless in Seattle: Setback for the WTO

There were also growing concerns in Canada that the latest round of trade talks, which commenced in Seattle at the end of November 1999, might extend to such services as education and health and thus threaten existing government support for these programs. A WTO background paper argues that a country permitting both private and public health institutions would probably be required to provide equal government funding to both; otherwise it would violate the WTO's national treatment obligation that requires governments to treat alike all economic actors, whether foreign domestic, public or private.[52]

The Seattle talks began against a backdrop of widespread public protests, with an estimated 50 000 people, representing such diverse groups as labour, the environment, churches, and the student movement, demonstrating in the host city. But more than the demonstrators kept trade delegates sleepless; the talks ran into difficulty and no agreements were reached. The issue of agricultural subsidies was a major stumbling block, as it has been in the past, but there were numerous other problems as well, including an overly ambitious agenda and considerable infighting.[53] More significant than the collapse of these particular talks, however, is the fact that opponents of the WTO may have won the battle for public opinion. Only 32% of Canadians (with similar numbers in other countries) claim to trust their own governments to protect their nation's interests in trade negotiations.[54]

---

[51]Lori Wallach and Michelle Sforza, *Whose Trade Organization*? as quoted in Silja J. A. Talvi, "World Trade or World Domination?" *Mother Jones*, November 24, 1999, available at web site *www.motherjones.com*.

[52]Thomas Walkom, "Squeeze Play," *Toronto Star*, November 13, 1999.

[53]James Baxter, "International trade talks collapsed under strain of divisions," *Kingston Whig-Standard*, December 7, 1999.

[54]Richard Gwyn, "Giving voice to our fears about Seattle trade talks," *Toronto Star*, November 28, 1999.

Concluding Observations

In 1945 the federal government for the first time formally accepted that it had a role to play in managing the economy of Canada in pursuit of the goals of full employment, price stability, economic growth, and balance of payments stability. For 25 years or so, it applied the fiscal and monetary policies of Keynesian economics with considerable success, presiding over a period of economic growth which allowed for, and was stimulated by, the provision of a number of income support programs. To a considerable extent, however, this success was part of a prolonged period of growth enjoyed by most Western nations in the post-war years and at least partly attributable to the stability provided by a fixed exchange rate system and a variety of institutions and arrangements put into place at the end of World War II.

The government's economic record in the last quarter of the 20th century has been much more uneven and there are widely differing views as to the appropriateness of the economic priorities which have prevailed. As we enter the 21st century, inflation has not been a concern for a number of years. The federal government has balanced its budget and is likely to have a substantial surplus in the coming years, and most of the provinces have put their fiscal houses in order as well. After years in the double digits, the unemployment rate is now down to about 7%. On the basis of these measures, one could claim success for the government's efforts over the past couple of decades, even if this success was hard earned.

Many feel, however, that this success was too hard earned, and has not been enjoyed by enough of Canada's population. Those concerned about our record in economic management point to such factors as a social safety net which has been seriously eroded because of reduced resources and a shift from universal to targeted coverage and a growing income disparity within the country. They point to a federal government so reduced in scope and activity that its expenditures now represent the same proportion of the Gross Domestic Product as they did in the early 1950s. They see a federal government also weakened by years of decentralization, largely to placate provincial demands and to counteract the separatist threat from Québec. They worry about a government seemingly at the mercy of currency speculators and under constant pressure from business interests to reduce taxes and social programs to be more competitive in the global marketplace.

However we characterize economic developments over the past half century, it seems clear that the government's role has become increasingly constrained. During the first quarter century following World War II, the government appeared to be taking positive initiatives, through both fiscal and monetary policy, to bring about desired conditions in the economy—or at least to moderate the excesses of normal business cycles. Since that time, the government's role has become increasingly passive and reactive. Under monetarism, it largely abandoned its economic policy making to the Bank of Canada and its single-minded pursuit of zero inflation. More recently, it reacted to the accumulated deficits of two decades by focusing on reducing expenditures and transfer payments. Instead of making things happen, the government's role seems reduced to reacting to things that have already been allowed to happen. Economic policy making also seems increasingly shaped by external considerations and the demands of global capital rather than by domestic considerations and the needs of Canadian citizens—reflecting more concern for Moody's than the public mood. New international agreements and organizations, such as the FTA and NAFTA, and the WTO, impose further constraints on the autonomy of governments.

> Government policies more concerned about Moody's than the public mood.

In light of these developments, a key question is whether or not the federal government still has the presence and the political will to pursue the economic policies needed by Canadians as we enter a new century with an improved fiscal position. How it responds is partly up to you, and the final chapter of this Guide will suggest a number of ways in which you can make your views felt.

The Last Word

Definition of Terms and Concepts

Automatic Stabilizers:
Any arrangement that automatically supports aggregate demand (that is, spending) when it would otherwise weaken and holds down this demand when it would otherwise expand too rapidly.[55]

Bracket Creep:
Additional tax burden incurred when income increased by inflation lifts a taxpayer into a higher tax bracket.

Consumer Price Index:
An index number for the price level, with weights based on the spending patterns of a typical urban household. It measures monthly changes in the retail price of a selected "basket" of about 300 commodities.

Deficit: (See also Public Debt.)
The amount by which the government's expenditures exceed its receipts during a specified time period, usually one year.

Fiscal Policies:
The government's use of its spending and taxing powers to stimulate or slow down the economy.

Foreign Exchange Market:
An exchange rate is the cost of one country's currency in terms of the currency of another's country. The Canadian dollar is expressed in terms of how much it costs to exchange it for an American dollar. Buyers and sellers of currencies operate in a foreign exchange market.

Gross Domestic Product (GDP):
The sum of the money values of all final goods and services produced in the economy during a specified period, usually a year.

---

[55]The definitions of a number of economic terms are based on those found in William J. Baumol, Alan S. Blinder and William M. Scarth, *Macroeconomics: Principles and Practices*, 4th Edition, Toronto, Harcourt Brace & Company, 1994.

Inflation:
A significant and prolonged increase in the price of goods and servic

Laissez Faire:
Literally, "to leave alone," a term reflecting the notion that government should play a minimal role, leaving most decisions to the private sector.

Monetary Policies:
Actions taken by the Bank of Canada to create "easy money" (reflected in lower interest rates) or "tight money" (higher interest rates) so as to stimulate the economy or slow it down.

OECD:
The Organization for Economic Cooperation and Development comprises 29 countries which produce two-thirds of the world's goods and services.

Protectionism:
The opposite of free trade. The use of tariffs and other trade barriers to discourage imported goods, thereby prompting consumers to purchase domestic products.

Public Debt:
The government's total indebtedness. The total of all net budget deficits (not offset by surpluses) accrued by government over time.

Stagflation:
An economic situation which combines elements of stagnation and inflation (high unemployment and high prices).

Tax Expenditures:
Revenues not collected by the government because of various tax concessions provided to individuals and organizations.

Unemployment Rate:
The number of unemployed people, expressed as a percentage of the labour force.

World Trade Organization:
It represents over 130 countries and negotiates rules for international trade, defined very broadly.

Points to Ponder

1. While government actions influence the economy, the economy has even more influence over government actions. Give examples to support either or both sides of this statement.

2. Are you one of the many Canadians who holds the view that excessive government spending is the main cause of our deficit and debt problems? Has this chapter caused you to reassess your view?

3. What are the potential advantages for Canada of the agreements and organizational arrangements which facilitate free trade in the world, and what are the potential drawbacks or dangers for Canada?

4. What grade (A, B, C, D or F) would you assign to the federal government for its management of the Canadian economy over the past 50 years, and why?

For Further Reading

The best source of information on government actions concerning the Canadian economy is found in Canada's media, its daily newspapers and news broadcasts and news magazines such as *Maclean's*. There are also a large number of economics textbooks which examine the issues touched on in this chapter, such as C. Michael Fellows, Greg Flanagan, and Stanford Shedd, *Economic Issues: A Canadian Perspective*, Toronto, McGraw-Hill Ryerson Limited, 1997.

Concerns about the impact of globalization and the growing power of transnational corporations are found in such sources as:
-   Murray Dobbin, *The Myth of the Good Corporate Citizen*, Toronto, Stoddart, 1998.
-   Final Report of the Standing Senate Committee on Social Affairs, Science and Technology, *Social Cohesion*, June 1999.
-   Linda McQuaig, *The Cult of Impotence: Selling the Myth of Powerlessness in the Global Economy*, Toronto, Penguin Books, 1998.

A great deal of information is available on the Internet, from sources such as:

- the Ministry of Finance at *www.fin.gc.ca.*
- the Bank of Canada at *www.bank-banque-canada.ca.*
- the Canadian Centre for Policy Alternatives, which, as its name suggests, provides analysis and alternatives with respect to government economic policies. It is at *www.policyalternatives.ca.*
- the World Trade Organization at *www.wto.org.*

Chapter 11

Where Do We Go From Here?

Objectives and Highlights

◆ To summarize key findings of this Guide.

◆ To identify specific actions you can take to participate as an informed citizen in a democratic society.

As Canada enters a new century, its political leaders wrestle with an apparently intractable "problem"—what to do with the increasingly large budget surpluses which are beginning to accumulate. Should they be used to expand or initiate government programs, to provide tax cuts, or to reduce existing public debt? How quintessentially Canadian! It should perhaps not be surprising that a country prepared to spend untold years agonizing over the minutia of constitutional reform would turn its new-found financial solvency into a problem rather than a success. Yet as silly or tedious as the debate sometimes sounds, it reflects an underlying and very fundamental question about the extent of the role which government should play in Canadian society.

It is noteworthy that even before Paul Martin issued his Fiscal and Economic Update on November 2, 1999, with its promising projection of steadily increasing government surpluses,[1] those on the right and left of the political spectrum "jumped the gun" with their critiques and suggestions. The *National Post* of October 30 contained a series of articles decrying the increased federal spending that was anticipated over the next five years. With titles like "Liberals plan $47B spending spree," "Whiners get help—but not taxpayers," and "Social programs will

---

[1]See Ministry of Finance, *1999 Economic and Fiscal Update*, available at web site *www.fin.gc.ca/update99*.

consume $9B over 5 years," these articles made clear their dismay that a substantial portion of accumulating government surpluses might go to increased program spending. In contrast, the Canadian Centre for Policy Alternatives released on November 1, 1999 an Alternative Fiscal and Economic Update which proclaimed that the federal government has ample fiscal room to fund major new investments in human services and public infrastructure without increasing tax levels and without threatening its balanced budget position. This debate over what to do with the surplus will continue to rage over the next several years (and probably as long as any surplus remains).

The Importance of Policies as well as Programs

Discussions about the surplus, and how much of it will go to program spending, certainly merit our attention. But they should not be allowed to obscure the importance of how governments exercise their policy making responsibility on our behalf. There are indications that program spending in areas such as health and education will expand again because of the government's improved financial position. But it is far from clear that our governments will initiate the kinds of policies which may be desired by large segments of Canadian society—especially when such policies are opposed by business interests and the domestic and international organizations which promote them.

For those concerned, as this Guide is, with the growing dominance of transnational corporations and mobile capital, the starting point for any change is a recognition that the so-called global economy is not the result of some natural and inevitable evolution, immune to intervention by government. To the contrary, it has taken its particular shape and characteristics as the result of a series of decisions made by governments, decisions that removed international controls that used to exist and that facilitated the free movement of goods and capital. While it will not be easy to reintroduce controls or constraints, especially through any one government acting on its own, it is only through such means that national governments will regain control over their domestic affairs. A few suggestions follow.

Changing the Rules of International Trade and Finance

Our government needs to be sensitive to provisions in Canada's free trade agreements which threaten Canadian sovereignty, and should use every opportunity to push for changes in such provisions. The rules of the World Trade Organization also pose an apparent threat to the sovereignty of member countries—as with the examples of national governments being unable to keep out suspected tainted beef or potentially harmful gasoline additives. Since the rules of the WTO have to be ratified in the parliaments of members countries, those countries have the power—if they could summon the political will—to reclaim more authority over these matters.

Whatever constraints free trade may impose on national governments, one can at least make a case that it generates widespread economic benefits. In contrast, the unfettered flow of capital has constrained national governments while mainly benefiting large investors and currency speculators. It is true that investment capital can be very important in financing the development of the economies of underdeveloped nations, just as British and then American capital helped to underwrite the development of Canada's economy over the past two centuries. But too often in recent years, such investment capital has flowed into developing countries at an almost overwhelming rate and then rushed out abruptly at the first sign of economic difficulties, contributing to great instability in those countries. Worse still, the response of the International Monetary Fund and others has been to bail out the financial institutions which got into trouble from their speculation by imposing harsh sanctions on the countries in difficulty.

Even more problematic has been the tremendous volume of currency speculation which now takes place in the world. Capital flows and the exchange of goods and services across borders will give rise to demands for various currencies, and their "exchange" is an entirely normal and predictable consequence. But most currency exchanges today do not relate to those real changes in economic activity. They arise because currency speculators hope to make quick profits by anticipating changes in currency values, or by prompting such changes by the very actions they take. In other words, if currency speculators believe that the Canadian dollar is going to weaken in value, they will exchange it for another currency whose value is expected to rise. The very fact that a substantial volume of Canadian dollars is dumped on the market creates an excess supply and, therefore, a drop in value—resulting in a self-fulfilling prophecy.

> Because of currency speculation, governments are often forced to pursue policies inappropriate for the domestic economy.

Quite apart from the questionable morality of speculators making profits from such activity, their actions constrain the actions of national governments. There is pressure to keep interest rates high so that capital will continue to be attracted to a country, even though such interest rates may be harmful to the domestic economy, contributing to slower growth and higher unemployment. Canada has experienced first-hand this unfortunate reality over much of the past 25 years or so.

One way of dealing with this situation is to introduce a tax on currency speculation, usually referred to as the Tobin tax after the American Nobel Prize winner who first advocated it some 30 years ago. In simplest terms, the idea is to impose a small tax whenever money is exchanged from one currency to another. If the tax is quite small, for example 0.2%, its proponents argue that it will discourage constant speculation without adversely affecting desirable capital flows. A tax of this magnitude will have no effect on long-term investment or on a one time purchase of foreign goods. But it will quickly become a punitive tax on funds which are shifted frequently from one currency to another in search of speculative profit. For example, a 0.2% tax on $100 000 amounts to an insignificant $200. But if that $100 000 is exchanged for another currency and then back, each "round trip" costs $400. If such exchanges occur an average of once a month, the tax adds up to $4800 in a year. If the money makes a round trip weekly, the yearly cost of the tax would be prohibitive at more than $20 000.[2]

The advantages of the Tobin tax are twofold. First and foremost, if it succeeds in reducing currency speculation, it returns more decision

---

[2]This example is from Linda McQuaig, *The Cult of Impotence*, Toronto, Penguin Books, 1998, p. 152.

making autonomy to national governments. Second, to the extent that it does not discourage such speculation, the resultant tax generates a very substantial sum of money each year (probably at least $100 billion) which could be used to address world poverty and other social ills.

Criticism of the Tobin tax usually falls into two main categories.[3] It is dismissed as an interference with the free flow of capital which will have adverse economic consequences. It is also rejected on the grounds that it is unworkable, that it would be impossible to get all the nations of the world to agree with such a measure. But McQuaig argues that the IMF, which is controlled by the world's dominant economic powers, could require all nations to impose the Tobin tax as a condition of membership. Since countries would not have access to IMF loans without such membership, they would feel obliged to institute the tax. Here again, it appears that there is a way to control excessive currency speculation, if there is a will.

What Can You Do?

What actions can citizens take to make their views and concerns known and to bring about the changed role for government that they desire? Whatever your views on how government should operate, you are apt to hold the view that one person can't make any impact—especially if your view is contrary to that of the financial and business interests which appear to hold sway. But you can make a difference, *if* you get involved. Whatever its faults, our government system is still a democratic one, in which the Canadian people have the ultimate say. While Tom d'Aquino may head an organization (the Business Council on National Issues) whose members have more than $1 trillion in assets, he still has only one vote like everyone else. If people exercise that vote, they can make dramatic changes.

---

[3]For a good exchange on this topic, see A. R. Riggs and Tom Velk, "The Tobin Tax: A Bad Idea Whose Time Has Passed," *Policy Options*, Montreal, IRRP, July-August 1999, pp. 53-57, Alex C. Michalos, "The Tobin Tax: A Good Idea Whose Time Has **Not** Passed," *Policy Options*, October 1999, pp. 64-67, and the response by Riggs and Velk in the same issue, pp. 68-69.

Look no further than the incredible results of the 1993 federal election. The Progressive Conservative Party, the party of Sir John A. Macdonald, the party which won back to back majorities in the 1980s, was reduced to two seats in the House of Commons. In contrast, look at the election results in Ontario in the summer of 1999, when only 62% of those eligible bothered to pass judgment on arguably the most radical and controversial government in the province's history. With 45% support from the 62% who voted, the Conservative government of Mike Harris was given a new mandate and a majority government by fewer than one-third of Ontario's electorate. Consider also the dramatic example of the actions taken by thousands of Canadians on the eve of the Québec referendum in October 1995. Their strong show of support culminating in the huge rally in Montreal is held by many to have been a key factor in avoiding (barely) a yes vote for separation and all of the disruptive consequences that could have followed from that. Canadian citizens also flexed their political muscles when they ignored the urgings of their political parties and most of the country's elite by decisively rejecting the constitutional amendment package known as the Charlottetown Accord in October 1992.

Concerted efforts can even make a difference in areas where citizens feel they don't have much influence, such as with respect to big business and the international sphere, as the following four examples indicate.

- In April 1998 the Multilateral Agreement on Investment (MAI) being promoted by the member countries of the OECD (Organization for Economic Cooperation and Development) was defeated, at least temporarily. Briefly put, the MAI was designed to broaden and deepen the foreign investor property rights first recognized and protected in the FTA and NAFTA. Its passage would greatly increase the volume and velocity of international capital mobility and would prohibit countries from treating foreign investment any differently than investment by their own citizens. The MAI would also reduce existing forms of state regulation which either impede the mobility of capital or attempt to cope with its consequences.[4]

---

[4]Ian Robinson, *The Multilateral Agreement on Investment and Provincial Government Powers*, Canadian Centre for Policy Alternatives, 1999.

- In December 1998, public opposition helped to persuade Finance Minister Paul Martin to reject, again at least temporarily, the bank mergers being sought by the Royal Bank and Bank of Montreal and the CIBC and Toronto-Dominion Bank.
- In March 1999 the House of Commons responded to public pressure by passing an NDP motion for an international tax on currency transactions, the so-called Tobin tax discussed above. The motion was not binding, however.
- In early December 1999, the WTO trade talks in Seattle adjourned in failure. The talks might not have succeeded under any circumstances, but delegates also had to contend with 50 000 protestors.

Three delays and one symbolic motion may not seem like great victories. Indeed, they may not be regarded as victories at all— depending on where you stand on the issue of government versus the marketplace. But these examples do illustrate that concerted efforts by concerned citizens can make a difference.

Specific Actions You Can Take

Listed below are a number of specific actions you can take, along with suggestions on how to make these actions more effective.

Cast Your Ballot

Only a little over 2/3 of those eligible bother to vote in federal and provincial elections, fewer than 40% in municipal elections, and only about 1/5 in school board elections. Municipal and school board elections in Ontario were shifted from December to November some years ago, on the grounds that inclement weather was affecting the voting turnout. When the right to vote is granted in previously dictatorial nations around the world, it is impressive to see the news reports of people lining up for hours, sometimes with gunfire around them, usually with threats of violence, all for the opportunity to have a say in their government. Yet democracy in Canada is apparently too fragile to withstand an early winter snowfall!

As discussed earlier in this Guide, the first-past-the-post electoral system we use in Canada often distorts the election results, with the result that the representation in the House of Commons (or provincial legislature) may not correspond to the popular vote cast. It has also been noted that strong party discipline makes it difficult for individual members of parliament to represent and respond to the interests of their constituents if these interests conflict with the official position adopted by the party. We have also discussed the influences pushing all political parties toward the centre of the political spectrum and making the choice available to voters at each election appear to be little more than one of tweedledum or tweedledee. All of these "imperfections" can be used as an excuse for political inactivity, but that is all they are— an excuse. Casting your ballot is the most fundamental political right you have, and one that should be exercised. Voting within the existing system of government doesn't preclude you pushing for changes and improvements in that system

Make Your Views Known

Important as it is, casting a ballot once every few years is a pretty passive and limited kind of involvement in the political system. That reality isn't an excuse for not voting at all, as some disillusioned Canadians claim. It is a reason for augmenting your voting with other acts of involvement between elections. Among the many steps you can take are the following:

Keep Informed on Public Issues and Government Activities

To be an effective participant in government, you must be an informed participant. People often complain that government is secretive, that it rushes through ill-considered legislative changes, that it doesn't consult enough. Yet there is ample evidence to show that even when governments consult, even when there is massive media coverage about public issues, the vast majority of Canadians remain blissfully unaware.

The sad reality is that most Canadians pay far too little attention to the activities of their governments. We can be roused on particular issues, especially when we feel personally threatened, but a sustaining interest is much more difficult to achieve. Yet most of us find time to keep track of the daily sports scores and to exchange comments about our favourite comedy show on television from the night before. It takes no more time or energy to keep track of the activities of our governments and it is hard to imagine a more important way to spend our time in a democratic society. Imagine the difference it could make if most people redirected the energy they expend in complaining about government into becoming informed about government.

As discussed in Chapter 4, however, becoming informed involves more than accepting at face value whatever version of events may be presented by the newspaper you happen to read or the news show you catch. For reasons already given, mainstream media outlets tend to reinforce the dominant ideology in society and to support the economic and political status quo. At the very least, you owe it to yourself to consult a variety of sources to gain insight into an issue. The fact that many sources of information are biased can be quite helpful—provided that you are aware of such biases and offset them with competing points of view. Those with access to the Internet can peruse with ease the contents of many newspapers and magazines as well as the web sites of various organizations which comment on public issues. Look at conflicting points of view and come to your own conclusions on these issues. The truth is to be found somewhere between the *Toronto Star* and the *National Post* or between the Fraser Institute and the Canadian Centre for Policy Alternatives—or if not the truth, at least a middle ground on many of the issues we face today. Consider the arguments and determine where you stand.

Exercise Your Informed Judgment

Knowledge is power, if it is used. Don't hesitate to contact your MP, MLA, or municipal councillor about issues that concern you. It is appreciated that there is a growing cynicism about government and a widespread view that once in power politicians forget about us until the next election. But how many people take the time to contact their elected members and to pass on their views and concerns? If you never try, how can you be sure that politicians are uninterested and unresponsive? We know that organized interests, especially business interests, devote a great deal of energy and resources to promoting their views to the government. If politicians seem insensitive to the concerns of "average citizens," is it because they so rarely hear from them?

Since most people pay little attention to most issues most of the time, when a politician receives 10 phone calls or letters it can seem like a groundswell of public opinion. Putting your concerns in writing is preferable, and is likely to generate a written response—even if it seems to be little more than a standard reply generated by a staffer. Here again, the Internet offers convenient access, making it possible to contact federal and provincial politicians and many heads of municipal council by e-mail. A written submission also gives you a better opportunity to demonstrate that your comments are based on knowledge of the issue in question and on informed judgment.

Don't forget the *Guide to Government* Directory included in Chapter 2. Photocopy that page, fill it in, and keep a copy by your phone or on your desk as a handy reference sheet when you want to contact someone in government.

Use your informed judgment, and add to it, by attending government meetings. Sitting in on "Question Period" in Ottawa or your provincial capital may be more entertaining than informative. But attending a meeting of a committee of the federal or provincial legislatures is quite another matter, and may not even involve much travel if it is a committee which holds hearings across the province or country. Often these committee meetings are fact-finding or are seeking a response to proposed government initiatives. Most of those who attend and present briefs are from organized groups with a vested interest in the particular issue. What about your interests as a citizen? Assuming that the government allocates sufficient time for the exercise, committee hearings can be a convenient way of accessing government.

Most accessible of all are meetings of your municipality or school board. But attending a meeting of your municipal council should extend beyond being part of a delegation to the council. The trouble with delegations is that those participating present their concerns during their allotted time and then leave the meeting. This brief appearance doesn't give you any indication about how your municipal council conducts its business. It doesn't give you any opportunity to see and hear your elected representatives in action. It provides no insight into the issues and challenges that require local action. Attending a meeting means just that; it means staying through the meeting, or a least a good portion of it, whether or not you (or your group) are on the agenda as a delegation or have already been heard.

Particularly informative can be municipal budget meetings, which are increasingly open to the public. What an opportunity to educate yourself in the pressures and priorities which are found in your local

> Municipal meetings, especially budget meetings, are not only accessible but highly informative.

community. A budget meeting will usually include high drama and low comedy, and a good mixture of pathos as well. It will be lengthy, confusing, ultimately exhausting. But it will also give you a new appreciation of the very difficult work done by your elected representatives. It will make you think twice before launching into the standard speech about all the waste in government. It might even make you concede, however grudgingly, that some increase in taxes now and then can be justified.

You can also use and augment your knowledge of government by becoming involved with political parties and candidates for office. Federal and provincial political parties have constituency associations, made up of local people from your community. Depending on how active the party is in your constituency, there are likely to be at least annual functions. Many are social events, also designed as fund-raisers and as a way of attracting new members. Attending such events is a way of participating in the political process while enjoying an evening out. You don't have to commit to a particular political party for life, or even for a day, in order to take part in this kind of gathering.

But if you find a political party whose views make sense to you, you will find it rewarding to join the local riding association and participate in its activities. Chief among these activities is the selection of a candidate to represent the party prior to each election. As a member, you will be eligible to vote in the selection process. You can also become more actively involved by working on behalf of one of the candidates, which provides valuable experience and an increased appreciation for the demands of political office. Even greater involvement, and insight, can be gained by campaigning on behalf of the candidate chosen by your party. When you campaign on behalf of someone who wants to win the nomination from a particular party, you come into contact with people who share a common belief in that party—even though they may differ as to the best candidate to represent it. Going on to the next stage and campaigning for the successful party candidate brings you into contact with the public at large, with people who don't like your candidate or party, even with people who don't like any candidates or parties (or people knocking on their door).

While parties aren't usually involved, campaigning on behalf of a candidate for municipal office can be an equally challenging experience. It is all too easy to criticize politicians but when you "walk a mile in their shoes" on the campaign trail you gain an appreciation of the process through which they go to attain elected office.

For those not comfortable with the "cut and thrust" of political competition and campaigning, another way of using and augmenting your knowledge is by seeking appointment as a citizen member of a board or committee. While such appointments are made by all levels of government, they are especially conspicuous at the local level. Most municipalities place ads in the local newspapers each fall, inviting applications from citizens interested in being appointed to serve on such bodies as planning advisory committees, industrial commissions, community centre boards and committees of adjustment. Being appointed to one of these local governing bodies is an excellent way of serving in government without the rigours of the election process. It allows public-spirited citizens to make an important contribution to their community and how it is governed.

Concluding Observations

When this Guide (in Chapter 1) stated a bias in favour of a continuing significant role for government, it did not advocate big government or free-spending government. It is entirely appropriate for citizens to demand that governments be careful with their money, just as it is reasonable to criticize examples of wasteful or excessive spending. It is also valid, indeed desirable, for citizens to be critical of shortcomings in the way our system of government operates, and to push for reforms—a number of which have been discussed in this Guide. But we must remember that, whatever its faults, we need our governments. We need them, as Walter Stewart reminded us in Chapter 1, "active and muscular enough to right the imbalances created by our marvellously efficient, monumentally unfair economic system."[5]

Fortunately, from the point of view of this Guide, there are reasons to expect public support for a greater leadership role from our governments.[6] This may seem surprising, since Canadians have become more cynical about government and more mistrustful, a pattern also evident in most Western democracies. There also appears to be somewhat less support for collective action by government on behalf of the less fortunate in society and more support for individual and family responsibility. This shift is reflected in the view that perhaps the social safety net has become too much of a comfortable hammock when it should act more as a trampoline, helping people to spring back on to their feet.

It is striking, however, that even though Canadians have doubts about their government, they do not see such alternatives as the marketplace, the family, or the volunteer sector as an adequate replacement. "[G]overnments are still identified as the prime agent for achieving societal goals."[7] When asked how they would redress the balance of power, Canadians don't call for a reduction in government power. Rather, they want the power of big business and the media reduced and the power of small business and the average citizen strengthened. They believe the economy is important—not when narrowly viewed in terms of dollars and markets, but when viewed as jobs, security and people; they want "to see the economy harnessed for the well-being of average citizens...."[8]

---

[5]Walter Stewart, *Dismantling the State*, Toronto, Stoddart, 1998, p. 16.

[6]The following discussion is largely based on Frank Graves, "Rethinking Government," in Leslie A. Pal (ed.), *How Ottawa Spends 1999-2000*, Toronto, Oxford University Press, 1999, which draws upon public attitudes measured by Ekos Research Associates.

[7]*Ibid.*, p. 43.

[8]*Ibid.*, p. 47.

After two decades of neoconservatism which attempted to diminish greatly the role and significance of government in our lives, there are signs that Canadians are receptive to a more active role for government —albeit under considerably changed conditions. The deficit and debt appear to be less of a threat, but there are growing concerns about the social costs of deficit reduction and of globalization, and fears of a loss of Canadian identity and autonomy. These feelings have prompted support for an increased role for government generally and the federal government in particular.[9] But it is support for a new style of government and governance that emphasizes fiscal discipline, sets measurable targets and is held accountable for their achievement, and promotes partnerships with other players rather than building traditional bureaucratic empires. Canadians are not in favour of a return to big, free-spending governments, but they also do not believe that problems such as child poverty and the growing gap between rich and poor can be solved by tax cuts and a minimal role for government.

You Can Make a Difference!

It may be fitting to conclude with a quote from that famous political philosopher Pogo, who is credited with the saying, *"We have met the enemy and they are us."*

Our governments are far from perfect. This Guide raises a number of questions and concerns about the functioning of our governments and the priorities they have chosen. But cliché or not, it remains substantially true that we get the kind of government we deserve.

If you don't pay attention, if you sit back and grumble, if you contribute to the problems instead of preventing them from arising in the first place, you should remember Pogo and look in the mirror when you want to allocate blame. If, instead, you take more personal responsibility for your actions and those of your governments, if you become an informed participant, *you can make a difference.*

---

[9]*Ibid.*, p. 54.

Index

A

Aberhart, William, 103
Administrative law, 122
Agencies, Boards and Commissions (ABCs). *See* Boards, local
Alberta, 26, 41, 45, 51, 97, 131, 176, 196, 199, 251, 259-260, 281, 283, 286, 287-288, 321
Allmand, Warren, 145
Amalgamation, 192-195, 271
Amberley, 268
Arbour, Justice Louise, 228
Asian Pacific Economic Cooperation (APEC), 108
Association of Municipalities of Ontario (AMO), 194, 263, 264, 266
Asymmetrical federalism, 257. *See also* Federal-provincial relations
At large elections (municipal) 26, 80
Atlantic provinces, 155, 160, 227, 244, 276. *See also* Maritime provinces
Automatic stabilizers, 311
Avalon, 192
Axworthy, Lloyd, 279

B

Backbenchers, 124, 141, pay of, 162-163, roles of, 160-161
Baker, George, 145
Bank of Canada, 54, 66, 245, 269, 313-314, 339
Barlow, Maude, 67, 329
Bastarache, Justice Michel, 228
Begin, Monique, 289
Bienvenue, Justice Jean, 220, 221
Bill passing process, 151-152
Binnie, Justice Ian, 228
Bloc Québécois, 43, 46, 48-49, 150
Boards, local, 29, 178-179
Bouchard, Lucien, 3, 43, 48, 211, 212
Bracken, John, 40
Britain, 54, 79, 131, 140, 143, 183, 205, 207, 215, 244, 292, 325
British Columbia, 17, 40, 41, 45, 103-104, 176, 179, 196, 251, 253, 255, 282, 329
British North America (BNA) Act, 205, 206, 207, 208, 223, 240. *See also* Constitution